The Biology of
the Autistic Syndromes

The Biology of the Autistic Syndromes

Mary Coleman, M.D.
Christopher Gillberg, M.D.

PRAEGER SPECIAL STUDIES • PRAEGER SCIENTIFIC

New York • Philadelphia • Eastbourne, UK
Toronto • Hong Kong • Tokyo • Sydney

Library of Congress Cataloging in Publication Data

Coleman, Mary.
  The biology of the autistic syndromes.

  Bibliography: p.
  Includes index.
  1. Autism—Etiology. I. Gillberg, Christopher,
1950-   . II. Title
RJ506.A9C64 1985   618.92′8982   84-26402
ISBN 0-275-91309-0

Library of Congress Catalog Card Number: 84-26402
ISBN: 0-275-91309-0

First published in 1985

Praeger Publishers, 521 Fifth Avenue, New York, NY 10175
A division of Greenwood Press, Inc.

Printed in the United States of America

The paper used in this book complies with the Permanent
Paper Standard issued by the National Information Standards
Organization (Z39.48-1984).

10 9 8 7 6 5 4 3 2

Contents

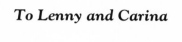

To Lenny and Carina

IMMINENT DISASTER

Even now I still feel frightened.

I was doomed ever since I can remember,
An autistic child.
Except at home.
So I never liked leaving home.

Everywhere I went I felt different,
An autistic child.
I hated everybody,
Except at home. That is the truth.

It was because I couldn't talk, I think,
And other children could.
I nearly ran away from home,
Because I thought they were dotty—

Dotty because they loved me.

Malcolm Gorst

Acknowledgments

This book is possible because of the support of many people. Most importantly, our main teachers have been the autistic patients and their families, whose admirable cooperation in clinical and research trials and detailed accurate reporting of their children's symptoms have greatly enhanced our understanding of the autistic syndromes. Without these patients, this book would not have been possible.

We also wish to acknowledge and thank the brilliant editorial assistance of Anne Shapiro and Mrs. Gun Jakobsson who are essential members of our team.

Much valuable help was also provided by the staff of the Göteborg Autism Treatment Centre [Furuhöjd] and the Göteborg Special School for Psychotic Children at the University Clinic of Child and Youth Psychiatry. Jno Randall of the Neurosurgical Department of George Washington University School of Medicine has been an essential adjunct to this work. Thanks are also due to John Wahlström, M.D. and other staff members of the Department of Clinical Genetics, University of Göteborg.

We also wish to thank our colleagues who helped us with conceptualization and manuscript preparation such as Ann Barnet, M.D., Harry Gruber, M.D., E. Fuller Torrey, M.D., Sarah Broman, Ph.D., and Maya Pines, a specialist in writing on neurological topics.

Our work has been backed up by the board of the Children's Brain Research Clinic, Washington, D.C.: Bruce Ashkenas, Jeanne Beekhuis, David Carliner, Brenda Clemons, Ph.D., Judith Downey, Julia Franklin, Margaret Joan Giannini, M.D., George Keeler, M.D., Irving Levine, Robert Marcus, Eleanor Norton, Richard Pei, Ph.D., Winifred Portenoy, Blanche Prince, M.S.W., and Curtis Seltzer, Ph.D. We also wish to thank the Stallone Foundation and Mrs. Barbara Herzberg of the Norton L. Smith Trust. Mrs. John Logan and the committee chairpersons of the

Nostalgia Gala Ball also have made a major contribution to this work. The committee chairpersons are: Barbara Gordon, Susie Groth, Olga Garner, Nancy Hines, Ann Randall, Peg Zensinger, Suzy North, Gloria Lemos, Wayne Zeigler, Howard McElroy, Beverly Kligman, Ann Wallick, Louise Garcia, John Toole, Virginia Bennett, and Virginia Prange.

Other foundations contributing to the work of the Children's Brain Research Clinic include: the April Trust, the Max and Victoria Dreyfus Foundation, Inc., the Albert Beekhuis Foundation, Lucas-Spindletop Foundation, Wallace Genetic Foundation, Community Foundation of Greater Washington, Inc., John McShain Charities, Inc., Public Welfare Foundation, Carl Zimmerman Trust, Eugene and Agnes E. Meyer Foundation, Laird, Norton Foundation, Commodity Exchange Center Children's Fund, the Morris and Gwendolyn Cafritz Foundation, Government Employees Insurance Company, Hechinger Foundation, and Queene Ferry Coonley Foundation, Inc.

The poem by Malcolm Gorst is taken from Ruth Sullivan's "Parents Speak" column in the *Journal of Autism and Childhood Schizophrenia*, 1977, vol. 7, p. 398.

1   Introduction

In 1938, a small five-year-old boy from Mississippi was brought to Baltimore, Maryland to the Johns Hopkins University office of the child psychiatrist, Leo Kanner. According to Kanner:

> I was struck by the uniqueness of the peculiarities which Donald exhibited. He could, since the age of 2½ years, tell the names of all presidents and vice-presidents, recite the letters of the alphabet forwards and backwards, and flawlessly, with good enunciation, rattle off the Twenty-Third Psalm. Yet he was unable to carry on an ordinary conversation. He was out of contact with people, while he could handle objects skillfully. His memory was phenomenal. The few times when he addressed someone—largely to satisfy his wants—he referred to himself as 'You' and to the person as 'I'. He did not respond to any intelligence tests but manipulated intricate formboards adroitly.

In the course of the next few years, Kanner observed ten more children who displayed similar behavior patterns and noted that they had in common "extreme aloneness from the beginning of life and an anxiously obsessive desire for the preservation of sameness." He reported these 11 cases in a scientific journal in 1943 (Kanner 1943), introducing to the world medical literature this group of children he labeled, "autistic."

Once the syndrome was identified, several earlier accounts of children, probably autistic, were found (Darr and Warden 1951; Vaillant 1962; Wing 1976). Actually, strange, mysterious and enigmatic children have been part of our culture throughout history. Some of them were known as feral children, suckled and reared by wolves or other wild animals. In Roman history, Romulus and Remus were thought to have

1

been cast into the Tiber River and somehow retrieved and reared by wolves until they could rejoin the human community in order to found Rome.

These legends are not confined to ancient history; such children have been a source of group fantasy in more recent centuries also. Victor, the wild boy of Aveyron, was first seen in 1797 running through the woods in the region of Lacaune, in south central France. He was captured, escaped twice, and recaptured when he was approximately 12 years old. The French physician, Jean Marc Gaspard Itard, devoted five years to teaching Victor, but eventually gave up his experiment (Lane 1976). The story of Victor has so caught our imaginations that it is the subject of many books and has been made into a movie.

The twentieth century has also had its feral children. The Reverend J.A.L. Singh discovered Kamala and her sister Amala, in 1929 in Midnapore, India. In this parish in India, the natives had been terrified by strange happenings and ghosts, and the Rev. Singh found that there were two wild children in the area. He reported that the children were reared by wolves and found in a wolves' den. Dr. Gesell of Yale University studied the reports on these children and in "what now appears like a jarring suspension of rationality" (Schopler 1976) reconstructed, from his imagination, how the well-known Gesell norms manifested themselves in the wolves' den (Gesell 1941). He described Kamala's successful adjustment to the wolves' den, an adjustment which had admittedly been constructed purely from his imagination.

The Rev. Mr. Singh's diary of Kamala also interested the psychologist, Dr. Bruno Bettelheim (1959). Bettelheim suggested that Kamala was not raised by wolves at all, but that she, like other feral children, behaved very much like autistic children in his school. However, just as Gesell had done before him, he used the tools of his discipline to project fantasy medical history on Kamala. He argued that the so-called feral children were actually autistic children who had been neglected and emotionally deprived by their mothers. Without having any medical history to rely on regarding Kamala and her sister, he concluded that there were no feral children, only feral mothers.

According to Schopler (1973), Kamala's place in the history of autism is significant, not because of the theories widely-published experts claimed about her and her origin, but because of the myths that have evolved from these same theories, resulting in confused and misguided implications for the treatment of autistic children.

In a story published by the Russian author Gorky in 1912, there is a description of a boy who meets many autistic criteria. In this story, Gorky has the child fathered by a monk, and makes the child an attractive, enigmatic individual in spite of his mental deficiency. Thus, Gorky is describing the time-honored notion that mentally deficient children may have a "peculiarly close relationship to the almighty" (Gorky 1964).

In every culture, people as a group project their feelings onto unusual members of the group and target them for inappropriate fantasies and myths. This has been true, particularly, of mentally handicapped children of all kinds, perhaps especially autistic children with their complex and unusual behavior patterns. These cultural projections are not limited to the uninformed and poorly educated; the written history of autistic children and their parents is replete with examples of inappropriate interpretations. It is the purpose of this monograph to examine what hard data exist regarding these children so that the medical profession can move forward with appropriate diagnosis, treatment and care of these children. They are not mystical, superhuman, subhuman, legendary, mysterious, occult individuals in possession of non-human traits. They are simply children who are in trouble because their brains are not functioning as they should.

Since the syndrome was defined by Kanner in 1943, there have been a number of areas of major disagreements regarding this patient population. One is how the diagnosis is arrived at and which children are included or excluded from the term "autistic." Differing points of view on diagnosis are reviewed in the next chapter and a working solution is suggested by the authors of this monograph. In this chapter, the controversies regarding the multitude of etiologies proposed as responsible for the symptoms in this patient group will be reviewed and discussed.

CONTROVERSIES ABOUT THE ETIOLOGY OF THE AUTISTIC SYNDROME

Kanner, who introduced the syndrome of autism, was a child psychiatrist deeply involved in the controversies in his field at the time. In the 1920s, theories of the parental causes of mental illness were being developed. Fromm-Reichmann's theory about schizophrenogenic mothers and Levy's theory about overprotective mothers are just two examples from that period. According to Victor (1983), Kanner, like many mental health professionals, was drawn into the conflict. His participation was said to be intense and he fought on both sides, foreshadowing the controversy about the role of parents of autistic children that was to follow. In 1941, during the period leading up to the publication of his paper on autism, Kanner published an article about mothers' destructiveness (Kanner, 1941a). In the same year, he published *In Defense of Mothers*, a book in which he sought to relieve mothers of guilt in relation to their children (Kanner, 1941b). This ambivalence toward mothers continued after he introduced the concept of autism.

In 1949, Kanner wrote:

> The vast majority of the parents of autistic children have features in common which it would be impossible to disregard.... Most of the parents declare outright that they are not comfortable in the company of people.... They are polite and dignified people who are impressed by seriousness and disdainful of anything that smacks of frivolity. (Kanner 1949)

He also described them as perfectionists, and as obsessive, humorless individuals who used set rules as substitutes for life's enjoyment. His most extreme statement was made to *Time* magazine, a popular magazine, available to friends, families and neighbors of autistic children. In this magazine, he reported "that children with early infantile autism were the offspring of highly organized, professional parents, cold and rational, who just happened to defrost long enough to produce a child" (*Time*, July 25, 1960). This was his view of the "refrigerator" type of parent about whom he had been lecturing.

During this period, Kanner criticized the blindness of colleagues (such as Van Krevelen [1952] and Benda and Melchior [1959]) who looked for physiological causes of autism rather than noting parental behavior. He found the evidence for parental causes over physiological causes to be "so obvious as to force itself on... an open-eyed observer" (Kanner 1948). Kanner also wrote that the condition usually could not be remedied because the parents sabotaged treatment. Therefore, unless the mothers could be helped by psychotherapy, the only hope for most autistic children lay in removal from the home and placement with foster mothers (Kanner 1952).

Yet this is the same Kanner who said:

Herewith I especially acquit you people as parents. I have been misquoted many times. From the very first publication to the last, I spoke of this condition in no uncertain terms as innate. (Kanner 1972)

Kanner was ambivalent about the etiology of autism, and here he was not alone.

Since his time there have been a great many etiological theories developed, mostly psychodynamic, which assume that the infant was normal at birth and attribute its development of symptoms to poor nurturing, particularly poor mothering (as reviewed by Hingtgen and Bryson 1972). Many additional theories have been developed by Fraknoi and Ruttenberg (1971); Williams and Harper (1973); Szurek (1973); Ekstein and Friedman (1974); King (1975); Massie (1978); and Victor (1983). These various theories have postulated that the parents of autistic children were deficient either in touching, in feeding practices, in speech practices and/or in eye-to-eye contact with the child, or were thought to project dehumanizing fantasies onto their infant. They were viewed as extreme personality types: either very depressed, or cold, or full of rage, or without a sense of self, or actually psychopathic (as reviewed by DeMyer et al. 1981).

In addition to the poor nurturing theories as a sole etiological factor, DeMyer points out that there are also two varieties of a combined nature-nurture theory of autism. In one version, autistic infants were seen as biologically deficient and the parents viewed as failing to give proper emotional support to the vulnerable infant. In another version, some infants were viewed as organically damaged and others as biologically normal. In this latter version, the parents of the "non-organic" infants were described as failing to a greater degree than the parents of "organic" infants. Examples in recent years of these theories are those developed by Despert (1971); O'Moore (1972); Miller (1974); Tinbergen and Tinbergen (1976).

One of the first authors to speak up prominently suggesting that the parents themselves may not be at fault and that there may be some other etiology to autistic symptoms was Rimland, a parent/professional who wrote the book *Infantile Autism: The Syndrome and Its Implications for a Neural Theory of Behavior* in 1964. Since then, in an attempt to address the large literature on parent deficits in child rearing, several investigators began studying parents of autistic children and comparing them to other control groups, using established scientific methodologies of obtaining data. Cox et al. (1975) investigated early stressful events and parental warmth, responsiveness and sociability in parents of autistic children compared to a matched group of parents of dysphasic children. (Dysphasic children have a delayed, usually aberrant, acquisition of language, but are not handicapped in any other major area of functioning.) The two parent groups did not differ in interpersonal relationships or ratings of emotional warmth and sociability, except that parents of autistic children spent more time with friends than parents of dysphasic children. This study suggested that parents of autistic children may be more, rather than less, sociable. Goldfarb et al. (1976) also failed to demonstrate parent group differences in psychopathology and functioning. McAdoo and DeMyer (1978a) decided to study the parents of autistic children who had an organic diagnosis versus the parents of children who did not have an organic diagnosis. They used as a tool the Minnesota Multiphasic Personality Inventories (MMPIs) and found no difference between the two parent groups.

A study of infant care practices was also done comparing the parents of autistic children and a carefully matched group of parents of normal children. In this study there was no difference in infant acceptance, warmth, nurturing, feeding and tactile or general stimulation (DeMyer et al. 1972). Using the Ferreira and Winter unrevealed differences task, Byassee and Murrell (1975) found similar family interactions in both normal families and families with an autistic child. Cantwell et al. (1978) compared families with autistic and dysphasic children and reported they were similar in quality and intensity, except that the autistic children received greater interaction. Using the Ittleson Center Scales, the authors found group similarities in spontaneity, decisiveness, anticipation, control, and meeting children's demands. Of interest because of earlier speculation regarding the use of language by the mothers of autistic children, the study by Cantwell et al. (1978) found the same linguistic clarity, complexity and grammaticality in the speech of the mothers. Other studies have also yielded no evidence that the speech of parents had any detrimental effect on their children (Frank et al. 1976; Cantwell and Baker 1978).

However, there were two studies which showed different results. Goldfarb et al. (1973) compared mothers of schizophrenics/autistics with mothers of normal controls and described them as inferior in labeling and describing objects. King (1975), using a rating system on chart descriptions, compared the mothers of autistics and controls and reported more "double bind" interactions in the mothers of autistics.

This entire literature on parents was reviewed in 1978 by McAdoo and DeMyer, and they concluded that, as a group, parents of autistic children: 1) display no more signs of mental or emotional illness than parents whose children have "organic" disorders, with or without psychosis; 2) do not have extreme personality traits such as coldness, obsessiveness, social anxiety or rage; and 3) do not possess specific deficits in infant and child care (McAdoo and DeMyer 1978b).

DeMyer (1979) also wrote a sensitive piece acknowledging the difficulties of rearing an autistic child.

Although autistic children are some of the most difficult children to assess and evaluate, several studies have shown that parents can be trusted in the information they provide about their child (Schopler and Reichler 1972; Wing and Gould 1978). Schopler and Reichler (1972) point out:

> Professionals, however, because of their distrust of parental judgment, frequently superficially reassure, or even worse, humiliate parents by labeling them overconcerned and overanxious, or blame the child's problems on parental management. Such criticism without appropriate evaluation and specific instructions in improved management can... leave parents on their own to cope with extremely difficult developmental problems, discouraging their seeking of further help, and harmfully delaying appropriate interventions.

To this day there are several myths in the field which tend to suggest that environmental factors cause autism. One is the myth that autistic children are from the upper social classes.

Kanner himself long believed that autism was a disease of the upper social classes (Kanner 1943, 1949). When Lotter (1966) published the first epidemiological study of autism and found a small, but statistically significant, excess of parents from the highest social classes, this single result was at once incorporated into the Kanner theory as unequivocal proof. There are, however, several reasons why the social class theory cannot be regarded as proven or even plausible. First of all, Lotter's finding really was that the majority of autistic children do *not* belong to upper and upper-middle class families. Second, the calculated statistically significant difference rested on the shaky basis of a single child! If one autistic child had belonged to social class III instead of II the difference with regard to expected frequency would not be statistically significant. Third, Schopler has provided evidence (1979) for a social class *referral* bias in studies of autism. Fourth and most importantly, there are at least six other epidemiological studies of autism (Brask 1970; Ritvo et al. 1971b; Wing 1980a; Gillberg and Schaumann 1982; Bohman 1981; Anderson and Wadensjo 1981) and all have shown autism to be almost equally distributed over social strata. Thus, one can only conclude that the bulk of the data suggests beyond any reasonable doubt that autism is *not* associated with social class. The few authorities who still maintain that autism is correlated with high social class rely on the Lotter study and clinically referred samples for their argument, and do so in the face of a host of epidemiological data and other clinically referred samples not indicating a social class bias.

Another myth is the "first or only child" theory. Several authors have reported an excess of first born children in autistic samples (Despert 1951, Kanner 1954, Rimland 1965, Deykin and MacMahon 1980, Pitfield and Oppenheim 1964). This has been taken by some as firm evidence for psychogenetic theories. Two considerations are of major importance in this connection: (a) there is no study suggesting that *a majority* of autistic children are first-born, and (b) there are several epidemiological studies that have not come up with results in support of the "first-born notion" (Lotter 1966; Wing 1980a; Gillberg 1984a). One study (Tsai and Stewart 1983) has suggested an increase among first and fourth or later-born children. This would be in line with biological hypotheses as both first and fourth or later-born children children are more at risk for pre- and perinatal hazards than second or third-born children. However, the results in this field are equivocal to say the least and cannot serve as a basis for any firm argument.

The notion that a number of autistic children are only children in a disproportionately large number of cases has no scientific support that we are aware of. However, should this prove to be the case in a comparative study, the explanation that immediately presents itself is that the massive handicaps of the child may cause the parents to refrain from trying to have more children, as has been confirmed by a number of parents.

More recently, the attempt to prove that autism does not have an organic basis has shifted. In 1981, a paper was written stating that the theory that autism is of organic origin is inconsistent with a review of the literature of the frequency of autism among Italian, Chinese, Hispanic, African and Israeli children (Sanua 1981). This author postulates that because of the family network available to various nationality groups and because of the isolation of mothers in nuclear families in the West, autism is seen more frequently in the West. The author suggests that the

Western family pattern prevents parental surrogates from compensating for the deficiencies of parents. However, this paper has several major weaknesses. For example, in the Israeli study, he quotes Kauffman (1972), who points out that he could identify eight out of 3,000 children as suffering from early childhood psychosis with autistic features. He didn't want to count them as autistic if they had seizures, an inappropriate assumption (see chapter 4). Since the incidence of autism elsewhere is somewhere around four to five per 10,000, what is being reported in this one paper is a much higher frequency than usual (25 per 10,000). However, we don't know what the incidence actually is, since no sound epidemiological studies are available from those countries. And, even if there were fewer cases of autism among Italian, Chinese, Hispanic, African and Israeli children, it still would not disprove an organic etiology, since the prevalence of organic diseases can vary in different groups. And example is phenylketonuria (PKU), an established etiology of the autistic syndrome (see chapter 16), which is found more frequently in people of European extraction than of African extraction (Therrell et al. 1983). Gillberg (1984d) has recently suggested that divergent findings in epidemiology in autism might be due, not only to different diagnostic criteria, but also to different etiologies in different parts of the globe.

This present monograph is a review of the known information regarding the organic etiology of the autistic syndrome. If we assume for the moment that the organic explanation appears to be the most reasonable explanation of the disease process in autistic children, the question then arises: Why do highly intelligent, well-educated professionals continue to espouse the psychogenic theory of autism?

Several possible answers come to mind. The first is that the authority figure who first defined the syndrome—Kanner—himself wrote a number of medical papers suggesting that the parents were a major factor in their child's disability. As the innovative psychiatrist who established the syndrome and brought it to the attention of the world, his point of view would tend to be taken most seriously.

Secondly, perhaps the most compelling reason why the psychogenic/nurture/environmental theory of autism persisted was that some reasonable parallels were drawn between autistic children and the animal experimental literature. As summed up by Harlow and McKinney (1971), the theoretical linkages between abnormal behavior in Rhesus monkeys and human beings were elucidated by experiments with monkeys producing two prime behaviors: total social isolation; and disruption of affectionate bonds between mothers and infants, or between peers. Harlow et al. (1955) were able to produce a syndrome in Rhesus monkeys that somewhat resembled the autistic syndrome by rearing infant monkeys from birth in a total isolation chamber where they had no contact with other monkeys or humans. The technique was effective in producing severe and long-lasting problems in monkeys, so that when they were removed from the chambers they spent most of their time huddled alone in a corner, rocking, self-clasping and refusing to enter into play or other normal social encounters with their peers. Some of them had self-abusive behaviors. It is not unreasonable to apply to children who share many of the characteristics of these monkeys the findings of the experiments.

For those who espouse an organic cause of autism, such a striking parallel in animal experiments and human behavior must be explained. The answer probably lies in a similar lack of sensory input whether of an exogenous and endogenous nature at an early developmental state. If a small infant is in a normal environment, but has an endogenous central nervous system impairment in the ability to process incoming sensory stimuli, the same effect might be achieved. Emotional nourishment, such as being hugged and kissed by a parent, is processed through the tactile sensory system, a system often impaired in autistic children who have tactile defensiveness. An infant's joy of visually exploring a mother's face depends upon a totally functional visual system, not a system relegated to avoidance of eye contact and fleeting glances. The pleasure of the parent's words and songs comes through the auditory processing system, a system so often impaired in autistic children that is has even been considered as a primary cause of autistic symptoms (Churchill, 1978).

But the autistic baby is not able to benefit from his environment and often is unable to send feedback messages through meaningful glances and smiles to his parents to further parent/child interaction. The nurturing environmental stimuli, just as essential for the organizational growth of a human brain as food is for the physical growth of the human body, are improperly processed by these children, thereby depriving them of much of the emotional and cognitive nutrients that they need in the first years of life.

A few individuals, who suffered from autism as children, as adults have been able to discuss their earlier experiences. The word common to all these accounts is "confusion": as one boy put it "I did not know what was wanted from me."

THE GOALS OF THIS MONOGRAPH

This monograph grew out of fifteen years' work with autistic children on the part of one of the authors (M.C.), and is a natural development from our earlier research monograph, *The Autistic Syndromes* (1976). In that volume, we described an extensive study of 78 autistic children and 78 age- and sex-matched controls performed in one week of 1974. So much new data came out of that study that ten years later we are still trying to sort out the meaning of many of the findings. Recently when suggestions were made to reprint that study, it seemed better to update rather than just to reprint it. Within the context of ten years' perspective, it became clear that a monograph which reviewed *all* the organic studies available on autistic children might be the most useful publication at this time. A great many important studies by other research centers have greatly enriched our understanding of these children, and a review that looked at all sound data available made the most sense.

The second author's (C.G.) interest in autistic children dates back to 1974 when he first became clinically involved with such patients. Three years later, he started a large-scale research project on autism in Sweden where psychogenic theories were prevailing at the time. The findings from his studies indicated organic dysfunction in autism. He had long encountered difficulty in trying to persuade the followers of the psychogenic "tradition" that autism might be a primary handicap in the child and not in the parents. In discussions with the first author, it soon became clear that the interest in the biological aspects of autism was mutual and that a book outlining current knowledge it this field was highly warranted.

This book attempts to review extensively all medical studies performed on autistic children to date. Because of diagnostic confusion in many older studies, it has not always been possible to sort out exactly who was being studied or if every child would meet our current definition of having an autistic syndrome. We did the best we could regarding this problem.

This book has few final answers. Many patients with an autistic syndrome do not yet have a well-defined disease entity. There are more research questions than final medical answers.

The goals of this book are severalfold. One is to review the known evidence that links autism with an organic problem in the central nervous system. A second is to examine comprehensively the known specific disease entities found in a subgroup of children with autistic symptoms. Also, we shall explore the medical literature regarding biochemical subgroups within the syndrome. We will recommend areas where every autistic child should have medical testing as part of an overall evaluation. We feel that every such child is entitled to a state-of-the-art medical evaluation in case either a specific or non-specific medical therapy might be selected for that individual autistic child based on his or her individual medical test results. And finally, by summarizing currently available studies in the areas of neurophysiology, neuroradiology, biochemistry, neuropharmacology and neuropathology, we hope to pinpoint limitations, suggest some relevant new questions, and stimulate further research in these areas.

Part I

Clinical Considerations

2

Clinical Diagnosis

Let it be spelled out at once: autism is not a single disease entity in the sense that, for instance, phenylketonuria is. Rather, the concept of infantile autism represents a comprehensive diagnosis, somewhat along the same lines as cerebral palsy or epilepsy. Many articles and books have already been written under the impression that infantile autism will eventually turn out to be a disorder with one single etiology, be it psychogenic or biological. There is now overwhelming evidence that the behavioral syndrome of autism represents the final (common?) expression of various etiological factors. And even within a purely behavioral/phenomenological framework of autism, one is struck by the complexity of the symptomatology and the difficulty in fitting all individual cases into one operational diagnostic model. Hence the title of this book: "The Biology of the Autistic Syndromes."

The term autism was coined by Bleuler (1911) to designate a category of the thought disorder that is present in schizophrenic syndromes. When Kanner (1943) described infantile autism (or rather autistic disturbances of affective contact in young children), he used the term differently, although with a special reference to schizophrenia which he at first thought was related to infantile autism, but later tried to distinguish clearly from the "Kanner syndrome." The use of the word autism in connection with this latter syndrome is somewhat misleading, implying as it does a (possibly non-existent) link with schizophrenia and also that the "extreme aloneness" (synonymous with "autism" according to Kanner) is at the etiological root, as it were, of the syndrome. In later years, some authors have, rather rhetorically, argued for the use of terms other than autism, but without much success. Autism, and inflectional forms of that word, will probably be used as a descriptive term for years to come in connection with children and adults who at one time in their life showed the marks of the "Kanner syndrome."

Kanner's very first description of autistic children in a scientific journal was accurate enough, and even though substantial progress has been made since 1943 as regards the pathogenesis of the autistic syndromes, no later study has given a more vivid or clearer presentation of them. Certainly, some development in diagnostic criteria has been made since then, most notably by Kanner himself together with Leon Eisenberg (1956), but also by Creak (1963, 1964); Ornitz (1971); Rutter et al. (1969); Rutter (1971, 1972a, 1978a); the Diagnostic and Statistical Manual of Mental Disorders (DSM-III 1980); Wing (1978, 1980b) and Tanguay (1984), but for a classic presentation of a typically autistic child one is well advised to study Kanner's first case in the 1943 paper.

THE AUTISTIC PERSON

The autistic syndromes (Coleman 1976) are variously referred to as childhood autism (Wing 1980b), infantile autism (Rutter 1978b) and childhood psychosis (Fish and Ritvo 1979). Of these latter categories infantile autism is the concept that has received the most attention and about which there is at least some consensus with regard to diagnostic criteria. However, several of the criteria considered necessary for this diagnosis are universally accepted also as the crucial features of childhood psychosis. In many quarters the label of childhood psychosis is considered a comprehensive diagnostic term, and infantile autism constitutes one of the subgroups. Some have argued for the abolition of the term "psychosis" in connection with the autistic syndromes and suggested the substitution of "developmental disorder." The move away from the schizophrenia/psychosis branch was clearly evidenced in the late 1970s when the leading scientific journal in the area changed its name from the *Journal of Autism and Childhood Schizophrenia* to the *Journal of Autism and Developmental Disorders.*

The criteria for infantile autism currently agreed upon by most authorities are:

1. early onset

2. severe disturbance of social relatedness

3. severe abnormalities of language development

4. elaborate repetitive routines

These four criteria account well with those set out by Rutter (1978) and the DSM-III (1980).

Many American authors (e.g. Coleman 1976; Ornitz 1983) would demand that a fifth criterion be met for a definite diagnosis to be made; namely, *abnormal perceptual responses to sensory stimuli*.

All these criteria need further elaboration. At first, however, before discussing specific criteria, we need to be aware that a majority of autistic children are also mentally retarded. We need to bear this in mind in order that distinctions between autistic and mental retardation "symptoms" are kept clear, whenever possible. A small minority of autistic children function in the normal IQ range. The behavior patterns unique to autism are often most clearly evident in such children.

Early Onset

With regard to the age of debut, most clinicians and researchers agree that the behavioral disorder must have begun prior to the age of 30 months (DSM-III 1980; Rutter 1978a). However, some would require an onset before the child's first birthday and others (e.g. Lotter 1966; Wing and Gould 1979) would allow the appearance of first symptoms to be delayed until the child's fifth birthday. Some authors have gone further still (e.g. Bohman et al. 1981) and have accepted cases with a debut up to the age of seven. Nevertheless, the age limit of two-and-a-half is widely accepted (Rutter 1978a). Evans-Jones and Rosenbloom (1978), while arguing that disintegrative psychosis forms a diagnostic category separate from autism, maintain that sometimes the psychotic symptoms typical of autism may begin before two-and-a-half years of age, and yet not qualify the child for a diagnosis of autism but rather for disintegrative psychosis (see the section on differential diagnosis). Even though the criterion of early onset rarely causes much dispute in controversies over diagnostic symptoms in autism, the description by DeLong and others (DeLong et al. 1981; Gillberg 1985) of typically autistic syndromes beginning in hitherto quite normal children between the ages of four and 14 years (in connection with herpes encephalitis) shows clearly that the matter cannot be regarded as settled.

In the great majority of cases with autistic syndromes, however, onset is quite clearly within the first few months of life. Wing (1982) has suggested that "infantile autism" is congenital in approximately 80 percent of the cases. In the remaining 20 percent there is either too scanty anamnestic evidence to form an opinion, or there are definite clues that the typical behavioral symptoms began sometime between the age of six and 20 months. Only rarely are there cases that commence around age 30 months.

Disturbance of Social Relatedness

The disturbance of social relatedness—as all other symptoms—has to be out of proportion in comparison with the often concomitant mental retardation. The central features of this disturbance seem to be a lack of reciprocity in social interaction with other humans and a failure to recognize the uniqueness and "specialness" of other human beings (Wing 1980b; Rutter 1983). Some children during the first two years of life (and, to a lesser extent, later also) display, in Kanner's words (1943), an extreme autistic aloneness. Others are described as "easy so long as they're left to themselves in their bed or in their room." Still others are "difficult," "terrible," or scream at all hours and need little sleep. Imitation and imitation play are deficient or lacking. Feeding problems and sucking difficulties are very common (Wing 1980b).

The typically autistic child avoids eye contact from before the end of the first year of life (Mirenda et al. 1983), gazes out of the corner of the eye and gazes only very briefly, does not show anticipatory movements when about to be picked up, resists being held or touched, and does not "adjust" himself to "fit" in a hug or something similar. Autistic infants often seem to lack initiative, and the interested curiosity and exploratory behavior seen in normal babies is often completely lacking.

Frequent responses include: "he was so happy if we left him all to himself, but started to scream as soon as someone picked him up"; "he was so stiff to hold"; or "I don't know what it was, but he just wasn't 'there'." There is an impression that humans, animals, and soft and hard objects are treated alike. There is some empirical evidence (Hobson 1982) that this may be one of the crucial dysfunctions in autism, at least after some years of development. Human beings are often treated by the child as if they were technical tools, there only for the benefit of the child to reach certain objects in the surroundings (exemplified by the child who leads his mother's hand, not by the hand but by the wrist, to his spoon, and then directs the spoon via his mother's hand/wrist to his own mouth). The autistic child does not usually come to his parents, brothers or sisters—or anybody else, for that matter—for help or comfort.

However, not all autistic children show these typical features and, to be sure, even in those who do, there is often a gradual decrease in the severity of the symptoms.

Typical of all in the early pre-school years is a failure to develop normal relationships with peers. This inability usually persists throughout childhood, youth and often into adult life.

As the child grows older, the abnormalities of social relatedness become less immediately obvious, particularly if the child is seen in his familiar surroundings. The resistance to being touched and held usually decreases with age, even though rough and tumble play is often preferred to gentle stroking. The gaze avoidance behavior may decrease. Some authors (Rutter 1978a; Mirenda et al. 1983) hold that it is not the amount of gaze contact which is abnormal in autism, but rather that—at least after the infant period—there is a qualitative difference, the gaze of autists being stiffer and lasting longer on an individual basis. Symptoms pertaining to the avoidance of visual or physical contact are often classified in the category of social abnormalities. However, several authors (e.g. Wing 1980b) would argue that these abnormalities are best dealt with in the context of abnormal sensory responses. Be that as it may, the result of the changes in the autistic child in these respects is that the child becomes somewhat more cooperative and easy to *relate to*. Unfortunately, the inability to play reciprocally with age peers remains sadly unchanged throughout the years in most cases, though this characteristic may not be as conspicuously apparent in the autistic latency age child as it was in that same child during the pre-school years.

In some cases and at some stages of development the disturbance of social relatedness takes on the form of a lack of selectivity and distance. However, even in autistic children with seemingly attention-seeking, distance-lacking behavior, the inability to reciprocate and the failure to treat humans as anything but objects are clearly evident. These hallmarks differentiate them from superficially similar behavior seen in emotionally deprived children.

Abnormalities of Language Development

Usually from a very early age, the autistic child shows major problems in the comprehension of human mime, gesture, and speech. Social imitation is lacking or deficient, and common early imitation play such as waving bye-bye or doing pat-a-cake is not elicitable. Some

(though by no means all) do not babble and some yield strange monot-
onous sounds instead of the varied babble patterns heard in normal
children.

It is often mentioned that abnormal babbling is a crucial symptom
of abnormal language development in autism. Actually there is no
sound scientific evidence to uphold such a view and many autistic
children have indeed babbled in what appears to be a normal fashion. In
fact, babbling and language development may be discrete functions, not
as intrinsically interwoven as hitherto believed (Zetterström 1983).

Almost without exception, autistic children are delayed in their
development of spoken language. This delay runs parallel with an
impairment in the understanding of language, which may vary from an
almost total lack of comprehension to more subtle deviances leading to
concrete interpretation. An example of this kind of concrete interpretation is provided by the 10-year-old speaking autistic girl (full scale
WISC IQ 100) who showed catastrophic anxiety when the nurse, about
to do a simple blood test said "Give me your hand; it won't hurt." The
girl calmed down immediately when another person said: "Stretch out
your index finger." She had understood, at the first instruction, that she
was to cut off her hand and give it to the nurse!

Many autistic children learn to follow simple instructions if given
in a particular social context, but appear to fail to grasp the meaning of
these instructions when given out of that context. Quite unlike deaf
children, autistic children make little, if any, use of mime or gesture.
Often they totally misinterpret human facial expressions and begin to
laugh when somebody cries or vice versa.

Approximately one out of every two autistic children fails to
develop useful spoken language. Almost all of these are mentally retarded.
Of those who do develop speech, all show major abnormalities of
speech development, such as sustained phases of seemingly noncommunicative delayed and/or immediate echolalia (present only during
short phases and integrated with the development of communicative
speech in normal children), avoidance of personal pronouns, sustained
pronominal reversal, usually with the substitution of "you," "he" or
the first name for "I," but also with confusion over the use of other
pronouns (thought to be a consequence of the echolalia), and repetitive
speech without talking *with* so much as *to* someone.

Some talking autistic children have a very good root memory and
can repeat whole conversations word by word. However, these same
children may have great difficulties or may not be at all able to extract

meaning from sentences based upon the order and meaning of the words (Hermelin and O'Connor 1970).

Many non-speaking autistic children may be able to imitate and sing songs with baffling accuracy and some may even know the words of the song without being able to repeat any of them without singing.

Relatively brighter autistic children may have some spontaneous speech. But rarely, if ever, do they communicate to others about their feelings and needs. They may, however, hold lengthy and detailed disquisitions on the subject of a given concrete experience, such as a dinner, or travelling on a bus, but will usually be unable to answer even simple questions about this same topic, in spite of having no difficulty at all "recreating," as it were, the whole journey from start to finish in his own very concrete, descriptive words.

There are often grammatical immaturities consistent with the overall developmental level of the child's speech (Bartak et al. 1975).

Typically there are peculiarities in respect to vocal volume and pitch, often with a tendency to use staccato-like or scanning speech. Problems of pronunciation arise when using spontaneous, but not echo, phrases (Wing 1966; Howlin 1982).

Elaborate Repetitive Routines

Autistic children often form bizarre attachments to certain objects, such as stones, curls of hair, pins, pieces of plastic toys, or metals. These objects are selected because of some particular quality (color, surface-texture) and are carried around by the child, who becomes frantic if anybody tries to remove them. Others line up toys or household equipment for hours on end. Round and spinning objects, such as wheels of toy cars, coins, gramophone records and tape recorders almost always hold a distinct fascination for autistic children. A majority of autistic children demand that certain routines be adhered to in a pathologically rigid fashion. One six-year-old autistic boy regularly demanded his mother to put the frying pan on the stove and to heat some butter in it, after which he would have cereal, tea and sandwiches, or ham and eggs. This "show," as it were, had to be put on every morning or he would scream for hours, refusing to eat altogether. Another autistic boy of seven would eat only if one leg of the father's chair was one inch away from one of the legs of the dinner table and his mother had one elbow on the table. An autistic girl of four would scream in rage if her mother did not always walk on the same pavement on her way to the post office. This phenomenon is sometimes referred to as "insistence on sameness."

It is often impossible to predict what environmental changes will cause the emotional outbursts. On the whole, it appears that minor changes tend to be more upsetting and to cause more severe temper tantrums than do major changes. For instance, a five-year-old autistic boy cried desperately for almost an hour until his mother realized that she had removed a book from one of the many shelves of the bookcase. When she put it back, he stopped crying within seconds. This boy, who was considered by his parents and professionals as unable to cope with even the smallest kind of environmental change, accepted going abroad or moving house without any outward reaction at all.

The "insistence on sameness" may also affect the verbal skills of the child, limiting superficially excellent language resources to the stereotyped repetition of certain questions with demands for standard answers.

Especially during the school years and after, some often relatively brighter autistic persons show unusual preoccupations, with, for example, weather reports, birthdays, or train schedules.

Various other ritualistic and compulsive phenomena are common. Some authors include less complex stereotyped behavior—such as simple stereotypies or toe-walking—among the elaborate repetitive routines. Even though some stereotypies, especially hand-flapping with flexion of the elbows and extremely "high" tip-toeing, appear to be rather typical of autism, most authors do not include these kinds of stereotyped behavior as *necessary* criteria for a diagnosis of autism.

Abnormal Perceptual Response to Sensory Stimuli

Perhaps the most characteristic abnormal perceptual response encountered in autistic children is that associated with sound stimuli. The child who acts deaf and does not react at all when an explosion is suddenly heard near by may moments later turn at the sound of paper being removed from a chocolate. Many autistic children cover their ears to shut out even "ordinary" noise levels. There may also be strange reactions, such as the covering of the ears or the eyes at a special sound.

Reduced or abnormal sensitivity to pain is also often encountered in autism. The classic example is that of an autistic boy who seemingly derives pleasure by biting the back of his hand. Many autistic children withdraw or squeal if touched or stroked lightly, but enjoy being handled roughly. Other kinds of tactile stimuli may give pleasure to a child who can stand for half-hours just feeling and scratching differently textured surfaces.

Abnormal responses to visual stimuli are probably present in a large majority of young autistic children who often give the impression of having difficulty in recognizing the things they see. People may ask the parents if the child is blind; in fact, every now and then autism is mistaken for blindness. The peculiarities of gaze reported in the section on abnormalities of social relationships could also be taken as evidence of abnormal perceptual responses (see Figure 2.1).

Autistic children often want to smell people and objects. This is a characteristic not usually displayed in normal development or in mental retardation.

By and large, clinical experience suggests that perceptions relating to auditory and tactile stimuli are more impaired in autistic children than are perceptions of visual and especially olfactory stimuli. The two latter functions make their first intracranial nerve connections at a much higher level in the nervous system than the two former. A preference for proximal stimuli has also been experimentally evinced in autism (Hermelin and O'Connor 1970). Masterton and Biederman (1983) have argued that proprioceptive input dominates over visual input in autistic children. They see this dominance as the effect of an alternative strategy to compensate for a lack of visual control over fine motor performance. In this context it is of some interest that certain autistic children, who otherwise yield good gaze contact, can talk coherently only when avoiding gaze contact.

Abnormal sensory responses are by many (e.g., most U.S. authorities and Wing 1980b) regarded as "primary" in autism and should in their view therefore be included among the diagnostic criteria. Oddly, neither the DSM-III (1980), nor Michael Rutter (1978a), whose criteria are currently most widely used internationally, attribute any special importance to these problems. However, Rutter (1978a, 1983), to be sure, does make mention of the "undue sensitivity to sound" which he found distinguished autistic from dysphasic children.

We would submit, therefore, on the available evidence (e.g., a Swedish total population study of autism in which the Rutter criteria were used and in which *all* children diagnosed as autistic in accordance with these criteria were found actually to be abnormal in their response

FIGURE 2.1. A seven-year-old autistic boy staring with fascination at his shadow, one of the many visual preoccupations of these children.

to auditory stimuli [Gillberg and Wahlström 1984]), that the criterion of abnormal sensory responses should be considered one of the five essentials for a diagnosis of infantile autism.

Other Common but Not Pathognomonic Symptoms

Hyperactivity is a very common symptom especially in young autistic children. Sleep problems are most often apparent in infancy, when the child may keep the whole family awake by crying, but may sometimes continue right through to adulthood. Many autistic children are awake for long periods each night. An almost total lack of initiative is a dominating problem in certain autistic children.

Food fads are the rule rather than the exception. Many autistic children have great problems chewing. Hard objects are sometimes orally preferred to soft ones. There are many other symptoms often or occasionally encountered in autism but which are not pathognomonic.

The self-destructiveness (head banging, wrist biting, chin knocking, cheek smashing, clawing, hair tearing, etc.) seen in many autistic children has been proposed as concomitant to the mental retardation, but in fact could not be, since such behavior is often seen even in normally intelligent autistic children.

Cognitive Profile in Autism

Most autistic children are mentally retarded. However, it appears that there are certain characteristics in the cognitive patterns of a majority of autistic children that differentiate them from non-autistic mentally retarded children. First, it is well established (e.g., Shah and Frith 1983) that some autistic children, though not all, show "islets of special abilities," particularly in the fields of root memory (e.g. numerical skills), music, art, and visuospatial skills (or skill with jig-saw puzzles). Second, they seem to have an impaired memory for recent events (Boucher 1981). Third, they perform better than mental-age-matched retarded and normal children in respect to "concrete" discrimination. However, tasks requiring "formal" discrimination are more difficult for the autistic child (Maltz 1981). Their concrete way of interpreting and solving problems is often evident throughout life, even in those few with relatively high intellectual functioning. It is the unusual cognitive profile of autistic children that has given rise to the wide-spread speculation that they are indeed of superior intelligence, and just hiding their phenomenal capacity behind a shell of autism. Unfortunately, a large body of research is agreed that this view is mistaken and that most autistic children, even those showing almost unbelievable splinter skills, are clearly mentally retarded. All have cognitive problems (Rutter 1983).

Summary of Clinical, Diagnostic Criteria

There are many children with two or three of the four criteria proposed by Rutter for diagnosing autism. What term do we apply to them? Are they "autistic," "autistic-like," "children with autistic features"? The matter can hardly be regarded as settled.

At the present stage we would argue for an umbrella definition, namely that of "the autistic syndromes." Based on the foregoing discussion all autistic syndromes in our view share these characteristics:

1. Early onset (before two-and-a-half years of age)

2. Severe disturbance of social relatedness

3. Abnormalities of development of communication, usually prominently noted in abnormalities of language development

4. Elaborate repetitive routines

5. Abnormal response to sensory stimuli

All symptoms have to be out of phase with the overall intellectual level of the child.

For a diagnosis of the "complete autistic syndrome" all symptoms have to be present.

In cases with three or four of the symptoms we suggest that "partial autistic syndrome" be diagnosed. Children showing only one or two should not be diagnosed as suffering from an autistic syndrome at all.

COMPLICATING HANDICAPS

Mental Retardation

A majority (approximately 67 to 81 percent) of all autistic children are definitely mentally retarded (Lotter 1966; Rutter 1978b; Wing 1980b; Bohman et al. 1981; Gillberg 1984a). This intellectual retardation was previously thought to be a secondary consequence of the affective disturbance, and Kanner (1943, 1949) himself believed that these were children with potentially superior intelligence. Now, several different lines of research have been followed and the results are in total agreement that a majority of autistic children are indeed mentally retarded (see Rutter 1983 for overview). This retardation is not caused by motivational factors in the child and remains relatively stable over the years with or without improvement with regard to the autistic behavior problems.

It goes without saying that the clinical picture of autism varies somewhat with the intellectual level. Severely mentally retarded autistic children (with an IQ of less than 50, who make up about half of all autistic children) behave differently from mildly mentally retarded or normally intelligent autistic children. Prognosis varies with IQ and level of speech development. The speech-language competence on the whole of course is closely correlated with the IQ level. Badly retarded children are less likely to have any speech at all, whereas more intelligent autistic children are the ones most likely to demonstrate a wide variety of elaborate repetitive routines and to exhibit islets of special giftedness in circumscribed areas, a symptom once mentioned as central by Kanner, but which obviously cannot be as conspicuous in the severely mentally retarded group.

Epilepsy

Some autistic children have early onset of seizures. Indeed, infantile spasms are often followed by the development of an autistic syndrome even in infancy (Taft and Cohen 1971; Riikonen and Amnell 1981). Rather more common, however, is the development of any type of epilepsy at or near the time of puberty. One third of all autistic children (Rutter 1970; Gillberg 1984e) develop seizures. It is a more common phenomenon among the mentally retarded autists, but it can occur at all levels of intelligence. Most of the autistic children who develop epilepsy in adolescence have not shown any outward signs of major neurological abnormality before. (For more details on epilepsy in autism, see chapter 4.)

Blindness and Deafness

It is often suggested that blindness (supposedly by way of sensory deprivation) may cause autism and that blindness and autism often coexist (Keeler 1958; Rapin 1979), but there is actually no good evidence to support this view. If autism and blindness are indeed associated, then the association might well stem from some kind of underlying central neurological deficit. The same goes for deafness. It is rather surprising that the interrelationship between autism and blindness/deafness has attracted so little attention. Many interesting hypotheses might be tested in connection with studies undertaken in order to elucidate this interrelationship. For instance, the relative importance of periodic sensory privation versus central brain damage could be evaluated in such studies.

Based on clinical experience, it would seem that deafness is more likely to show a primary connection with autism than blindness is. Throughout childhood, most autistic children show deviant reactions to sound, whereas deviant reactions to light appear to be less conspicuous, at least in later childhood. Furthermore, among autistic individuals there are more clinically proven cases of deaf than blind people.

Other Handicaps

The autistic syndromes are but a behaviorally defined set of collections of symptoms and it is therefore quite possible to diagnose any kind of handicap in connection with autism. However, cerebral palsy (Schain and Yannet 1960) is only rarely seen in concurrence with autism and related disorders (Gillberg 1984a). Tuberous sclerosis (Lotter 1974), neurofibromatosis (Gillberg and Forsell 1984), achondroplasia (Gillberg and Andersson 1984), Moebius syndrome (Ornitz et al. 1977, Gillberg and Winnergård 1984, Coleman, unpublished data), Laurence-Moon-Biedl syndrome (Gillberg 1984a) are but a few of the handicaps described in connection with autism. Later in the book, we will return to a consideration of the possible implications of these connections. (For further details on associated handicaps see chapter 18.)

DIFFERENTIAL DIAGNOSIS

Here we need only be concerned with those neurological, developmental and psychiatric syndromes that may cause diagnostic confusion. Often, a whole list of conditions, such as rubella embryopathia, tuberous sclerosis, infantile spasms and so on, is presented in the section of differential diagnosis. Since we consider autism to be a set of purely behavioral syndromes, regardless of underlying pathology, we will not enter into such a discussion at this stage.

Deafness

Deaf children may occasionally show some, though rarely all, autistic features, in which case they should in our view be diagnosed as deaf and autistic.

Blindness

Several authors (Wing 1980) have attested that certain cases, which have been diagnosed as blind for several years, were in fact seeing and autistic. Children with documented blindness and autism, like deaf children, should be diagnosed as both blind and autistic.

Mental Retardation

Some mentally retarded children are very autistic-like in their behavior without fulfilling all the necessary criteria for a diagnosis of autism (Gillberg 1983b; Haracopos and Kellstrup 1978; Wing and Gould 1979). Conversely, autistic children more often than not are themselves mentally retarded. Sometimes the dividing line is indeed obscure and the allocation to diagnostic category haphazard. The studies by Wing (1981b) are essential reading for anyone interested in this dichotomy.

Emotional Deprivation

Retarded children reared in certain institutions (especially if looked after by a number of caretakers) display, like autistic children, abnormalities of affect, language and behavior. However, closer inspection usually makes differential diagnosis easy, since such children are indiscriminate rather than aloof, language-delayed rather than deviant, and show totally different kinds of behavioral problems. Also, positive environmental stimulation usually leads to quick development in these cases quite unlike the relatively minor changes seen in autism in connection with such stimulation.

Infant Depression

Children who have developed normally in the first year of life or so and who are then separated from their primary care-giver for an extended period sometimes develop major signs of depression (Spitz 1946). They first protest, then show sadness and withdrawal, but finally slowly adjust to the new situation. There is possibly an increased risk of depression in adult age (e.g. von Knorring 1983).

Asperger's Syndrome

Thought by many to be a certain kind of personality variant, the Asperger's syndrome (Asperger 1944; van Krevelen 1971; Wing 1981c; Gillberg 1984b) has many similarities with autism. The main difference is that Asperger persons are not quite so handicapped as autistic persons, and language skills, although impaired, are better developed.

Other Childhood Psychoses

In the latest edition of the DSM-III (1980), the term "Childhood Psychosis" has been replaced by "Childhood Onset Pervasive Development Disorder." Though signifying a more positive approach to autism than the "psychosis label" (with all its overtones of schizophrenia, "insanity," withdrawal from the cruel outside world and so forth), it seems premature totally to discard the earlier terminology of "Childhood Psychosis."

There are instances of *disintegrative psychoses* commencing around the age of three and usually characterized by restlessness and hyperactivity during the first half-year or so before the child becomes very much like an autistic child. There are also occasional instances of *childhood schizophrenia* (showing up in hallucinated, thought-disordered children who have little in common with most autistic children). These cases probably, unlike autism, represent the early onset form of schizophrenia and rarely, if ever, commence before the age of 7 or 8 years. Only rarely does one come across the kind of child (originally described by Mahler and Gosliner 1955) who shows a "clinging" attachment to the mother and in other respects too exhibits an overall arrest of development at the so-called symbiotic stage. These cases are extremely rare—in the author's experience constituting something like 1 to 2 percent of all childhood psychosis cases—and it is doubtful as to whether they should be grouped a separate diagnostic category, since most of the cases may readily be classified in other categories, with the added feature of the conspicuously clinging behavior. Some authors seem to think that this kind of *symbiotic psychosis* is a common disorder and also that the cause underlying the behavior is found in the symbiotic relationship between mother and child. Not only is there no proof whatsoever for such a relationship; Margaret Mahler herself—the original proponent of the syndrome—considered some inherent defect in the child to be necessary for the development of this condition.

Comprehensive Differential Diagnosis

The comprehensive differential diagnosis in respect to autism, other childhood psychoses, Asperger's syndrome, emotional deprivation and infant depression is shown in Table 2.1.

TABLE 2.1. Differential Diagnosis in Cases with Early Onset Disturbance of Social Relatedness.

Syndrome	Social relationships	Language	Behavior	Other	Age of onset and course
Autistic syndromes	Period of autistic aloneness; lack of reciprocity; comprehension of human mime and gesture impaired; people treated as objects	Concrete interpretation of language; muteness; echolalia; reversal of personal pronomina	Obsessive insistence on elaborate routines; special stereotypies of hands and arms; toe-walking; lack of interest; failure to meet demands; resistance to change; passivity and overactivity alternating	Abnormal auditory perception	From birth (minority during first 2½ years); chronic; usually life-long handicap
Asperger's syndrome	Gradual realization that child is uninterested in peers, formal contact	Concrete interpretation of language in spite of superficially well-developed skills	Much like autism though circumscribed interests (astrology, etc.) often more conspicuous	Mild autism? "Personality" trait	Often not obvious until the age of 3-4 years; chronic; fair (though restricted) prognosis
Other childhood psychoses*	Regression to level of echolalia or muteness		Partly same as autism; often extreme degrees of overactivity without purpose	Confusion; variable abnormality of auditory perception	30-50 months (small minority in the 4-10 year age range); chronic; usually life-long handicap

TABLE 2.1. (continued)

Syndrome	Social relation-ships	Language	Behavior	Other	Age of onset and course
Deprivation syndrome	Lack of reticence and distance; always in pursuit of contact; understands human mime and gesture; people not objects	Delayed (not deviant) language development	Extreme overactivity; eats garbage; drinks toilet-water	Quick amelioration if early stimulation	6-30 months; sensitive to environmental change; fair prognosis if early stimulation
Infant depression	Initial autism followed by accepting relationship with new caregiver; ambivalence upon return to primary caregiver	Initial regression	Apathy followed by adjustment to new demands	Amelioration on return to normal milieu; normal auditory perception	8-30 months; highly age-dependent; fair prognosis if promptly treated; risk of depression in adult life

*Includes childhood schizophrenia which has a set of symptoms coinciding with those of adult schizophrenia.

It is hoped that the difficulty of diagnosing the autistic syndromes has not been understated in the foregoing pages. There are still many unresolved problems. In an era when operational criteria and interrater reliability of judgment have come into focus and taken the step from research methodology to clinical necessity, it may seem obsolete to speak of such a thing as experience. Even child psychiatrists only infrequently encounter classic Kanner autism cases. The cases fulfilling Wing's criteria for "the triad of language and social impairment" occur more frequently, but only those working among the mentally handicapped are likely to be aware of the actual number. Clinical experience is a prerequisite seldom mentioned in chapters or articles dealing with the diagnosis of autism, and yet this fundamental element is of utmost importance. There is inevitably a "gestalt measure" inherent in the whole concept of the autistic syndrome. The experienced clinician will have no difficulty in selecting the group of children in which those with autistic syndromes will be found. He may have some trouble deciding whether to diagnose infantile autism or atypical pervasive developmental disorder, but the Wing category will be easier to discern. The clinically inexperienced researcher on the other hand may have no major difficulty in deciding that a mildly mentally retarded four-year-old autistic does fulfill DSM-III criteria for infantile autism, but will altogether miss the possibility that a normally intelligent eight-year-old with much communicative speech belongs in that same diagnostic category also. Diagnostic studies concerned with childhood psychosis require the "gestalt acumen" of the experienced clinician just as much as everyday clinical work with autistic persons does.

Diagnostic difficulties/confusions have been eloquently discussed by Waterhouse (Waterhouse et al. 1984), who concluded that (1) there is some evidence that diagnostic subcategories not mentioned in the DSM-III exist, (2) there is a need for classification concerning the relationship between the cognitive and conative profile of children classified as autistic, and (3) a subdivision of the autistic syndromes into one group of "early childhood onset pervasive developmental disorders" and another group of "other similar syndromes" should be made either in accordance with some age of onset limit or in accordance with some specific symptomatology, but not on the basis of both.

The term "the autistic syndromes of childhood" may, by some, be taken as further evidence of the diagnostic problems relating to the area. However, at the present stage, it is our contention that this label accords best with the current state of knowledge insofar as comprehensive categories are needed. This wording makes clear that on balance there is, as yet, no hard evidence that there exists a qualitatively unique behavioral or etiological syndrome of autism. In the future it may be possible to make a definite distinction between "inborn" and "later acquired" forms of autism (roughly corresponding to "infantile autism" and "childhood onset pervasive developmental disorder"/"other childhood psychosis") on some more clearcut criterion than the rather arbitrary 30-months onset limit. As time goes by, we will also be able to distinguish between etiological and behavioral subsyndromes, and eventually "the autistic syndromes" will in all probability be replaced by a number of different syndromes.

3   Clinical Course and Prognosis

Autism, like any other developmental disorder, shows changes with respect to prevailing symptomatology with age (Rutter 1978a; Wing 1980b; Ornitz 1983; Waterhouse et al. 1984). This needs emphasizing again and again, especially since many autistic children develop in rather different directions. Children who could scarcely be distinguished behaviorally at age one-and-a-half may by the age of ten have developed completely different personalities and symptoms. This is one of the reasons why early recognition and observation is essential for establishing a precise diagnosis. Several years later it may even be impossible to say in retrospect that the child was ever autistic. We have followed individual children who at age three showed all the characteristics of Kanner autism, but who five years later were only slightly odd, had some peculiarities of spoken language, and who had several peers of his own age group. By the time the child reached the age of eight, most people would find it hard to believe that he had ever been autistic. The same observation has been made by Chess (1977) in her follow-up of autistic children with rubella embryopathy.

Infancy

There are extremely few observational records available on autistic children during their first years of life. Such evidence as there is—combined with anamnestic data from parents and other caretakers—suggests that unspecific symptoms such as lack of initiative, hyperactivity, sleep problems and feeding difficulties are often the first to be recognized. Peculiarities of gaze appear possibly to be the most obvious specific early symptom of autism. We have performed a total population study of autism, looked at the medical records from the newborn period, and interviewed the parents in detail in retrospect (Gillberg and Gillberg

35

1983, and Gillberg and Dahlgren 1984). Both of these lines of research have suggested to us that many autistic children have gaze abnormalities apparent already at the maternity clinic, although nobody can spell out explicitly just what is the matter. The child appears not to see whoever comes near; his gaze appears "empty and inwardly focused."

There is no "response," "no smile." Later in the first year it becomes obvious that the child lacks the normal anticipatory reactions typical of healthy children who want their parents to pick them up. The abnormal response to sound is often obvious in the second half of the first year, and many autistic children have been thought deaf by persons outside the immediate family (who *know* they cannot be). There are either major sleep problems (reversed day-night rhythm or a great reduction in the need to sleep) or the child is described as "almost too good, never wanting any attention." Feeding problems (both in breast- and bottle-fed infants) are the rule, with the child either displaying sucking difficulties, or holding his head in stiff and strange postures, or actively turning away.

Most autistic children are extremely behaviorally deviant even during this first year of life. They may engage in their stereotyped hand movements and be completely passive, not interested in exploring their environment, indeed, showing no initiative whatsoever, and already fiercely protesting when demands are made or routines changed. Some, though by no means all (perhaps not even the majority), reject body contact. Most prefer to be left alone.

Towards the end of the first year, the autistic child's lack of initiative and interest in exploring the environment comes into focus. The child will not look for things which disappear out of vision like normal children of that age will do. One-finger pointing is rarely achieved until several years later.

Although still a matter of dispute, it appears that a small number of autistic children develop quite normally during the first year. Wing has suggested (Wing 1980b) that perhaps 70 to 80 percent of all autistic children are definitely abnormal from birth. Even in the group with an apparent setback, careful, detailed, retrospective history-taking with the parents often reveals that there have been early developmental delays and abnormalities (Wing 1971).

She is also of the opinion (Wing 1982)—as are the present authors—that there are at least two modes of presentation during the first year. On the one hand there is the "model baby" ("there wasn't a baby in the house") who appears content just to be left alone. On the other hand there is the "terrible baby" who screams round the clock, who refuses to be fed or held, and who has trouble sleeping. In themselves, some of these children might not be so different from each other after all. It could be that the main differences lie in the style of approach made by parents and others. The "model baby" who is left to himself and therefore appears to be content might, if constantly "disturbed" (approached) turn into the "terrible baby." On the other hand, as in mental retardation where the same differences occur, innate personality characteristics or the effect of disease processes on the brain might provide the explanation.

Walker (1976) in his comparison of 76 autistic with 76 normal subjects found that hypertelorism, low-seated ears, and partial syndactyli of the second and third toes differentiated between the groups. Campbell et al. (1978d) found that ear anomalies (low-seated, malformed, asymmetrical, or soft and pliable ears, and adherent lobes) and mouth anomalies (high palate, tongue furrows, and smooth-rough spots) differentiated 52 autistic children from siblings and controls. Lurks et al. (1980) also found significantly higher anomaly scores for autistic children compared to their siblings. These findings are the beginning of approaches designed to identify autistic infants in the first week of life.

Preschool Years

From ages one to five (and especially from about two-and-a-half to five) the typically autistic behavior pattern is usually most clearly evident. For most families these years (or possibly, in some cases, the years of puberty) are the hardest to cope with. The fearful temper tantrums associated with the more extreme forms of insistence on sameness are usually at a peak during this period. Also, most autistic children learn to walk on time or only a few months late, and from the time they first start walking they are even more difficult to handle. Many are hyperactive and destructive and move about constantly. Others are engaged in repetitive activities, such as endlessly listening to tape recorders (a favorite activity for many). Some are fascinated by a particular object, such as a set of keys, and will be furious if deprived of it (Figure 3.1).

Around the age of one-and-a-half, most normal children develop some kind of communicative, spoken language, and begin to show a greater interest in other children. The autistic child almost invariably fails to do any of these things and so is, perhaps in all its severity for the first time, recognized as abnormal. Many normal—and autistic—children

FIGURE 3.1. A two-year-old autistic boy about to put his hands over his ears, a common mannerism in these children.

experience the birth of a sibling at about this age. It has become "popular" to attribute the autistic child's withdrawal to the psychological trauma supposedly connected with this birth. Careful anamnesis will reveal, however, that the child has already displayed abnormal characteristics, and it is only the demands on normal development, which he cannot live up to, and the comparison with a normal sibling, which make his abnormalities so much more conspicuous.

In a few cases of autism, it does appear that normal development precedes a period of regression to an autistic state at about the age of one-and-a-half years. However, it is quite unclear what proportion of all autism cases they represent. There is also something to be said for grouping them with the cases of disintegrative psychosis.

During the later preschool years, the autistic child's active avoidance of other children is usually very prominent and contributes to the impression of "extreme autistic aloneness," a term coined by Kanner himself.

Early School Years

During the so-called latency years (about the age of six to eleven years) most autistic children gradually become somewhat less difficult to manage. The social aloofness often tends to subside somewhat and they become more cooperative. As a rule they no longer totally avoid other children, even though they cannot relate to them in a manner appropriate to their age.

The degree of language development at age five is one of the most significant prognostic factors. Two autistic children who might appear equally behaviorally deviant around the age of three may be very different at seven; the one could appear almost as deviant as at age three and without useful language skills, whereas the other could appear odd and peculiar but in possession of useful speech and much less deviant than during the preschool years.

On the whole, hyperactivity and temper tantrums are not as frequent during the school years as earlier, and therefore parents, siblings, and teachers usually have a relatively calmer period. Also sleep problems do not tend to take on such dramatic guises and although the autistic child may still have a greatly reduced need for sleep, he may now be able to occupy himself at night and leave the other family members to rest.

There are, of course, many exceptions to this rule, and some autistic children, especially the more severely mentally retarded, have major behavior problems throughout the school years.

An interesting recent observation has been made by Lindquist (1981), who found that those autistic children who showed the most extreme degrees of bizarre behavior during the preschool years were those who had the best adjustment prognosis in school age. This unexpected finding must be interpreted with caution. However, in this one respect it resembles adult schizophrenia, in which bizarre and "productive" symptoms in the acute stage indicate a better prognosis (Ottosson 1983).

Puberty and Adolescence

Problems associated with puberty have long been disregarded or dealt with summarily in descriptions of the development of autism. To be sure, a rather small minority of autistic children improve perceptibly during the teen-age years (Kanner 1971). However, a much larger minority show severe aggravation of the symptoms or even outright deterioration in puberty. Apart from those few, often relatively brighter autistic children who improve markedly during puberty, the majority go through their teens without more problems than are usually associated with puberty in normal children. However, in the mentally retarded group of autistic children, marked physical changes sometimes occur, so that, pretty, bright-looking autistic children may come out of puberty looking more deviant and "mentally retarded." Also, many autistic youngsters who have not been affected by seizures in childhood will develop epilepsy before adult age. As many as one-fourth to one-third of all autistic children (Brask 1970; Rutter et al. 1971; Gillberg 1984) will as adults be affected by seizures. The risk of epilepsy is higher among the mentally retarded autists but is raised in the normally intelligent ones also.

There has been much controversy as to whether to include children with obvious brain dysfunction in the category of infantile autism. Some would still argue for the exclusion of those with major neurological impairment. The onset of epilepsy in adolescent autistic children who previously had shown no signs whatsoever of neurological dysfunction (even in children without previous EEG abnormalities) demonstrates the impossibility of such a position. At the present time, there is still no way of predicting in early childhood (the time when autism is most often diagnosed) just who will experience seizures in adult age.

Brown (1969), Rutter (1970), and Gillberg (1984e) have all described cases of autistic children who show deterioration in adolescence. According to their studies, an estimated 10 to 30 percent of the autistic population can be expected to show cognitive and behavioral deterioration in puberty accompanied by a regression and reappearance of many of the symptoms typical of the preschool period. In the Rutter (1970) series, half of those who deteriorated showed simultaneous neurological symptoms, but this finding has not been confirmed by others so far. Gillberg and Schaumann (1981) have suggested that high maternal age, female sex, and a family history of affective disorders might increase the risk of symptom aggravation/deterioration in puberty.

There may be problems associated with the growth of sexual functions and awareness (Gillberg 1984e). Masturbation in public, naive approaches, and childish touching of other people are rather common, especially in boys; whereas problems with menstruation, such as smearing blood or tearing up underwear, are relatively rare.

Adult Age

There have only been a few scientific reports published pertaining to the topic of adult autism (Kanner 1973; Wing 1983; Gillberg 1983b), but there is growing clinical concern with the continuous psychiatric and psychosocial needs of autistic adults (Schopler and Mesibov 1983). It has long been recognized that a small fraction of all autistic persons develop into rather normal, or highly original, though not psychiatrically ill, grown-ups. The vast majority, however, have major difficulties coping even with the ordinary routines and stresses of everyday life. It is estimated that 75 to 85 percent of those diagnosed in childhood as suffering from autism will turn out to have a poor, or very poor, psychosocial prognosis (see below).

Wing (1983) has recently outlined three major groups of autistic adults: (1) "the aloof group," (2) "the passive group," and (3) "the active but odd group." In a study by Gillberg (1983b) further evidence for the existence of these rough categories was found.

The aloof adult group comprises those individuals who retain much or some of the characteristics of autistic aloneness. They will still prefer to be alone and even to withdraw actively from the nearness of other human beings. It may not be as obviously apparent in adult age, but the aloofness shows in the company of others in that the autistic individual does not readily react to other people's questions or approaches. He may quietly withdraw to the seclusion of his own room, where he may play his records or just sit and rock incessantly to and fro. If disturbed he may forcefully push the intruder out of the room, after first having appeared oblivious to the other person's presence for several minutes. Adult autistic persons of this type cause problems mostly if demands are made. They may be quite easy to "handle" if left completely to themselves. On the other hand, this quickly leads to the deterioration of both acquired and self-help skills.

The passive group may also, at first glance, appear aloof. However, approaches by both strangers and well-known people are accepted in a quite friendly manner. They may have " automatic" imitation skills enabling them to participate in some social activities without appearing extremely odd, just so long as reciprocal social interaction is not demanded. As a group, the passive autistic adults are those who have the most skills and are most likely to be able to lead relatively independent lives. Change of routine, at least if introduced in abrupt ways, may be very upsetting to this group of autistic adults, as well as to the aloof and active groups. Because of the overall friendly attitude of the passive autists, disturbed behavior in connection with change may be especially alarming; and, unless those living with or caring for these individuals are informed, may lead to tragic mistakes, such as expulsion from a group or admission for psychiatric treatment.

The active, but odd, group is by far the most difficult. On the surface, grown-ups in this group appear totally unlike those in the other two groups, but there is the same lack of reciprocity in all three. The active, but odd, autistic adult tends to approach other people with physical touching (if mute) or constant repetitive questioning. The endless monologues or questioning may seem rather harmless, but any one who has been confronted with it for any length of time, and learned that answering leads to even further repetitions of the same questions, knows how wearing and frustrating this behavior is.

Within these three groups there is, of course, considerable variation, some persons sometimes showing characteristics of more than one "type," with personality differences naturally playing an essential role in all cases.

Periodicity in Autism

There are several clinical accounts (Coleman 1976, Wing 1983, Gillberg 1984a) acknowledging a periodic intensification of symptoms in the autistic syndromes. This periodicity may be particularly prominent in puberty (Komoto et al. 1984b). However, after thorough interviewing of the parents it is often evident that it has been present from the onset in infancy. Gillberg (1981) has suggested that affective illnesses might be more common in the families of autistic than of normal children. There is evidence from several different sources that this might be the case (Rutter et al. 1971; Folstein and Rutter 1977; Lotter 1967), even though previous authors generally seem to have attributed conditions such as recurrent depression in the parents to reactions against the handicapped child rather than vice versa. Thus, it is possible that a hereditary trait of periodicity exists in some cases of autism in which parents and other relatives have shown major affective disorders.

Overall Prognosis

There are a number of follow-up studies reporting on the overall prognosis for "autistic/psychotic" children. These have been closely examined by Lotter (1978). However, only a handful of studies (Eisenberg, Johns Hopkins, USA, 1956; Creak, Great Ormond Street, UK, 1963; Rutter, Maudsley Hospital, UK, 1970; DeMyer et al., Indiana, USA, 1973; and Lotter, Surrey, UK, 1974) have presented enough detail to allow firm conclusions. These studies all yield remarkably consonant results. A poor, or very poor, outcome with regard to social adjustment (characterized by limited independence in social relations) was seen in 61 to 73 percent of the cases followed up to pre-adolescence or adult age. A good prognosis (with near normal or normal social life and acceptable functioning at work or school in spite of minor difficulties in social relationships and oddities of behavior) was seen in 5 to 17 percent of the cases. In the studies mentioned, 39 to 54 percent of the autistic persons had been placed in institutions at follow-up.

All the follow-up studies mentioned (as well as the one by Goldfarb from Ittleson Center, USA [1970]) agree that the absence of communicative speech at age five is indicative of a worse long-term overall prognosis. However, the best predictors of outcome are IQ ratings at the time of diagnosis (Rutter 1970), and the educational functioning in early childhood (DeMyer et al. 1973). Other important prognosis variables include a lack of reaction to sound in early childhood (poor outlook), milder forms of behavioral problems, and the amount of schooling and teaching of specific skills (better outlook).

It would appear from the foregoing discussion that making a reliable prognosis on the basis of diagnostic data obtained at about the age of five years would be rather easy. However, there are several problems.

On the bright side, however, is the, so far unexplained, tendency for a small minority of autistic children to grow out of their extreme behavior/cognitive problems almost completely—with or without treatment.

Then, there are the many problems associated with IQ testing. First, in the preschool years it may be very difficult to test an autistic child at all. However, pre-test personal knowledge of the child and special testing skills or experience by the child psychologist reduce the problems of testing to a minimum. Freeman (1976) has argued that it is usually possible to accomplish reliable testing of a preschool autist. Also DeMyer and co-workers (1973) showed that a simple index of educational attainments was a stable predictor of educational outcome. Perhaps such measures (or the Vineland interview) could be added to the test battery in order to strengthen the predictive validity of the IQ factor. Further, it appears that IQ is predictive of overall long-term prognosis only for those with ratings below 50. All of those who have an IQ of less than 50 before age five are likely to have a poor, or very poor, prognosis. Of those with an IQ greater than 50 it is much more difficult to make a reliable prediction of outcome. Nevertheless IQ on the whole remains as stable throughout childhood for autistic as for normal or mentally retarded children (Rutter 1983).

Speech as a prognostic indicator is useful for group effects but not always for individual children. Even in those who show no intelligible speech at five years of age, there may later be major speech development and a fair overall prognosis. Occasionally you will come across a child, who unexpectedly starts to talk or communicate at age ten or even later. One typically autistic individual, examined by one of the authors, said nothing for 27 years and then started to write long communicative sentences using a pocket-size typewriter (Sanua 1983).

The minority of children who show deterioration in puberty (Brown 1969; Rutter 1970; Gillberg and Schaumann 1981) constitute another problem. As yet we have no sure way of knowing in advance who they are. It is possible that high maternal age, female sex and a family history of affective disorder might all point in the direction of pubertal aggravation of symptoms, but so far, nothing definite is known in this respect.

For the most part, we must retain a cautious attitude when discussing prognosis with the parents. The majority of autistic children will show deviances and psychiatric handicap conditions throughout life, but others will improve enough to make it possible for them to lead an almost independent adult life. The problem in the individual child is that there is no sure way of knowing to which of these two groups the child will later belong.

4   Epilepsy in Autistic Patients

Dimension of the Problem

Authors from all over the world agree that autism is associated with epilepsy (Schain and Yannet 1960; Lotter 1967; Rutter 1970; Kanner 1971; Ornitz 1973; Fish and Ritvo 1979; Wing 1980b; Bohman et al. 1981; Shirataki et al. 1982; Gillberg 1984e). Epilepsy in autism is reported in every seventh to every third child, the frequency rising in accordance with the length of the follow-up period. Kanner, in his first follow-up of the Baltimore children before puberty, found one of the eleven children to be affected by epilepsy, whereas in adult life, two (18 percent) were said to suffer from epilepsy (Kanner 1971). Similarly, Rutter (1970), Lotter (1974), Corbett (1982) and Gillberg (1984e) have all found an increase in the rate of epilepsy with increasing age. The rise in frequency is particularly pronounced around the time of puberty (Rutter 1970; Gillberg 1984b). Clinical experience indicates that the rate of epilepsy will continue to rise, albeit at a very slow rate, perhaps throughout the entire life span.

The rate of 14 to 42 percent (mostly 25 to 35 percent) for epilepsy among autistic adults (all intellectual abilities counted) should be compared with 0.5 percent among the general population (Corbett 1983b), 3 to 6 percent among mildly mentally retarded subjects (Rutter et al. 1970) and 18 to 32 percent among the severely mentally retarded (Corbett 1983). Thus, the incidence is decidedly higher than among the normal population and may even be somewhat higher than among indiscriminate groups of the mentally retarded. At the present stage the latter point is arguable, even though the reported prevalence figures from various studies do suggest a difference. Epilepsy is definitely more common among the more severely mentally retarded autists (Rutter 1970, Corbett 1983), but it is not uncommon in mildly mentally retarded autistic youngsters and possibly occurs in above-base-rate frequencies in relatively brighter autism cases also (Gillberg and Wahlström 1984).

Already at this stage, we may sum up some of the existing evidence by saying that (1) the association between autism and epilepsy is indisputable and suggests brain dysfunction in many cases of autism, (2) there is a steep rise in the frequency of epilepsy around the time of puberty (possibly steeper than in cases of uncomplicated mental retardation), suggesting hormonal influences on the development of epilepsy, and (3) it appears that the connection between autism and epilepsy might be rather specific, and not only mediated via the common denominator of mental retardation. The latter statement is speculative at the present stage, but the possibly higher rate of epilepsy among autists than among the mentally retarded, and its appearance in association with puberty argue in its favor.

It should be mentioned here that many children with autism, showing no gross signs of neurological damage—apart from mental retardation and autism—in infancy and early childhood, unexpectedly develop epilepsy around the time of puberty.

Type of Epilepsy

Given the ample evidence that autism is associated with epilepsy, it is surprising that so little descriptive literature discusses the type or severity of this associated handicap. Corbett has recently (1982) surveyed the area, but no study is yet available detailing the subcategories of epilepsy in autism.

Nevertheless, there is evidence that children with infantile spasms (West's syndrome) have an increased risk compared with normals of developing autism or autistic-like behavior (Knobloch et al. 1956; Schain and Yannet 1960; Kolvin et al. 1971; Taft and Cohen 1971; Riikonen and Amnell 1981; Corbett 1982). This increase is not produced merely by way of mental retardation as is evinced by the higher rate of autism in West's syndrome (16 percent according to the Riikonen and Amnell study) than in mental retardation (4 percent in severe mental retardation according to Gillberg 1984a), and underlined further by the fact that a small proportion of children with West's syndrome do not become mentally retarded. However, infantile spasms are also associated with tuberous sclerosis, which, in turn, is associated with infantile autism. The nature of this trifold connection is poorly understood, but it is reasonable to assume that tuberous sclerosis (whether clinically diagnosed or not) causes both infantile spasms and autism.

With regard to epilepsies other than infantile spasms, no population-based frequency figures exist in autism.

Psychomotor Epilepsy

Corbett (1982) has suggested that psychomotor epilepsy with temporal lobe affliction might be more frequent in autism than commonly recognized, and that underreporting may be due to diagnostic difficulties arising when these complex seizure disorders affect noncommunicative children. This is in line with the experience of one of the authors (CG), who has published a case report of an autistic latency-age girl with a complex seizure disorder accompanied by "absent staring spells" (very uncharacteristic) and temporal lobe discharge on the EEG (Gillberg and Schaumann 1983). Her autistic behavior—and the staring spells—promptly disappeared after treatment with valproic acid.

The relationship between psychotic development and psychomotor epilepsy is further illustrated by the follow-up studies of Ounsted and his associates in Oxford, England, who found "temporal lobe epilepsy" to predispose to later psychosis in boys with a left-sided EEG abnormality (Lindsay et al. 1979).

Minor Motor Epilepsy (Myoclonic Epilepsies of Early Childhood)

Excluding the infantile spasms category, the myoclonic epilepsies of childhood (Lennox 1945; Gastaut et al. 1966) have not regularly been reported as common in infantile autism. However, some authors have described classic cases of autism in connection with minor motor epilepsy (Boyer et al. 1981, Gillberg et al. 1984c), and it appears that in clinical practice with severely mentally retarded autistic persons, minor motor epilepsy is relatively common. Gillberg and his associates (1984b) have described an autistic boy with severe and frequent minor motor seizures who became seizure-free on medication with valproic acid, and thereafter quickly grew out of his most severe autistic and language disturbances.

Petit Mal Epilepsy

Petit mal epilepsy, another form of subcortically generated epilepsy, has been reported to masquerade as autism in an eight-year-old boy who had almost continuous 3 c/s spike and wave activity on the EEG (Gillberg and Schaumann 1983). This boy improved dramatically—both psychiatrically and neurologically—with ethosuximide monotherapy. Otherwise, petit mal has not been mentioned frequently in literature on autism.

Grand Mal Epilepsy

Grand mal is the most common form of epilepsy in an unselected population. There are several statements (e.g. Corbett 1982) that it is also the most common variant of epilepsy in autism, but there is actually no good scientific evidence to support this notion. A detailed population-based study of epilepsy in autism is highly warranted.

Autism, Epilepsy, and Other Disorders

A number of disease entities that are found in patients with autistic syndromes predispose to seizures. Thus, if an autistic child develops seizures, these entities should be specifically sought for if the child has not already had a firm diagnosis, or, at least, an adequate workup.

If an infant displays the infantile spasms syndrome, there are a variety of possibilities to be considered (Jeavons and Bower 1964). Those also included (to date) in the autistic syndrome are tuberous sclerosis, neurofibromatosis, phenylketonuria and minor hydrocephalus.

In seizures appearing at a somewhat later age, the differential diagnosis changes. If the autistic child is a girl, Rett's syndrome should be considered; 71 percent of this group develop epilepsy and the median age of onset is four years (Hagberg et al. 1983). If the autistic child is a boy, the possibility of the fragile-X syndrome, which often coincides with autism and sometimes with epilepsy, should be considered. It has been suggested that brainstem dysfunction–muscular hypotonia–psychomotor epilepsy–autism might be specifically associated with this chromosomal syndrome (Gillberg and Wahlström 1984). Purine disorders are associated with seizures in children (Coleman et al. 1974), so purine metabolism should be evaluated in autistic children who develop epilepsy.

Antiepileptic Treatment in Autism

There are no adequately controlled studies relevant to the topic of anticonvulsive pharmacological treatment either in autism or in epilepsy in association with autism. However, clinical experience indicates that some of the best antiepileptic drugs (especially phenobarbitone and the benzodiazepines) may be detrimental to the autistic-epileptic child's behavioral status.

Drug treatment aimed at alleviating a seizure disorder in autism should be tried only if the child has two or more seizures a year, and even here an individual decision has to be taken in each case. Reduction of environmental stimuli may sometimes serve as an adjunct. It appears that drugs with supposedly "psychotropic" properties (e.g. valproic acid and carbamazepine) might be of special benefit to this group, since behavior is only rarely—though sometimes—negatively affected (Figure 4.1).

FIGURE 4.1. Five-year-old boy with typical Kanner autism diagnosed at age two-and-a-half. Severely mentally retarded and suffering from almost continuous minor motor epilepsy (alternating with seizure-free days) at diagnosis, he has become seizure-free, developed speech, and grown out of autistic syndrome after treatment with valproic acid. Chromosomal culture has revealed an XYY karyotype.

In the autistic child with no clear-cut clinical signs of epilepsy, but with unclassifiable spells of absentmindedness, "rolling" of the eyes, etc., and an EEG with epileptogenic discharge, we would suggest a three to six-month trial with a suitable anticonvulsant drug.

If the autistic child with epilepsy is also in need of neuroleptic drug treatment, which is often the case in puberty, haloperidol, pimozide and thioridazine appear to be the most useful, because of their lack of epileptogenic properties. (Also, see Chapter 21.)

Coleman has suggested that epilepsy in autism might sometimes be specifically associated with abnormalities of purine metabolism (see chapter 16). Therefore, in cases with the combination of epilepsy and autism, disorders of purine metabolism should either be ruled out or treated appropriately.

It is quite possible that research into the area of anticonvulsive treatment in autism might prove valuable. The possibility of a connection between autism and psychomotor epilepsy (Corbett 1982; Gillberg and Wahlström 1984) makes scientific trials of such drugs highly warranted.

Summary

In conclusion, one can only be amazed that so little scientific progress has been made in the field of epilepsy in autism, particularly since the association has been amply documented for the last 15 years or so. Autism *is* associated with epilepsy, and the nature of this association needs much more elucidation in the near future.

Part II

Review of the General Literature

5   Epidemiology

Prevalence

Victor Lotter performed the first major epidemiological study of autism (Lotter 1966, 1967) and found "nuclear autism" in 2.0/10,000 children in the former county of Middlesex, England (corresponding to 15 cases altogether). He made a thorough search of all schools and other institutions known to care for eight- to ten-year-old children in one way or another, and even now his investigation is by many considered "standard." Lotter also found "non-nuclear autism" (closely resembling classic Kanner cases) in another 2.5/10,000 children. Still another group, corresponding to 3.3/10,000, was identified which contained individuals with a few, but not all, of the characteristics of autism.

Prior to Lotter, Rutter (1966) had discovered 4.4 psychotic children per 10,000 in the eight- to ten-year-old population in Aberdeen.

Lotter's findings of four to five clearly autistic/childhood psychotic children per 10,000 have since been confirmed in three different epidemiological studies: in Århus, Denmark (Brask 1970), London, England (Wing and Gould 1979), and Göteborg, Sweden (Gillberg 1980, 1984a) (Table 5.1).

The National Institutes of Health Perinatal Collaborative Prospective Study (Torrey et al. 1975) also found the same frequency. Clinically based surveys (Treffert 1970; Steinhausen 1983, unpublished data) have come up with somewhat smaller numbers, but the figures are not widely discrepant.

There are, however, some epidemiological studies which do not fit the four to five per 10,000 standard perfectly. First, in a study of a handicapped child population (under 15 years of age) by Wing, she mentions that the "triad of language and social impairment" (see above, chapter 2) occurs in 21/10,000 children (including both "nuclear" and

TABLE 5.1. Epidemiological Studies. Prevalence (Number of Children per 10,000 Age-specific) of Autistic Syndromes and Closely Related Disorders. Sex Ratios in Brackets (Boys to Girls).

Author of study (year)	Nuclear autism[1]	Non-nuclear autism— Other psychosis	Autism— Clearcut psychosis combined	Asperger's syndrome	Total psychotic behavior— Triad of language and social impairment
Lotter (1966)	2.0 (2.8:1)	2.5 (2.4:1)	4.5 (2.6:1)	–	7.8 (2.0:1)
Brask (1967)	–	–	4.3 (1.4:1)	–	–
Wing et al. (1976)	2.0 (6:1)	2.9 (10:0)	4.9 (15:1)	0.6[2] (3.8:1[3])	21.2 (2.6:1)
Gillberg (1980, 1984a)	2.0 (3.3:1)	1.9 (1.1:1)	4.0 (1.8:1)	0.4[2] (3:1)[3]	69[4] (7:1)
Bohman et al. (1981)	3.0	3.0	6.1 (1.6:1)	–	–

[1]Social aloofness and elaborate repetitive routines, both to a marked extent

[2]Minimum figure, study not adequately designed to find all cases

[3]Sex ratio computed on basis of clinic referral sample

[4]Figure obtained from another study different from that used for remaining figures in this row (Gillberg 1983)

"non-nuclear autism"). Second, in an epidemiological study of perceptual, motor, and attentional deficits in unselected seven-year-olds, Gillberg (1983c) found that 69/10,000 children were affected by "psychotic behavior" (closely related to Wing's triad). Third, Bohman and his associates (1981) in the northern-most part of Sweden found 6.1/10,000 children with "childhood psychosis." Finally, there are now reports from Japan that "autism" occurs in 16/10,000 children born in Toyota, Japan (Ishii and Takahashi 1982).

What sense can one make of these partly conflicting findings? First of all, the possibility remains open that different diagnostic criteria have been applied in different studies. This issue has already been discussed in the chapter on diagnosis and will not be elaborated upon at any length here, except to say that the studies reporting lower figures are more likely to have focused on the most severely handicapped and typically autistic children. The low-frequency studies reported above all conform to acceptable epidemiological standards, and there is little reason to assume that any large percentage of children considered autistic by the authors of those studies would have been missed in the screening or diagnostic procedures. Also, the studies which have presented their case-finding methods in the greatest detail (Lotter 1967; Wing and Gould 1979; Gillberg 1984a) agree that childhood psychosis/autism cases occur in a frequency of four to five children per 10,000 and that "nuclear autism" represents about half of that number.

The two Swedish epidemiological studies of childhood psychosis, performed in the same era and by authors who have discussed diagnostic criteria and case-finding methods in some detail, are of particular interest in this context. The study of Gillberg (1984a) in Göteborg, a large industrial town on the Swedish south-west coast, thus yielded a figure of 4.0/10,000 age-specific prevalence (with 2.0/10,000 classic Kanner autism with early onset social aloofness and elaborate repetitive routines) for childhood psychosis total. Gillberg also reported a large number of mentally retarded children with quite similar, though not typical, symptomatology. Bohman and co-workers (1981, in Swedish), on the other hand, reported an age-specific prevalence of 6.1/10,000 (half of which were typically autistic) from a rural area in the northernmost part of Sweden. In other comparable epidemiological Swedish studies, mental retardation has been shown to be more frequent in rural areas. It is quite possible that the same is true of autism, either because of some common genetic or other organic etiological factor which is more common in rural districts, or because of the well-known link between autism-mental retardation, or both, or possibly because of some as yet unidentified factor. In a Scandinavian-Finnish study of twins (Gillberg 1984f), preliminary findings indicate that childhood psychotic twins are considerably more prevalent in northern Scandinavia and Finland (with their almost exclusively rural areas) than in southern parts of these countries (which are more "urban" in character). The conclusions regarding rural-urban differences in autism can only be tentative at the moment, and the results of the reported studies need confirmation. At any rate, the differences between the Gillberg and the Bohman studies are relatively small and may, of course, prove to be of chance significance only. However, if there is a real difference, this would also argue in favor of classifying autism with the developmental rather than with the usual psychiatric syndromes of childhood. Unspecified psychiatric abnormality is much more frequent in urban than in rural areas, in sharp contrast with our findings in autism.

The study by Wing and Gould reporting 21/10,000 cases with the "triad of language and social impairment" (that is, the combination of disturbance in (1) social relationships, (2) language, and (3) behavior including autistic or autistic-like features) is one of the best epidemiological studies in the field of childhood autism so far. These authors have used clearly defined criteria and the prevalence in typical autism cases corresponds with that of most other studies. Other authors have pointed to the similarity between autism and other kinds of disturbances of social relatedness in mental retardation (e.g. Corbett 1983a), but the Camberwell study is the only one so far (with the possible exception of the Danish study from institutions for the mentally retarded, Haracopos and Kellstrup 1977) in which this "borderline" group has been awarded the status of a scientifically based prevalence figure. In a study of perceptual, motor, and attentional deficiencies in Swedish seven-year-olds, Gillberg (1983c) found an age-specific prevalence of a high 69/10,000 children with "psychotic behavior" including autism. Thus, the Wing London prevalence is possibly a minimum one. "Psychotic behavior" (closely related to the triad of language and social impairment) may actually be five to ten times as common as clear-cut cases of childhood psychosis.

The only really problematic study to date in respect to epidemiology is the Japanese screening (Ishii and Takahashi 1982), which yielded an age-specific prevalence of 16/10,000 for "early infantile autism." The case-finding method has not yet been presented in detail. Differences in diagnostic criteria could account for the vast discrepancy between this study and all others. The Wing "triad" or the Gillberg "psychotic behavior" category cases could have been included under one "early infantile autism" rubric. On the other hand, there is the possibility that real frequency differences between Eastern and Western countries may exist. It has recently been suggested that the etiology of autism in various parts of the globe may vary considerably (Gillberg 1984d), and this could account both for varying frequency figures and for seemingly conflicting results in studies on etiology. It would be of great theoretical interest to have the Japanese authors elaborate in some detail the methods they have used in order to resolve some of the issues discussed and to renew faith in future claims of representativeness made by the Japanese groups.

Mental Retardation

All studies to date (Lotter 1966; Brask 1970; Rutter and Lockyer 1967; Wing and Gould 1979; Gillberg 1980; 1984a, Bohman et al. 1981, Ishii and Takahashi 1982; Steinhausen et al. 1983) agree that a vast majority of autistic/psychotic children are also mentally retarded and test reliably (Clark and Rutter 1979; Rutter 1983) in the IQ range of less than 70. Seventy-five to ninety percent of the children included in various studies are described as mentally retarded, whereas only about ten percent are of normal or, in very rare instances, superior intelligence. A majority of the Kanner autism cases, in spite of severe overall mental retardation, have an "islet" of special ability, which does not represent a "signal symptom" of hidden superior talents but is rather to be taken as the only intact functioning area in an otherwise extremely deviant child (Shah and Frith 1983).

Epilepsy

Most authors (Rutter 1970; Brask 1970; Lotter 1974; Gillberg 1984a) agree that one-quarter to one-third of autistic children develop fits at some time before adolescence. The epileptic seizures are of all kinds, but infantile spasms and the psychomotor variant are possibly relatively more frequent than in other epilepsy populations (see above, chapter 4 on epilepsy in autism).

Other Handicaps

There are several references in the literature (e.g. Keeler 1958; Fraiberg 1977; Rapin 1979; Wing 1980) to the high incidence of blindness and deafness in autism. However, there is really no hard epidemiological evidence to support this view and, although clinically credible, claims for a connection between visual-auditory deprivation and autism await scientific appraisal.

Epidemiological studies strongly suggest that neurofibromatosis and tuberous sclerosis are associated with autism (Lotter 1974; Gillberg and Forsell 1984).

Cerebral palsy is rare in autism (Wing 1980b; Gillberg 1984a). However, Moebius syndrome with bilateral facial nerve paralysis is possibly associated (Ornitz et al. 1977; Gillberg and Winnergård 1984). The facial nerve paralysis leads to severe handicaps in eating, talking, and swallowing. The etiological link between the two syndromes is probably mediated via brainstem damage.

Asperger's Syndrome

In chapter 2, Asperger's syndrome was mentioned. This "autism-related" diagnostic category has recently been surveyed by Wing (1981) who found 0.6/10,000 children with both Asperger's syndrome and mental retardation. Wing states that about 20 percent of "her" Asperger's cases were mentally retarded. An educated guess about the total prevalence for Asperger's syndrome would then be approximately 3/10,000 children.

Sibling Rank

There is still no clear consensus with regard to birth rank of autistic children. Early studies (Despert 1951; Kanner 1954, Rimland 1965) suggested a high number of first-born children, but later reports have yielded conflicting results (Lotter 1967; Wing 1980a; Gillberg 1981). On balance, it seems reasonable to assume that the Tsai and Stewart (1983) position of more first and late-born (number four or later) children in autism may turn out to be correct.

Social Class

From as early as Kanner's first account of autism (1943) there has been a notion—which sometimes has taken on mythological qualities—that autistic children tend to come from high social classes (see discussion in chapter 1). Kanner himself in all probability saw a highly selected population of autistic children. Lotter is the only one of the students of epidemiology in autism who has found a *slight* social class bias. Wing (1980a), Bohman et al. (1981), and Gillberg and Schaumann (1982), on the basis of epidemiological studies, all agree that autism occurs in all social classes and with normal distribution across classes. Schopler and coworkers (1979) are also of the opinion that the social-class bias seen in some clinical samples is due to a number of referral/selection factors. Brask (1967) in Denmark claims that there was no social-class bias in her Danish study, but unfortunately she does not put forward any real evidence in support of this claim. However, the fact remains that of the five published population studies of autism only one has come up with a *small* over-representation of the higher social classes. The epidemiological study by Gillberg in Göteborg, Sweden, is currently being extended to cover a larger population. Preliminary findings point in the direction of a slight over-representation of the lowest social class. Taken together, the bulk of the evidence definitely does not favor a high social-class bias in autism, and it is hoped that the endless pointless arguments about social class in autism will come to an end. There is nothing very substantial to suggest that autism has anything to do with social class. The possibility remains that among the relatively brighter autistic children the social class might be somewhat raised. This, however, could hardly be more significant than the finding that among the normal child population high intelligence and high social class are associated.

Sex Ratios

Boys outnumber girls in all studies of autism at a ratio of 1.4 to 4.8 boys for every girl (Kanner and Eisenberg 1956; Lotter 1966; Brask 1970; Rutter 1970; Wing 1975; Bohman et al. 1981; Gillberg 1984a). The Gillberg study suggests that the overrepresentation of boys is marked only in the classically autistic group.

Wing (1981a) and others before her have documented that the overrepresentation of boys with autism is markedly less pronounced in the severely mentally retarded group. Thus, in her group of 74 children with the triad of language and social impairment, the boy/girl ratios were 1.1:1, 3.1:1 and 14.2:1 in IQ ranges of 0–19, 20–49 and greater than 50, respectively. In Gillberg's study (1984a) among the typically Kanner autistic children (n=26) the ratios were 2.5:1 and 3.8:1 in those with IQs of less than 50 and more than 50, respectively. In short, these trends suggest that autistic girls are, on the average, more severely brain damaged than autistic boys.

Summary

Most epidemiological studies agree that autistic syndromes occur somewhere in the range of four to five children per 10,000. Nuclear Kanner autism cases possibly constitute half of this group. There is a larger group of mentally retarded persons with autistic features. Two-thirds to four-fifths of autistic children are definitely mentally retarded, and only about one in ten is of normal intelligence. Epilepsy is common in autism, affecting about one in three of adult age. A number of associated handicaps and conditions are common in autism. Girls are much less frequently affected by autistic syndromes than boys. This is particularly true in the relatively brighter group with IQ levels above 50.

The exact epidemiological figures obtained are, of course, highly dependent on the case-finding method and the diagnostic criteria used. Most of the studies surveyed in this chapter are agreed with regard to diagnostic criteria. However, the case-finding methods vary considerably. It is therefore quite surprising that frequency estimates have been so close. This might indicate that nuclear autism cases do exist as a separate disease entity. However, the well-known phenomenon of the association between autism and mental retardation illustrates that the issue of the specificity of autism has not yet been solved.

Finally, one needs to keep in mind that if different epidemiological studies produce somewhat differing prevalence figures, this might be due not only to diagnostic differences but also to discrepancies in etiology. Gillberg (1984d) has suggested that just as mental retardation frequencies vary from one country to another (because of varying etiology), so the prevalence of autism may fluctuate from one part of the globe to another (for example, PKU is common in Scandinavia but rubella in pregnancy is becoming extremely rare, whereas in developing countries the opposite applies).

6   Twin and Family Studies

Twin Studies

Kanner (1943) was the first authority in the field of childhood psychoses to suggest some sort of constitutional—which could include a genetic—predisposition in children who later developed the typical symptoms of autism. Except for the literature survey by Rimland (1964) who found case reports of eleven monozygotic twins reported to be concordant for autism, there is, quite remarkably, only two published studies, and one further study in progress, of a series of monozygotic and dizygotic twins and autism (Folstein and Rutter 1977; Gillberg 1984f; Ritvo et al. 1984). There were a number of single studies of twin pairs in the fifties, sixties and seventies, but only a handful of these (Bakwin 1954; Ward and Hoddinott 1962; Vaillant 1963; and McQuaid 1975) dealt with sex-matched pairs or presented sufficient data in respect to zygosity, probability, and description of clinical characteristics. There are also two studies of single opposite-sexed pairs (Böök et al. 1963; Kotsopoulos 1976). The results of these seven studies are equivocal. There are at least twelve other studies of single twin pairs in which at least one twin is autistic (see Folstein and Rutter 1977 for a review). Most of these document concordance for autism in monozygotic twins, but cannot serve as a firm basis for conclusions.

The most obvious reason for the comparative lack of twin studies in autism is the rarity of the disorder and the relative rarity of twin births. Thus, in the whole of Great Britain, Folstein and Rutter (1977) found only 21 sex-matched pairs in which at least one twin was autistic and in which those cases with known causative disorders had been excluded. Gillberg (1984f), in a preliminary report from a study of autism and related conditions among twins in Scandinavia and Finland, found 30 sex-matched pairs identified on the basis of at least one childhood psychotic twin. These studies are thorough and together

61

encompass a total screening population of some 20 million children and adolescents.

Ritvo, in a survey of familial autism in the US, so far has reported on 40 pairs of twins, in which at least one is afflicted with autism (Ritvo et al. 1984).

The British study yielded results consonant with the hypothesis which links autism with heritable language-related cognitive deficiencies. Of 11 (eight male, three female) monozygotic (MZ) twin pairs, four (all male) were concordant for "typical" (Kanner) or "atypical" autism (later debut or not such striking behavioral oddities as in the Kanner group with elaborate repetitive routines). In another five MZ pairs, the non-autistic twin showed either speech-language disorders (in some cases reminiscent of autistic-like language disorders, such as echolalia and reversal of pronouns, and late onset of speech, or an "uneven" IQ profile with low verbal scores or general intellectual retardation. Of the ten (seven male, three female) dizygotic (DZ) twin pairs none was concordant for autism, but in one pair one twin had autism and the other had displayed speech delay, echolalia, repetitive speech and a borderline IQ (74 [fullscale] and 60 [language]).

Folstein and Rutter (1977) also noted that in their *discordant* twin pairs (n=17), neonatal hazards (hemolytic disease, asphyxia, convulsions, second twin born more than 30 minutes after first, and multiple physical anomalies) affected the autistic twin in six out of 17 cases, but not the non-autistic twins. Altogether, 12 of the 17 autistic twins in the discordant pairs, compared with none of the 17 non-autistic twins, had non-optimal perinatal factors when compared with their co-twin.

Finally, in the English study on twins, there were no major differences within the twin pairs with regard to psychosocial factors. In summary, Folstein and Rutter concluded that autism often requires a heritable cognitive defect involving language to develop, but that it can occur on the basis of brain damage alone.

The Scandinavian/Finnish study on twins is currently in progress. Preliminary data (based on diagnoses made by treating doctors, but not yet in all cases confirmed by the researchers) point in the direction of a high concordance rate in MZ pairs and a much lower (perhaps nil) rate of infantile autism in the DZ pairs. With regard to "cognitive defects of any kind" (for example, learning disorders, mental retardation, severe speech-language disorders, or autism), the concordance rate in the sex-matched MZ pairs (16 pairs) appears to be 100 percent, compared with 21 percent in the sex-matched DZ pairs (14 pairs).

In the Ritvo study (Ritvo et al. 1984) from the US—in which families with more than one autistic sibling or with twins (one or both autistic) were enrolled after an advertisement in a newsletter—concordance for autism was seen in 22 of 23 MZ pairs (96 percent) and in 4 of 17 DZ pairs (24 percent).

Thus, the preliminary findings of the Scandinavian and US studies are in general accord with those of the British study. On this combined evidence, it appears likely that in some cases a predisposition to developing autism is inherited whereas in others autism follows specific brain lesions. Clinical evidence, and results from a population study in Göteborg, Sweden (Gillberg 1984a) suggest that, in still other cases, a combination of hereditary and brain-damaging factors may be crucial in the genesis of autism. Ritvo (Ritvo et al. 1984) has suggested that his concordance rates fit a model for autosomal recessive inheritance in some cases of autism (see the special section on autosomal recessive inheritance treated later in this chapter).

Autism in Siblings

Family studies, attempting to sort out possible genetic and constitutional factors, are also very few. The most valid are population-based studies, such as those by Lotter (1966) and Gillberg (Gillberg and Wahlström 1984). These two studies have indicated a 50 to 100-fold increase in the risk rate for developing autism in the siblings of autistic children; this means that two to five percent of the siblings of autistic children are themselves autistic. A number of clinic-based studies have indicated the same raised frequency of autism in siblings (Rutter 1965; Kanner and Lesser 1958; Creak and Ini 1960). In a study based on questionnaires from 4,200 families who voluntarily mailed them in, Rimland found approximately 1.6 percent of the families showed multiple incidence, even excluding twins (Coleman and Rimland 1976). Somewhat out of line with most other studies is the work of Spence et al. (1973) who found a high rate of nine percent in a study of 47 families. In none of these studies were data published regarding the subgroups of the autistic syndrome in the families where siblings were affected. Thus, in genetic counseling of families of autistic children, these data can provide an overall guideline, but are, by definition, out of date. The specific disease entity, with its specific genetic patterns, is the information needed to give accurate genetic counseling to families of autistic children.

Autism in Families

If genetic factors are responsible in some families for autism, the questions that arise have to do with the frequency of genetic illness in autism and the pattern of inheritance. Coleman and Rimland (1976), on the basis of a clinical sample of 78 cases, were among the first to measure the prevalence of autism in the extended family of cousins and other relatives. They found an 8 percent incidence. Gillberg in his epidemiological study from Göteborg, Sweden (Gillberg 1984a), also found that 8 percent of the families showed multiple incidence (parents, siblings, aunts, uncles, grandparents and first cousins were surveyed). But this kind of work is still in its infancy. Because of the dominance of males over females with the syndrome, the possibility of an X-linked recessive mechanism seems logical. In fact, one subgroup of autism has been identified as having such an X-linked recessive pattern (see chapter 13).

Some evidence in favor of the fragile-X (q27) chromosome abnormality being important in the genesis of autism in such a subgroup is provided by a recent study of triplets (Gillberg 1983a). Identical triplets (11-year-old boys) all showed the classic combination of symptoms typical of Kanner autism, moderate mental retardation, and the fragile-X (q27) abnormality. In a total population study of autism including 25 families with autistic children (Gillberg and Wahlström 1984), one family, or four percent, had two brothers with autism and normal to near-normal intelligence. One of them had psychomotor epilepsy. Both showed the fragile-X (q27) abnormality. In a clinic-based sample of 19 families with autistic children, the same authors found another family—representing five percent—with two autistic brothers. Both of these were moderately to severely mentally retarded and one had psychomotor epilepsy. Both had the fragile-X (q27) syndrome with the typical physical appearance and the chromosome abnormality (Figure 6.1).

From the Swedish chromosome studies (see chapter 13) comes evidence that in certain families other chromosome abnormalities may be important.

Evidence is building to suggest that there is also an autosomal recessive subgroup (or subgroups) with autism. In the Coleman and Rimland (1976) study, the conclusion was that the data most closely fit this autosomal recessive pattern.

The international family study referred to previously is presently going on at UCLA (Ritvo et al. 1982; 1984). An international "bank"

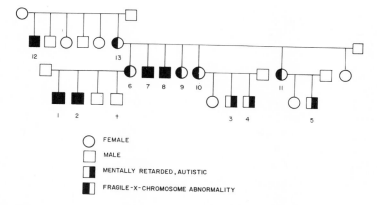

FEMALE

MALE

MENTALLY RETARDED, AUTISTIC

FRAGILE-X-CHROMOSOME ABNORMALITY

FIGURE 6.1. Family with several autistic-fragile-X positive males. Case 1, severely mentally retarded ten-year-old boy with classical Kanner autism. Case 2, his brother, moderately mentally retarded with autism and psychomotor epilepsy, 14 years old. These brothers have one healthy brother. One elder brother was stillborn. Their mother is fragile-X positive (6), shy, and has articulation problems. Two of her brothers are fragile-X positive (cases 7,8) moderately mentally retarded and autistic adults with aloofness, insistence on sameness and echolalia. Three of her four sisters are fragile-X positive (cases 9, 10, and 11). Two of the three fragile-X positive sisters have two moderately retarded sons and one mildly retarded son, respectively, all three of whom are autistic (cases 3,4 and 5). These three boys have not yet been chromosomally examined. The maternal grandmother (13) is fragile-X positive and to this day retains speech/language problems. One of her brothers is moderately mentally retarded and autistic (case 12), and he shows the fragile-X chromosome abnormality. The great-grandparents are dead.

of autistic, multiple-incidence families is being reported from the Neuropsychiatric Institute. In October 1983 (Ritvo et al. 1983b) there were 308 families with at least one autistic child and at least one first- or second-degree relative with autism (n=120) or with some other kind of developmental disorder (n=188). Naturally, this study is not as reliable for percentage data as the previously mentioned epidemiological studies because of the large number of possible selection factors (for example, all cases have responded to an advertisement). Nevertheless, the large number of families, and the detailed analysis of the data make this study highly interesting. The results of the twin part of the Ritvo study add further strength to the "partial heredity" argument.

Now, as mentioned above, the Ritvo study also contains a large number of non-twin, multiple-incidence families with autism. Ritvo has considered four different genetic mechanisms to account for the bulk of the data (Ritvo et al. 1983): (1) gonosomal recessive, (2) polygenic threshold, (3) dominant, and (4) autosomal recessive inheritance. In conclusion, Ritvo states that the autosomal recessive model is consistent with his findings, but that the sex ratios in the multiple-incidence families are the same as in the populations studies. However, this ratio could reflect that a subgroup of autistic children might have a predominant, rare X-linked syndrome, viz. the fragile-X (q27) chromosome abnormality.

From the UCLA family study come other potentially important results regarding shared parental HLA antigens (Stubbs et al. 1984). The hypothesis is that heterozygosity between parents with regard to human leukocyte antigens (HLA) is important for the protection of the fetus from the mother's immune system, but that, in autism, where onset is from birth or shortly after, and mothers often suffer from pre-eclampsia or have an increased incidence of spontaneous abortions, homozygosity might be more common. The parents of autistic children (52 families) were compared with the parents of normal children (83 families). In the experimental group, 77 percent shared at least one HLA antigen compared with 22 percent in the control group ($p < .0001$). This research is only just beginning, but might prove to be very fruitful for the understanding of the genesis of some of the autistic syndromes.

Autosomal Recessive Inheritable Autistic Syndromes

The family studies, in particular those of the Ritvo group, indicate a subgroup of familial autism among the autistic syndromes. Obviously, the fragile-X (q27) chromosome abnormality is responsible for a number of the autistic syndromes occurring in several males within the same family. However, there are also multiple-incidence families in which both boys and girls are affected. Thus, in the Los Angeles study (Ritvo et al. 1983) of 42 families with two autistic children, in 28 (a full two-thirds) both were male, in 11 there was an autistic brother and an autistic sister, and in three families both were female. So far, Ritvo has only analyzed for the occurrence of the fragile-X (q27) chromosome abnormality in a minority of the cases and found it to be present in one family with two autistic boys. The family pedigree data in the Ritvo study are consonant with an autosomal recessive inheritance model. If allowance is made for an important fraction of the 28 families with two male autistics to be accounted for by the Martin-Bell syndrome, the remaining cases fit an autosomal recessive construct almost perfectly.

The study by Coleman and Rimland (1976) also suggests the existence of an autosomal recessive inheritable autistic syndrome. Their results too lend support to the notion of both a sex-linked (the Martin-Bell group) and an autosomal recessive subgroup of hereditary autism. It is possible that these groups might be distinguishable by means of physical characteristics (for example, large ears and testicles at least in postpubertal Martin-Bell cases), but so far no conclusive evidence in this respect exists.

In this context, some mention should also be made of the metabolic disorders (see chapter 16) linked with autism. These disorders have turned out to be autosomal recessive (or sex-linked recessive in a few cases). Thus, one would expect that the metabolic etiologies of autism will contribute to the genetic subgroups.

7   Preconception, Prenatal, and Perinatal Studies

Children who are found with a disease entity whose symptoms often become apparent in early infancy are in a group of patients where the preconception and the prenatal histories of the parents may have direct relevance to the child's illness. In this chapter, evidence from the literature reviewing preconception and prenatal histories of the parents of autistic children will be summarized.

PRECONCEPTION FACTORS

In 1976, at the Children's Brain Research Clinic in Washington, D.C., 78 autistic children were studied, along with 78 age- and sex-matched controls (Coleman 1976). One of the criteria for eligibility to participate in the project for both the patient and the control was an elaborate six-page questionnaire to be filled out by the parents. The information was, of course, retrospective. Since the patients and controls ranged up to the age of 22 years, some very old information was required, and thus the questionnaire—particularly concerning preconception and prenatal history—was bound to be incomplete. However, since the limitations of this retrospective study might be assumed to apply equally to the parents of both the autistic children and the control children, there was nevertheless a value in raising certain basic questions.

An analysis of the preconception history showed that there were two areas where there was a statistically significant difference between the information provided by the parents of autistic children and that supplied by the parents of control children.

One of these areas was exposure to chemicals. In 20 families of the autistic patients (or 24 percent of all parents participating), an unusual amount of exposure to chemicals had occurred during the preconception period. In fact, in four of these families, both the mother and the father had been exposed to chemicals, mostly with both parents working professionally as chemists. However, since the parents of the autistic children who participated in this project were self-selected to participate in one of the first large biochemical studies ever performed on autistic children, it is possible that chemists, familiar with biochemical problems, might have selectively joined in this particular study.

In an attempt to answer this question of self-selection by the parents, a second study was done by another investigator. This new study took a group of 20 unselected autistic patients who were enrolled in a residential setting that could provide necessary services. These were compared with 20 retarded, nonautistic children in the same setting, and with a control group of 20 normal children in the nearby community. The parents of all three groups then filled out an elaborate preconception history questionnaire. Felicetti (1981), who did this study, reported that parents who had been exposed to chemical toxins accounted for 21 percent of the autistic group compared with 2.7 percent of the retarded control group and 10 percent of the normal control group, again a statistically significant finding, in spite of the relatively small number of patients under study. In this second study, five of the parents of the autistic children were found to be professional chemists.

The best type of research for producing accurate information is a prospective study. Such a study was the Collaborative Perinatal Study at the National Institutes of Neurologic Diseases and Stroke (Niswander and Gordon 1972) where 55,908 pregnancies were followed prospectively, starting in early pregnancy, and continuing until the child was born and then reached seven years of age. From among this group, fourteen children were identified who conformed to the syndrome of infantile autism. Torrey et al. (1975) matched this autistic group of fourteen children with two control groups: one of normal children and one of neurologically and behaviorally normal children with low IQ's. The controls were matched in race, sex, habitat (that is, they were from the same section of the country), and socioeconimic factors. Marcus and Broman (in preparation) tabulated the preconception occupations of the parents of the autistic children and of the two control groups. They found an increase in occupations that involved exposure to chemicals in the parents of the autistic patients.

These studies raise the question about preconception exposure factors in parents of autistic children. What would be useful next is a prospective study of a population of chemists and workers exposed to chemical toxins. Moreover, future studies need to have a much greater number of participants so that the results will not be skewed by small numbers. Until then, the "chemical connection" in autism remains a challenging hypothesis.

In the 1976 study at the Children's Brain Research Clinic, the other statistically significant difference found was that between the parents of autistic children and the parents of controls regarding the presence of hypothyroidism in the preconception history. In this study, five fathers and eleven mothers of the autistic patients reported having thyroid disease prior to conception, and in two cases, both parents (both father and mother) had a diagnosis of hypothyroidism at some time prior to the conception of the child. In the control group, one father and three mothers reported a diagnosis of hypothyroidism. These differences were statistically significant. Although thyroid disease, per se, has not been reported as increased in autistic patients (see chapter 19), the finding does have another possible implication. Many cases of hypothyroidism in adults are caused by autoimmune disease, and the role of autoimmune factors in autism is currently an active area of research (see chapter 8).

The study group from the Collaborative Perinatal Study of N. I. H. who had prospectively identified 14 autistic children and controls (Torrey et al. 1975) evaluated a number of preconception factors determined from the records and the mother's memory at the time of the pregnancy. In the Torrey et al. study (1975), the variables that were looked at included the mother's history of irregular menstrual periods and dysmenorrhea, previous x-rays, past illnesses, transfusions and immunizations, and the maternal age at the time of delivery. They also included the history of stillbirths and spontaneous abortions prior to the birth of the studied child and in the subsequent seven year period. In none of these variables was any statistically significant difference found between the parents of the autistic children and the two sets of controls.

In 1983, Funderburk et al. looked again at some of the questions addressed by the Torrey study using a larger patient group, this time in a retrospective study. They studied 61 patients, 51 of whom either met the criteria of autism or had autistic features or language disorders not specified. The other ten patients had a diagnosis of either classic or atypical psychosis. For control data, these authors used three previously reported surveys of normal infants born during the same period as the patients in the study and in comparable statewide or metropolitan areas. Comparing their patient group to the three published controls, they found that 13.1 percent of the parents of autistic or psychotic children had experienced a problem with infertility, and 11.5 percent with more than two spontaneous abortions. The increased rate of infertility and spontaneous abortions was considerably higher in the sample population than in the control populations where infertility affected only 3.7 percent and more than two spontaneous abortions 5.2 percent.

In 1983, Gillberg and Gillberg reported a study of 25 children with a diagnosis of autism in the region of Göteborg, Sweden and compared them to children of the same sex, born in the same obstetrics department. The pre- and perinatal conditions under which these children were born were evaluated, using an optimality/reduced optimality concept of Prechtl (1980). One factor studied of the preconception history was the record of more than two spontaneous abortions prior to the pregnancy of the index child. Not found in the control group, this history was present in one mother of an autistic child.

Regarding the mean maternal age, the Gillberg and Gillberg (1983) study also showed a statistically significant increase in maternal age (over 30 years of age) in the autistic group, confirming an earlier study by Gillberg (1980). Maternal age is an area where the medical literature is divided. In addition to Gillberg and Gillberg, Allanen et al. (1964), Treffert (1970), and Finnegan and Quarrington (1979) all found evidence of increased maternal age in their surveys. In contrast, Lotter (1966), Torrey et al. (1975) and Wiedel and Coleman (1976) have reported no differences in maternal age between the parents of autistic patients and controls.

One assumption suggests that the disparities in these reports are based on differences in the diagnoses of the autistic syndrome, a problem confronting all the material reviewed in this book. Another possibility is that, since autism is a syndrome of many etiologies, different subgroups of the syndrome vary in number from one study group to another. Gillberg (1984d) recently has suggested that the etiologies of the autistic syndrome may show wide regional variation, as is the case with mental retardation syndromes.

Increasing maternal age is associated with a large number of central nervous system syndromes of childhood, ranging from Down's syndrome (Pueschel 1982) to minimal brain dysfunction (Gillberg et al. 1982). As knowledge advances, the relevant question will be which of the many diagnostic subgroups of the autistic syndrome are associated with older maternal age.

PRENATAL FACTORS

Prenatal events that occur during the gestation of a child who later is diagnosed as autistic have been studied in several surveys.

The study from the Collaborative Perinatal Study of the National Institutes of Neurologic Diseases and Stroke (where 14 autistic patients were identified in a prospective study of 55,908 pregnancies) is the only prospective study of these variables in the medical literature. The study looked at 15 factors and identified a single prenatal event which appeared to be significantly associated with the subsequent development of infantile autism; namely, maternal uterine bleeding during pregnancy. Of the 14 mothers in the study, nine (64 percent) had some bleeding compared with five (36 percent) of the low IQ control group and four (29 percent) of the normal IQ control group. The authors note that the distribution by trimesters was probably as important as the incidence of bleeding in these mothers. There was a significant amount of early and especially mid-trimester bleeding among mothers who subsequently delivered autistic children. The difference in mid-trimester bleeding was significant at the level of $p < .01$. In the other control groups, mid-trimester bleeding was extremely rare.

There have been a number of retrospective studies which examine perinatal complications associated with autism (or autism and childhood schizophrenia) (see chapter 15). Sometimes the studies have not singled out gestational bleeding as an individual variable, and are accordingly very difficult to interpret. In the study by Harper and Williams (1974), gestational bleeding was separated out as a sign of threatened abortion, and was said to occur significantly more often among autistic, than among physically ill children, but not more frequently among autistic than among emotionally disturbed children. The retrospective Deykin and MacMahon (1979) study of 163 autistic children compared with an unaffected sibling control group found 16 percent maternal bleeding in the gestations of the autistic children, but only 7 percent for their siblings. In the study by Gillberg and Gillberg (1983), bleeding during pregnancy was one of the single factors found significantly more commonly in the autistic than in the control group. The Campbell et al. (1978b) study found a spectacular 71 percent bleeding before the third trimester, compared to 49 percent for siblings.

To date, bleeding during pregnancy, particularly during the mid-trimester, is the main finding that seems to stand out from the literature regarding gestational factors related to autism. There are, of course, many autistic children whose mothers did not bleed during pregnancy. (Torrey et al. [1975] cautions that it is difficult to interpret a result in any individual case since, in their study, the only woman who had a confirmed case of rubella during pregnancy and also bled in the third trimester had a child who was in the group of normal IQ controls!) In the Funderburk et al. (1983) study referred to earlier, increased gestational exposure to hormones was noted. In some of the autistic cases, the reason for the administration of hormones appears to have been maternal bleeding, although it does not account for all the cases of administration of progesterone/estrogen or cortisone compounds.

Theoretically, it is interesting to speculate on the meaning of mid-trimester bleeding. If bleeding occurs at a time when or shortly after the lesion occurs to the fetus, it might help suggest why many autistic children are so normal in appearance. If, in fact, the insult that struck the central nervous system of these infants occurred after the first trimester, then the injury occurred after the formation of the face was more or less complete. However, the second trimester is a very important time for brain differentiation and growth. This would explain, then, how there could be brain problems in such normal looking, attractive children whose pictures are seen throughout this book.

In the Gillberg and Gillberg (1983) Swedish study, signs of clinical dysmaturity and pre- or postmaturity were other single factors that were significantly more common in the autistic than in the control group. These authors found, however, that if one looks at the overall picture such as is seen in the optimality/reduced optimality concept, one gets a clearer picture of the perinatal complications in autistic children. In the Gillberg and Gillberg study, 48 percent of the cases with infantile autism had reduced optimality scores above the 95th percentile for the control group. In their study, both boys and girls had equally high values. One very interesting finding of these authors was that all autistic children showing reduced optimality in the peri- and neonatal period also had reductions in prenatal optimality.

At this stage of understanding of the problem, the optimality concept is helpful. In this careful study of autistic children, almost half may give evidence of sub-optimal conditions in the pre- and perinatal period. Since Swedish obstetrical and neonatal care is uniformly organized and data recording is done in accordance with highly structured manuals, this study, based on careful records, is useful in again emphasizing the multiple organic factors that may underlie the clinical symptoms in patients with the autistic syndromes.

In understanding these results, it is interesting to compare recent investigations of reduced optimality in cerebral palsy (Kyllerman 1982). These findings reveal that children with infantile autism, although having reduced optimality in the perinatal period, are not so heavily affected on optimality scores as those suffering from dyskinetic cerebral palsy. Although cerebral palsy is the syndrome generally thought to be associated with asphyxiation during the birth process, there is pathological evidence to suggest that a major portion of the central nervous system's lesions present at birth are due to processes of *prenatal* origin that have occurred well in advance of labor (Towbin 1969). Like autistic children, the majority of children later diagnosed as having cerebral palsy are of normal birthweight and term gestational age (Ellenberg and Nelson 1979). Thus, in this chapter, where we emphasize the evidence that there is a suboptimal perinatal period in many autistic patients, we do not necessarily imply that birth injury per se, rather than earlier gestational events or metabolic predisposition, puts a fetus at risk for perinatal morbidity.

IN UTERO STUDIES

Prenatal diagnosis of some of the genetic subgroups that are associated with autism is now a reality. In the case of chromosomal syndromes, it has been demonstrated that the fragile-X chromosome can be identified in cultured amniotic fluid cells (Jenkins et al. 1981; Shapiro et al. 1982). It also can be detected prenatally through fetoscopy using short term leukocyte cultures (Webb et al. 1981).

In the metabolic subgroups found in the autistic syndromes, the identification of a specific enzyme abnormality is possible if the enzyme is present in fibroblasts. Even in the case of phenylketonuria (where the enzyme in error—phenylalanine hydroxylase—is a hepatic enzyme not present in fibroblasts), the possibility of prenatal identification has been announced using recombinant DNA techniques (Woo et al. 1983).

8   Biochemical Studies

There have been many attempts to define the biochemistry of autistic children, and these studies will be reported in this chapter. The difficulties in interpreting these studies are enormous, however, because of the diagnostic problems within the syndrome. As with studies in schizophrenia, many studies have been done with autistic children in which they were lumped into a single category and compared either with normal controls or with other types of psychotic children. Very few studies have looked for subgroups within the syndrome of bio-chemical abnormalities.

Since children with many different types of autism were studied as a group, and since the goal was simply to discover some final common pathway or some final mechanism in autism that might explain the symptom complex, these studies are very difficult to interpret.

The main results of these studies have produced two predominant patterns. In one pattern of results, a finding is found with some consistency, but certainly not in every case, and when compared with other groups studied, there is great variability in the data. Examples of this kind of result are those in blood serotonin and serum free fatty acids. This pattern can be a sign of a syndrome rather than of a single disease entity.

In the other pattern the results are flatly contradictory, for example, in the platelet uptake of serotonin. In many cases, the studies were done by well trained investigators using well established techniques in good laboratories. The answer to interpreting these studies may not lie so much in refining the laboratory techniques as in learning how to sort the patients into different clinical or biochemical subcategories which can then be studied as more homogeneous groups. In studying this patient group, many of the right biochemical questions have yet to be asked. The day could come when it may be considered as limiting to study the biochemistry of an undifferentiated group of children with "autism" as it is today to study the biochemistry of an undifferentiated group of children with "mental retardation."

STUDIES OF SEROTONIN AND ITS METABOLITES

One of the first biochemical studies done on autistic patients examined levels of serotonin (5-hydroxytryptamine, 5-HT) in the blood (Figure 8.1). 5-HT is present in several different body tissues: the enterochromaffin system of the gastro-intestinal tract, the spleen, the platelets in blood, and the central and peripheral nervous systems. Studies in rats by Fuxe and his co-workers (1968) have shown that the 5-HT nerve cell bodies are mainly localized in the raphe nuclei of the lower brainstem; some are also found surrounding the pyramidal tract and in the medioventral part of the caudal tegmentum. No 5-HT cell bodies are found in the spinal cord, the diencephalon or the telencephalon. The axons from the 5-HT nerve cell bodies extend throughout the nervous system with 5-HT terminals concentrated in the visceral nuclei of pons and medulla, reticular formation, hypothalamus, thalamus, amygdala and septal area.

When 5-HT is measured in the blood, it is not a direct measure of central nervous system serotonin. Haverback and Davidson (1958) studied an adult patient with resection of the large and small intestine and demonstrated that 97 percent of his whole blood 5-HT and 75 percent of his urinary 5-HIAA originated from the intestines. In our laboratory, we studied the whole blood level of a newborn who died at

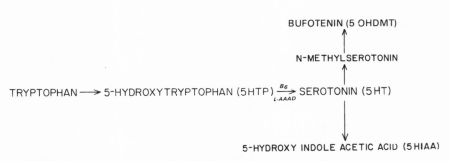

FIGURE 8.1. Metabolic pathway of serotonin. The enzyme and co-enzyme discussed in text are marked on diagram.

seven days of age with agenesis of the gastrointestinal system. The 5-HT level (0.5 ng/ml) was the lowest we had ever recorded (Coleman and Mahanand 1973). Serotonin synthesized outside the central nervous system does not cross into the brain because of selective active transport ("blood brain") barriers. CNS 5-HT is made de novo from tryptophan. Bertaccini (1960) has shown that in the rat the total removal of the gastrointestinal tract has very little effect on brain 5-HT, in spite of decreasing serum, spleen and lung 5-HT levels.

Thus, serotonin in the brain is not directly measurable. In the blood, almost all the serotonin is in the platelet. However, the platelet in the blood may be used as a partial model for a neurone-containing 5-HT (Paasonen 1968). Both cells (platelet, neurone) transport 5-HT by an energy-dependent process, store it in subcellular organelles of similar electron-microscopic appearance and metabolize 5-HT in a similar way (Pletscher 1968; Born and Gillson 1959). In autistic patients, studies have primarily been of whole blood or platelet serotonin or of the end product of the serotonin metabolic pathway—5-hydroxyindole acetic acid (5-HIAA). Inside the platelets, serotonin is bound to ATP in a micelle formation (Berneis et al. 1969).

The first description of serotonin in autistic patients was by Schain and Freedman (1961), who described elevated levels of endogenous serotonin in whole blood in six out of 23 patients with autism. The patients were a group of withdrawn, disturbed children with a variety of neurological and psychiatric diagnoses, including hydrocephalus. In 1970, two papers were published by a research group in Los Angeles (Yuwiler et al. 1970; Ritvo et al. 1970), confirming that serotonin in whole blood tends to be elevated in cases "variously diagnosed as early infantile autism, atypical ego development, symbiotic psychosis and certain cases of childhood schizophrenia." Although they noted increased platelet counts, this did not account for the elevation of serotonin. They also did a careful study of circadian rhythm of serotonin levels in their patients, but this did not account for the abnormal results either. In a large study of 72 autistic patients diagnosed by the criteria used in this book and compared with 71 age- and sex-matched controls, a statistically significant elevation of serotonin was again confirmed in whole blood by Goldstein et al. (1976). In addition to these studies using whole blood, other studies using platelet methodology (Campbell et al. 1975; Hanley et al. 1977; Takahash et al. 1976) have also confirmed a predominant pattern of elevation of serotonin in autistic patients, as did several serum studies (Suemitsu et al. 1974; Hoshino et al. 1979).

In all these studies, a consistent finding appeared to be an unusually great variability exceeding that of controls (Table 8.1A). In fact, a careful examination of the data indicates that, in addition to a large number of autistic patients with high serotonin levels, there was also a significant subgroup with low levels. In the 1974 paper by Campbell et al., one autistic patient was reported to have the lowest level in the study, lower even than any control. In the large study reported by Goldstein et al. (1976), 25 percent of the patients had serotonin levels below their age- and sex-matched controls. Again, the striking finding in this study was the great variability in the results. In the Yuwiler et al. (1971) study, although the mean showed elevated levels of serotonin in a small sample of only seven children, two of the seven had low serotonin levels.

Thus, the findings confirm that, in addition to the high serotonin group of patients which is more fully discussed in the literature, there is a smaller subgroup of patients who have distinctly low levels of this amine.

In an attempt to understand why serotonin levels in the blood of these children were abnormal, studies have been done regarding the mechanism of uptake and binding of serotonin in platelets. Siva Sankar et al. (1963) studied the mechanisms in the platelets for uptake of serotonin and found them decreased. Twelve years later, Yuwiler also studied the uptake mechanism and found it within the normal limits (Yuwiler et al. 1975). In a more recent study, Rotman et al. (1980) found the uptake elevated.

Thus, all three possibilities are reported!

Studies also have been done on the efflux of serotonin out of platelets. Two early studies by Boullin and co-workers (Boullin et al. 1970; Boullin et al. 1971), using the E-2 Rimland Diagnostic Checklist for clinical diagnosis, found the efflux of serotonin out of the platelets increased. In a later study by Yuwiler and co-authors (1975), using other clinical criteria for diagnosis, the efflux was found to be within the normal range.

The amino acid precursor of serotonin, tryptophan, was also studied in the serum of ten autistic children, compared with both child and adult controls (Hoshino et al. 1979). There was no significant difference between the mean serum-free tryptophan concentration in the children and their controls (adults) even though this was the same patient group where the authors had reported an elevation of serum serotonin levels. The authors did note, however, an abnormally elevated

TABLE 8.1.   Studies of Biogenic Amine Pathways Reported in Patients with Symptoms of Autism.

A. Serotonin and its metabolites

Biochemical	Medium	Result	Authors
Serotonin (5-HT) endogenous level	whole blood	great variability and predominantly elevated	Schain & Freedman 1961
	"	"	Yuwiler et al. 1970
	"	"	Ritvo et al. 1970
	"	"	Goldstein et al. 1976
	platelets	"	Campbell et al. 1975
	"	"	Hanley et al. 1977
	"	"	Takahashi et al. 1976
	serum	"	Suemitsu et al. 1974
	"	"	Hoshino et al. 1979
5-HT uptake	platelets	decreased	Sankar et al. 1963
	"	WNL[1]	Yuwiler et al. 1975
5-HT efflux	platelets	elevated*	Rotman et al. 1980
	"	elevated*	Boullin et al. 1970
	"	"*	Boullin et al. 1971
	"	WNL	Yuwiler et al. 1975
5-hydroxyindoleacetic acid (5-HIAA)	CSF	high level after probenecid*	Cohen et al. 1974
	"	low level after probenecid*	Cohen et al. 1977b
	"	WNL*	Winsberg et al. 1980
	"	WNL[1]	Gillberg et al. 1983
Bufotenin (5-OHDMT)	urine	present in 83% of patients	Himwich et al. 1972

TABLE 8.1 (continued)

B. Catecholamines and their metabolites

Biochemical	Medium	Results	Authors
Dopamine (DA)	platelets	greater variability in uptake and efflux	Boullin & O'Brien 1972
		uptake slightly elevated*	Szekely et al. 1980
Norepinephrine (NE)	plasma	elevated endogenous level	Lake et al. 1977
Epinephrine (E)	urine	decreased	Young et al. 1978
	"	"	Young et al. 1979
Homovanillic acid (HVA)	CSF	WNL[1] (tendency to elevation)*	Cohen, et al. 1974
	"	"	Cohen et al. 1977b
	"	"	Winsberg et al. 1980
	"	elevated	Gillberg et al. 1983
	urine	"	Garreau et al. 1980
	"	"	Lelord et al. 1978
3-methoxy-4-hydroxy-phenethylene glycol (MHP6)	urine	decreased	Young et al. 1978
	"	"	Young et al. 1979
	plasma	WNL	Young et al. 1981b
	CSF	WNL	Young et al. 1981b
Hydroxymetoxyphenyl-glycol (HMP6)	CSF	WNL	Gillberg et al. 1983
Homoprotocate-chuic acid	urine	present in 88% of patients	Landgrebe & Landgrebe 1976

C. Enzymes of the biogenic amine pathways

Enzyme	Medium	Result	Authors
Dopamine-beta-hydroxylase (DBH)	serum	decreased	Goldstein et al. 1976
	plasma	"	Lake et al. 1977
	plasma	WNL[1]*	Belmaker et al. 1978
	serum	"	Young et al. 1980
Catechol O methyl transferase (COMT)	RBC	WNL	O'Brien et al. 1976
	"	"*	Belmaker et al. 1978
	"	"	Giller et al. 1980
	fibroblasts	"	Giller et al. 1980
Monoamine oxidase (MAO)	platelet	WNL	Boullin et al. 1976
	"	"	Campbell et al. 1976a
	"	"	Roth et al. 1976
	"	"	Cohen et al. 1977b
	"	"	Lake et al. 1977
	plasma	WNL*	Belmaker et al. 1978
	platelets (type B)	"	Giller et al. 1980
	fibroblasts (type A)	"	Giller et al. 1980

[1]WNL—within normal limits

*compared with children with psychiatric or neurological diseases rather than normal controls concentration of serum free tryptophan in two of the children who were markedly hyperkinetic and aggressive in behavior.

In another approach to studying serotonin in autistic children, Cohen et al. (1974) published a study on cerebral spinal fluid levels of the end product of serotonin (5-hydroxyindoleacetic acid [5-HIAA], using the probenecid method in autistic children. However, as with all techniques, the probenecid method has limitations (Cowdry et al. 1983). The Cohen group reported that compared with epileptic children, autistic children were reported to have higher levels of 5-HIAA in their spinal fluids. However, when they redid the study on a larger number of autistic children and other controls, they found a *low* level of 5-HIAA in the cerebral spinal fluid of the autistic children (Cohen et al. 1977b). Winsberg et al. (1980) also found a low level of 5-HIAA after probenecid. More recently, Gillberg et al. (1983) have found an endogenous level of 5-HIAA that is not statistically different from controls.

Again, three different results comprising the three possibilities are reported.

The major pathway for the metabolism of serotonin results in the formation of 5-HIAA, and the overall degradative process is composed of two steps: first there is the oxidative deamination of 5-HT to 5-hydroxyindoleacetaldehyde; this is then catalyzed by the enzyme, monoamine oxidase (MAO), to 5-HIAA. Serotonin is also converted to other compounds, including bufotenin, a minor metabolite. Though there is an enzyme in the brain which could N-methylate 5-HT to bufotenin, the enzyme has a relatively high Km, so it was thought that the enzyme level may never reach a concentration in which this enzyme may be physiologically significant, except in cases of inhibition of MAO. In 1972, Himwich et al. decided to look at bufotenin levels in the urine of autistic children. They already found bufotenin and two other N,N dimethyltryptamines in the urine of several chronic schizophrenics who were receiving a monoamine oxidase inhibitor. They then reported that five of the six subjects with "a possible diagnosis" of infantile autism provided positive results for bufotenin, while at the same time six normal children and normal adults failed to excrete any of these compounds in their urine samples. There is no mention that any of the autistic children were on any drugs inhibiting MAO. A later study revealed that some of the normal parents of the autistic patients also were positive for bufotenin (Narasimhachari and Himwichy 1975).

High endogenous levels of serotonin in the blood have been reported in a large selection of patients with various mental retardation syndromes (Partington et al. 1973). In some of these groups, particularly in the leukodystrophies or in the patients with infantile spasms after their seizure syndrome has ended, autistic features can be present (see chapter 4). A review of the literature (Campbell et al. 1974) and our own practices suggest that the very high serotonin blood levels tend to be associated usually with low intelligence quotients.

In fact, serotonin can sometimes give an indication of the success of therapeutic intervention in a patient with an abnormal blood serotonin level, for example, in thyroid disease. Serotonin is related to thyroid function in two ways: the mesencephalic centers that regulate endocrine activity are affected by central nervous system levels; and serotonin is present in the thyroid gland itself. Infants with hypothyroidism have abnormally high serotonin values (Coleman 1970). Early initiation of thyroid replacement therapy in patients with infant hypothyroidism can be of value in ameliorating the retardation seen in untreated children. In one such case, the serotonin level fell down into the normal range seven days after therapy was started (Coleman and Hur 1973). The same principle in reverse can be seen in low serotonin patients such as those with phenylketonuria. Placement of the patient on a special low phenylalanine diet can result in marked improvement of the usually quite low serotonin level, moving it up toward the normal range (McKean 1971).

At the present time, the mechanism that causes high serotonin levels in many autistic children and relatively low levels in another small subgroup of autistic children is unkown. It is likely that it will be best understood when the underlying biochemical or structural mechanism causing the disease process in the particular autistic child is worked out. For example, high serotonin levels in the blood do not necessarily mean high serotonin levels in the brain. One child with leukodystrophy had a number of well documented high blood levels during life, but was found to have a low level of 5-HT in the central nervous system on autopsy (Coleman et al. 1977). In the case of patients with low serotonin levels, it is now understood that one factor in the low blood serotonin level in phenylketonuric children is due to interference with the metabolic pathway by the presence of an abnormally large number of other aromatic amines (minor metabolites) of the phenylalanine pathway (McKean et al. 1962). In other disease entities, undoubtedly, there are other factors.

Although one current therapeutic attempt in autism (the fenfluramine studies [see chapter 21]) is based on lowering serotonin in the brains of children who have high blood serotonin, the desired therapeutic effect may not be necessarily related to lowering blood levels of serotonin.

In the case of disease entities associated with mental retardation, a larger number have high serotonin levels, but only a few show low serotonin levels (Coleman 1978b). This pattern (the majority with high levels, the minority with low) is the same pattern we currently see in the autistic syndromes. This pattern is one of a number of factors that have led to our understanding that autism is a behavioral syndrome of multiple etiologies rather than a specific disease.

CATECHOLAMINES AND THEIR METABOLITES

Another area where a great deal of work has already been done in autism is that of catecholamine metabolism (Table 8.1B).

The catecholamine pathway is a metabolic pathway where enzyme errors are known to occur that adversely affect the brain (see Figure 8.2). An error in the first enzyme in the pathway, phenylalanine hydroxylase, causes the disease phenylketonuria (PKU). A significant number of these patients have autistic symptoms (see chapter 16). An immaturity in the second step of the pathway can cause a neonatal tyrosinemia, which includes, among its symptoms, later learning disabilities and other CNS problems (Menkes 1972). Following these two amino acids in the pathway are the three active amines—dopamine, norepinephrine and epinephrine. The first two are vital for good brain function. However, we have no model system (such as a particle in the platelet binding serotonin) that is easily available in the blood for studying these two amines in living patients, so they must be studied even more indirectly than serotonin can be studied.

Because of the interest with the serotonin binding system in platelets of autistic patients, an attempt was also made to study dopamine

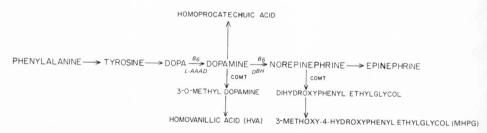

FIGURE 8.2. Metabolic pathway of catecholamines. Enzymes and co-enzymes discussed in text are marked on diagram.

binding in platelets. In 1972, Boullin and O'Brien studied both uptake and efflux from platelets of dopamine and found greater variability but without specific findings. A repetition of the uptake studies in 1980 by Szekely et al. showed a slightly elevated uptake in autistic patients compared with other psychotic children, but the authors expressed significant technical doubts about the value of platelets for the study of dopamine transport.

The other catecholamine thought to have a major role in brain function is norepinephrine. In 1977, Lake et al. studied plasma norepinephrine levels in autistic patients in both the reclining and standing position, and found an elevated endogenous level. These levels, of course, are outside the central nervous system and their relevance to brain function is unknown. Young et al. in both 1978 and 1979, in examining epinephrine, a minor metabolite inside the central nervous system but of major importance in the rest of the body, found decreased levels of this amine in urine specimens.

The end product of dopamine metabolism is homovanillic acid (HVA). There have been a number of studies of cerebral spinal fluid levels of this metabolite (Figure 8.3). The earlier studies by Cohen et al. (1974 and 1977b) found that autistic children do not differ from other diagnostic groups in the spinal fluid levels of this metabolite. However, they noted that the more severely impaired children, especially those with greater locomotor activity and more severe stereopathies, tended to have higher levels. This group also reported cerebral spinal fluid HVA levels in monozygotic twin autistic boys. The more disturbed twin, with more stereotypies and greater hyperactivity, had the higher level (Cohen et al. 1977b). Winsberg et al. (1980) also studied HVA in cerebral spinal fluid. In 1983, Gillberg et al. found a statistically significant difference of mean HVA concentration in a study of 13 autistic children when compared with controls (see Figure 8.3). In this study, a group of children with mental retardation, but without psychotic or autistic behavior traits, were also evaluated and had HVA values within the normal range, so the authors drew the conclusion that the high HVA levels were not specifically associated with the lack of cognitive function.

Elevations of HVA in urine also have been reported by Garreau et al. (1980) and Lelord et al. (1978 and reviewed by Garnier et al. 1983).

An end product of epinephrine metabolism (MHPG) has also been studied in urine, plasma, and cerebral spinal fluid by the Yale group of investigators (Young et al. 1978, 1979, 1981b). They found decreased

FIGURE 8.3. Six-year-old autistic boy with high CSF levels of HVA. Child has severe mental retardation, hyperactivity syndrome, cow's milk intolerance and abnormal auditory brainstem evoked potentials.

levels in the urine in association with the decreased epinephrine levels mentioned above. However, they found plasma and cerebral spinal fluid within the normal range. A study of HMPG (MHPG) by Gillberg et al. in 1983 also found cerebral spinal fluid within the normal range.

In the large study of autistic children with age- and sex-matched controls done at the Children's Brain Research Clinic, thin layer chromatography was performed on the urine of 74 autistic subjects. Eighty-eight percent of the patients were found to have homoprotocatechuic acid (3, 4-dihydroxyphenylacetic acid) in the urine (Landgrebe and Landgrebe 1976). Most literature on this compound reports it as present only after MAO inhibitors are given. This is a minor pathway in catecholamine metabolism, and one that is more likely to show up if there is a blockage in the enzymatic step (DBH) between dopamine and norepinephrine (see Figure 8.2). It is interesting that this is the same group of patients in whom DBH was first demonstrated to be depressed in the serum (Goldstein et al. 1976) (see below).

ENZYMES OF BIOGENIC AMINE PATHWAYS

Enzymes of these biogenic amine pathways have been studied in autistic patients (see Table 8.1C). The three enzymes studied, dopamine beta hydroxylase (DBH), catecholamine O methyl transferase (COMT) and monoamine oxidase (MAO) are all part of the catecholamine pathway. Monoamine oxidase is also involved in the serotonin pathway and elsewhere in central nervous system metabolism.

DBH is a possible index of the activity of the sympathetic nervous system in an individual. DBH is stored with norepinephrine in the granular vesicles of nerve endings of the sympathetic nervous system, as well as in the chromofin granules of the adrenal medulla. At the time that norepinephrine is released into the blood, DBH is released with it, and that is why it is possible to measure it in the plasma.

The results of the study of serum DBH in autism are complicated to interpret. The initial report in the literature of the largest group of patients studied (76, with age- and sex-matched controls) showed a decrease in the serum level (Goldstein et al. 1976). The same finding was replicated a year later in a smaller group of patients who were studied by a different laboratory, but were diagnosed by the same investigator (Lake et al. 1977). In third study, in which serum DBH in autistic patients was compared with that found in normal controls, 22 patients were involved (Young et al. 1980). In this study, although the value showed a trend toward lower levels in the autistic patients compared with both controls and all the patient groups studied, the sample did not show statistical significance. The investigators did report that they found a lack of relationship between age and serum DBH activity in autistic children, a phenomenon which is not seen in normal individuals or in any of the other groups studied to date. In contrast with these three studies that compared autists with normal controls, one that compared autistic children with psychotic children indicated similar plasma DBH levels in both groups (Belmaker et al. 1978).

Dopamine beta hydroxylase levels are very complicated to interpret because there is a familial factor. Members of the same family tend to have similar levels, and occasionally there are some families where no level at all can be determined, which skews any study. In the study by Young et al. (1980) a monozygotic pair of twins was studied and their serum DBH activities were virtually identical; on the other hand, a single dizygotic pair of twins did have some diversion of DBH levels.

The familial factor in DBH activity and the great range of levels among completely normal people make any interpretation of serum DBH as an index of sympathetic nerve activity unreliable (Schanberg and Kirshner 1976). Blood pressure also appears not to be directly related to DBH levels, so it is clear the interpretation of these enzyme levels is extremely complex.

Catecholamines are inactivated by O-methylation via the enzyme catechol O methyl transferase (COMT). The enzyme is available in red cells and has been studied by three groups, all of whom found that the level was in the normal range (O'Brien et al. 1976; Belmaker et al. 1978; Giller et al. 1980). COMT also has been studied in fibroblast preparations by Giller et al. (1980). In his small sample of five autistic patients no abnormality was reported.

An important degradation enzyme in the biogenic amine pathway is monoamine oxidase, which is involved in both the catecholamine and serotonin pathways. A number of studies have been done on monoamine oxidase in platelets, plasma, and fibroblasts, and all studies agree that the results were within the normal range (Boullin et al. 1976, Campbell et al. 1976a, Roth et al. 1976, Cohen et al. 1977b, Lake et al. 1977, Belmaker et al. 1978, Giller et al. 1980).

CYCLIC AMP

Also related to studies on biogenic amine pathways are the studies on cyclic AMP. Cyclic AMP could be considered as a possible reflector of post-synaptic receptor activity because it is believed to act as the "second messenger" inside the cell itself for neurotransmitters such as serotonin and the catecholamines. Cyclic AMP is found in high concentration in the brain with enzymes for synthesizing or degrading it. It is also found elsewhere in the body, mainly in the liver, kidney, lung, and adrenal glands.

In 1978, Belmaker et al. in Israel studied cyclic AMP in the plasma of eight autistic children and found no statistical difference between the levels of those children and children with other types of psychiatric diagnoses, although they were elevated compared with adult control levels. In 1979, Hoshino et al. in Japan studied plasma cyclic AMP concentrations in 20 autistic children, and then compared them with the results in ten normal children and 23 normal adults. They reported that the autistic children had an elevated plasma cyclic AMP concentration, when compared with both groups. Furthermore, they reported that a positive relationship existed between plasma cyclic AMP concentrations and the amount of hyperkinetic behavior in the children. The authors also reported a positive correlation between serum serotonin and plasma cyclic AMP concentration. A second study by the Israeli group (Goldberg et al. 1984) compared autistic and pervasive developmental disorder adolescents with normal adolescents, and again confirmed an elevation of cyclic AMP in the plasma of the patient group. An additional interesting finding was that plasma cyclic GMP, a nucleotide stimulated by different neurotransmitters such as acetylcholine, was not elevated.

DISCUSSION OF THE BIOGENIC AMINE STUDIES

If one looks at the studies of catecholamine and serotonin metabolites in autistic patients, one can observe a pattern that suggests a problem of diagnosis in this patient group. Many studies either are contradictory or show great variability, suggesting that a heterogeneous rather than a homogeneous group of patients is being studied. In 1977, Cohen and Young, reviewing the literature, pointed out that the two Boullin studies reporting increased efflux in autistic patients (Boullin et al. 1970 and 1971) offered "a finding often cited as the only replicable biochemical abnormality of childhood autism." Undoubtedly it was because both studies were conducted on patients clinically diagnosed by the same investigator using exactly the same diagnostic criteria. Since that time, other studies have been replicated, such as the average overall elevation of whole blood serotonin (multiple authors), the urinary decrease in MHPG and epinephrine (Young et al. 1978 and 1979), and the depression in serum dopamine beta hydroxylase (Goldstein et al. 1976; Lake et al. 1977). Elevations of HVA are also fairly consistently reported (multiple authors). What all these replicated studies have in common, apart from those on whole blood serotonin and HVA, is that the patients studied in each case were diagnosed by the same clinical criteria and by the same clinical investigator. In the case of the DBH replication by Goldstein et al. (1976) and Lake et al. (1977), although the patients were diagnosed by the same clinical investigator, the laboratories doing the work were in different sections of the United States and were unrelated. This again lends relevance to the concept that the difficulty of interpreting laboratory studies in autism is related more to the diagnosis of relatively homogeneous populations within the syndrome by particular investigators rather than to primary problems in methodology in the laboratory. The laboratory results must be understood in the light of this clinical methodological problem. In attempting to sort out the syndrome, with various subgroups, the clinical diagnostic problem must work hand in hand in with laboratory studies in an attempt to establish sound data based on replicable subgroups. That is, subgroups must be replicable both clinically and biochemically.

It is interesting that rare metabolites of both the serotonin pathway and the catecholamine pathway have been found in the urine of autistic children. In the case of the serotonin pathway, it is bufotenine, and in the catecholamine pathway, it is homoprotocatechuic acid (see Figures 8.1 and 8.2). In both cases, these rare metabolites were not found in the urine of the normal controls. What this could possibly suggest, when combined with all the other information concerning the serotonin and catecholamine pathways, is that there is a partial block of some enzymatic levels which results in the backup of inappropriate metabolites through minor pathways. (It is worth noting that initial identification of minor metabolites in the urine is the method through which the ultimate enzyme error in phenylketonuria (PKU), one of the metabolic etiologies of the autistic syndrome, was worked out 30 years ago.)

Studies of cerebral spinal fluid levels of serotonin and catecholamine metabolites also must be interpreted in terms of male/female differences. Cerebral spinal fluid HVA levels are higher in males than females (Leckman et al. 1980; Shaywitz et al. 1980). Cohen et al. (1982) has suggested that male children are more sensitive to disorders affecting the dopaminergic system. Also, a catecholamine enzyme, COMT showed the opposite trends according to sex (O'Brien 1976). However, in a recent study of male and female children with a diagnosis of autism, Gillberg et al. (1983) found that girls tended to have higher values of HVA, HMPG and 5-HIAA. One possible explanation is that girls tend to have a more severe form of autism (see chapter 2), so that the severity factors may override any gender factors involving any individual patient.

Again, it is important to note, within the groups of males and females, that there are undoubtedly different diagnostic subgroups.

AMINO ACIDS, AMINO COMPOUNDS AND ORGANIC ACIDS

It is now well established that one error in amino acid metabolism (phenylketonuria) can produce autistic-like symptoms in many of these children (see chapter 16). Histidinemia described in autistic children (Rutter and Bartak 1971) is now known to be a benign variant rarely associated with clinical symptomology (Levy et al. 1974). Spinal fluid amino acids have been reported as normal as a group, although two children had elevations of arginine. (Winsberg et al. 1980). A study by Perry et al. (1978) of amino acids in plasma and CSF of autistic children showed no known disease entities. Their CSF studies looking at amino compounds did reveal an elevation of the ethanolamine in autistic children. This interesting finding needs further replication. A study by the same group of organic acids by gas chromatography found many unidentified peaks, many of them large. Further identification was not possible.

Although the value of hair analysis has not been established, an amino acid analysis was done on the hair of 61 autistic children, then compared with samples from 15 control children by Johnson et al. 1974. No significant difference in hair amino acid composition between autistic and control children was noted.

In 1980, Trygstad et al. presented preliminary evidence that autistic children may have specific urinary peptide patterns. In a second study involving some of the same investigators (Gillberg et al. 1982), an extended investigation was undertaken which compared patients having infantile autism with five other control groups. The first group of children had psychoses; the second, attentional deficit syndrome; the third, minimal brain dysfunction; the fourth, mental retardation with psychoses. The fifth group was made up of normal controls. Chromatographic patterns were studied using a gel filtration column with a UV absorbency red and 280 nm. Six main types of chromatographic patterns were identified. Of the autistic children, 54 percent showed a distinct pattern that was not seen in any other cases, except in 17 percent of the children with other psychoses. Only 8 percent of the autistic children showed a pattern that was seen in over 95 percent of the normal children and 93 percent of the mentally retarded children without psychoses. The ultraviolet absorbency peaks of the chromatogram possibly corresponded to peptides or to protein associated peptide complexes.

The work of Lis et al. (1976) is also based on ultraviolet absorbent components of urine as obtained on high resolution ion exchange chromatography. In the case of the Lis paper, the ultraviolet absorption was monitored at 254 and 280 nm. Lis had interpreted his results as showing abnormalities in autism that fitted into three groups: abnormal excretion of 2-Py (the end product of the nicotinic acid pathway), abnormal excretion of hippurate, and abnormal levels of various purine metabolites. (Purines are discussed in chapter 16.)

In recent years, both the mechanism of the action of endorphins and the neurophysiology of underlying mental diseases point to the importance of small peptides in studies of abnormal behavior disorders. Hyperfunction of any pathway or part of the central nervous system could result in an overflow of peptides to the body fluids and urine. Peptides play a major role in the effective functioning of animals at all levels, from enzyme stabilization to homeostatic mechanisms governing essential functions such as eating, sexual behavior and temperature regulation. It is also well established that peptides, when exogenously administered, can affect neurotransmitter release uptake and metabolism, and also have behavioral consequences in animals (Reichelt et al. 1981).

In a recent study, Gillberg and co-workers (1984a) examined 20 autistic children and found evidence of raised CSF levels of endorphin fraction II in those children who were self-destructive and appeared to have a relative insensitivity to pain. This is an important area for future studies.

CARBOHYDRATE METABOLISM

There have been two approaches to the study of carbohydrate metabolism in autistic patients. One was concerned with free fatty acids (DeMyer et al. 1971), and was inspired by similar studies that were being done at the time in adult schizophrenia. In this study of free fatty acids in carefully selected autistic patients and controls, there was no statistically significant difference. The significance lay rather in the phenomenon that has been observed elsewhere in studies of autistic patients—far greater variability than in the controls.

A second approach involves the measurement of lactate and pyruvate levels in the serum of autistic children. Four children having the coexistent syndromes of autism and lactic acidosis have been described in the literature; one appears to have a deficiency of the pyruvate dehydrogenase complex (PDHC) (Coleman and Blass, 1985). Since lactic acidosis indicates some abnormality in the utilization of sugar, this suggests that autism can be associated with the family of disorders having to do with carbohydrate metabolism (see chapter 16).

CO-ENZYME AND OTHER VITAMIN STUDIES

The B group of vitamins function as co-enzymes to many neuro-transmitter pathways in the brain and other important pathways. Little work has been done in this area regarding the evaluation of baseline vitamin levels, but such literature as exists will be reviewed.

Thiamine (Vitamin B₁).   No actual study of thiamine levels in the serum has been reported in autistic children. In fact, the only literature available is an analysis of thiamine intake. In two studies of autistic children compared with non-autistic children (Shearer et al. 1982; Raiten and Massaro, in press), no difference was found in the mean daily intake of thiamine-containing foods by the autistic patients. In these two studies, Shearer et al. evaluated the intake of 12 autistic patients and controls while Raiten and Massaro worked with a larger sample of 40 autistic children and 34 controls. Since thiamine may be involved in enzyme complexes causing lactic acidosis (see chapter 16) this area needs further study.

Riboflavin (Vitamin B₂).   In 1979, Sankar (1979) studied the plasma levels of several water-soluble vitamins in 125 children admitted to a child psychiatric unit. He selected out a group of patients whom he labeled autistic, and found that the plasma riboflavin levels were no different from those of the other groups, which included mentally deficient children, non-autistic schizophrenic children, and those with behavioral disorders.

Shearer et al. (1982) studied the riboflavin intake of autistic patients. When he compared the 12 autistic patients with their controls, he found that the children consumed a significantly lower amount of riboflavin-containing foods than the control children. This was an interesting finding, particularly because none of the other vitamins studied was consumed in any statistically significantly different manner. In an attempt to understand this result, he evaluated the foods consumed according to the U.S. Department of Agriculture's food groups. He found that autistic children consume significantly fewer servings from the milk group than control children; this appeared to explain, from an intake point of view, the lower consumption of riboflavin-containing foods by autistic children. In the Shearer et al. (1982) study, there was no information regarding medications. Pelliccione et al. (1983) have shown that neuroleptic medications may adversely affect riboflavin metabolism. However, the Raiten and Massaro (in press) study found no such difference in riboflavin consumption in their study; again presence or absence of medication was not noted.

Nicotinic Acid (Vitamin B₃). Nicotinic acid is measured in patients by studying the amounts of the end products of the nicotinic acid pathway. In 1970, Lis et al. reported that some children with autistic tendencies excrete in their urine subnormal amounts of the end product of the nicotinic acid pathway, N-1-methyl-2-pyridone-5-carboxylamide (2-Py). In a repeat study in 1976, Lis et al. again found a group of autistic children who appeared to have low excretion levels of 2-Py. Here they reported that seven out of 19 children appeared to display this low level (Lis et al. 1976).

The daily intake of niacin in autistic and control children was also studied by Shearer et al. (1982) and Raiten and Massaro (in press). They report that autistic children ingest a normal amount of this particular vitamin.

Niacinamide has been given to autistic children as part of high vitamin regimes (Rimland 1973). But because vitamins competing for similar active transport systems were given together, it is difficult to know how to interpret the data. In 1970, Greenbaum reported on an evaluation of niacinamide in "childhood schizophrenia" and found no significant behavioral improvement.

Pyridoxine (Vitamin B₆). Plasma levels of pyridoxine, the co-enzyme of the second step of several biogenic amine pathways (described above), were studied by Sankar (1979). Taking the patients he labeled as autistic, he found no statistically significant difference between the plasma levels of these patients and other children admitted to a child psychiatric unit. Rimland (1973) also reported that pyridoxine was in a vitamin cocktail that local physicians gave to autistic patients. (For a full discussion of this work and following studies, see chapter 20.)

Pyridoxine is the co-enzyme of the L-aromatic amino acid decar-boxylase (L-AAAD) step in the biogenic amine pathways of serotonin and the catecholamines (see Figures 8.1 and 8.2). Pyridoxine is the co-enzyme of this later step of the pathway, that is, not the first or rate-limiting step of the pathway. Any effectiveness of a co-enzyme of a non-rate-limiting step of a metabolic pathway requires massive phar-macological doses of the co-enzyme actually to alter the amount of the next metabolite produced. For further information on the pyridoxine therapy in autism see chapter 20.

Vitamin B12. Serum levels of vitamin B12 were studied by Lowe et al. in 1981. The autistic patient group was compared both with normal controls and non-autistic neuropsychiatric patients and no abnormality was found.

Folic Acid. Serum and red blood cell folate, and cerebral spinal fluid levels of folate in autistic patients were also studied by this research group and no difference was found when compared with a group of non-autistic psychiatric patients (Lowe et al. 1981). They also reported that a subgroup of their patients received folic acid supplements without evidence of clinical improvement. The future role of folic acid supplementation in fragile X patients remains to be determined (see chapter 13).

Ascorbic Acid (Vitamin C). Sankar in 1979 studied the plasma level of ascorbic acid in both autistic patients and other children with psychiatric diagnoses. No significant difference was found in the ascor-bate levels in autistic patients, although it can be seen from the data in the paper that the autistic children in this group did have a slight trend toward lower levels compared with other patient groups.

Ascorbate was also one of the vitamins studied by Shearer et al. (1982) when he measured the mean daily intake of foods eaten by autistic children compared with controls. He found no difference in the intake of foods containing ascorbic acid in the autistic and control group. Raiten and Massaro (in press) found a slight increase in foods containing ascorbic acid but felt the result was not significant when corrected for MAR (Mean Adequacy Ratios).

Vitamin A. There are no published results on the levels of vitamin A and carotene intake in autistic patients compared with controls. At the Children's Brain Research Clinic in Washington,

D.C., vitamin A levels have been recorded in nine autistic patients who had minor or major steatorrhea and the results indicate no gross difference between the levels in patients and commercial laboratory controls. Raiten and Massaro (in press) found a slightly increased intake of fat and a slightly decreased intake of fat-soluble vitamin A in their study of nutritional intakes. Again, when corrected for MAR (Mean Adequacy Ratios) they did not conclude that their findings were significant.

Vitamin D. There is no published literature on vitamin D levels in autistic children. In the Children's Brain Research Clinic in Washington, D.C., the serum levels of 1,25 dihydroxy vitamin D_3 have been studied in autistic patients who have hypocalcinuria. To date, in a sample of 14 children, none with autism and hypocalcinuria has been found to have a level outside the commercial laboratory reference range for 1,25 dihydroxy vitamin D_3.

DISCUSSION OF VITAMIN LEVELS

Studies of vitamin levels in autistic patients have obviously been undertaken in the hope of finding some abnormal levels, even though vitamin therapies are usually based on abnormal metabolite or enzyme levels, rather than co-enzyme (vitamin) levels. In pediatric neurology, there are a number of disease entities with metabolic errors whose treatment depends on the use of vitamin therapy (usually in pharmacological doses) in an attempt to enhance enzyme function by using the co-enzyme (vitamin) (Stanbury et al. 1978).

One of the problems of pharmacological therapy in neurology using vitamins is the difficulty of enhancing co-enzyme levels in the central nervous system, even if one is able to elevate them in the serum. Ordinarily, the homeostatic systems between the plasma and the brain maintain relatively constant brain concentrations of vitamins such as ascorbate, except at very high or very low concentrations. In addition, it is difficult to maintain high plasma levels because of the regulatory mechanisms in the gut and the kidney. These homeostatic systems provide an "ultrastable" environment for the brain (Spector 1977) and often break down only in cases of extreme nutritional deficiency or when disrupted by diseases such as meningitis.

Nevertheless, if metabolic abnormalities can be identified, a rational therapeutic approach of the administration of a co-enzyme is indicated in autistic patients as in other neurological patients because, in any single individual, it is possible that the usual active transport systems and other homeostatic mechanisms may not have their standard level of function. One such vitamin therapy has already been demonstrated to be of value by three double-blind studies with autistic children (see chapter 20).

MINERAL AND ION STUDIES

Magnesium. In 1973, Saladino and Sankar reported that magnesium levels were lowered in the erythrocytes of a child psychiatric patient group compared with normal controls. In 1976, in the large study at the Children's Brain Research Clinic in Washington, D.C., 59 autistic children and 65 control children were studied for serum magnesium levels (Coleman et al. 1976a). There was a significant difference between the control and autistic serums ($1.98 \pm .21$ for controls and $1.66 \pm .26$ for autistics). These values have a $p < .001$ and a t of 7.13.

This serum finding of statistically lowered magnesium levels was the only positive finding in the serum in the many variables tested in this large study. This raises a question about whether there is a problem with magnesium absorption or binding, or whether there are enzyme systems among the etiologies of the autistic syndrome that utilize extra magnesium, or whether there is some abnormal renal handling of magnesium in one or more subgroups of the syndrome. Magnesium is, in fact, involved in several of the metabolic enzyme systems already identified as abnormal in one or more autistic children (see chapters 16 and 20).

Magnesium is the second most abundant intracellular cation. This element is essential for the production and transfer of energy for protein synthesis, for contractibility in muscle and for excitability in nerve. It is essential in a number of enzymatic functions in the central nervous system. The metabolic requirement for magnesium is related to the dietary factors such as protein, calcium and phosphorus (Seeling 1971).

A review of literature shows that in magnesium deficiency, there are nonspecific signs and symptoms. Often magnesium deficiency occurs clinically as part of a more complex nutritional disturbance and it is difficult to sort out what is specific to magnesium deficiency. In general, however, severe deficiency is associated with anorexia, growth failure, increased stooling, apathy, irritability, and, at a later stage, with hallucinations and confusions. Ocular signs that have been observed in cases of magnesium deficiency include lateral deviation of gaze, oculogyric crisis, fixed staring and fluttering of the upper eyelids. Also associated with this syndrome are occasional episodes of spastic twitching, weakness, flaccidity and various seizure patterns. Sweating, pallor, or a dusky appearance are also described (Caddell 1974). In studies on the brains of animals, magnesium deficiency selectively affects white matter more than gray matter (Chutkow 1974).

Magnesium depletion can occur with a number of problems such as loss of gastrointestinal fluids, malabsorption, hypoparathyroidism, maternal diabetes and congenital biliary atresia. Patients receiving large doses of vitamin D in the therapy of vitamin D resistant rickets may develop hypomagnesemia and convulsions. Burn patients treated with daily saline baths sometimes develop hypomagnesemia. Lowered serum magnesium is also seen in children with depressive symptoms (Pliszka and Rogeness 1984). Could low serum magnesium be a secondary reaction in some of the very sensitive autistic children who perceive their differences from other children (as described by the author of the poem at the beginning of this book) or could a magnesium deficiency cause depression in the first place?

It is difficult to be sure that an individual has adequate magnesium levels by current testing. Plasma and serum values of magnesium are helpful when they are low, but magnesium-deficient patients may have normal plasma levels (Harris and Wilkinson 1971). So much magnesium is intracellular that only one percent can be tested in extracellular fluids of the body. Erythrocyte magnesium is probably an index of the body stores of magnesium at the time when the erythrocytes were formed, since they do not reflect acute change. The age of the cell population is important in evaluating such results since reticulocytes contain eight times more magnesium than mature cells. Urinary magnesium in a person with normal renal status is low when the individual's magnesium is depleted, or when the oral magnesium intake has been sharply curtailed for at least three days.

Metabolic turnover studies, which are difficult under the best of circumstances and almost impossible with autistic children, provide the best means of studying magnesium. Parental magnesium load tests may be the most feasible of the diagnostic tests available and retention of more than 40 percent of such a load has been interpreted as indicating magnesium depletion.

Since magnesium is lost in the processing of many foods, this is an area where evaluation is indicated in the case of autistic children. It is of interest that, in animal experiments, magnesium deficiency in the presence of high thiamine levels can result in significant elevation of blood serotonin (Itokawa et al. 1972).

Calcium. Magnesium is a mimic/antagonist of calcium (Levine and Coburn 1984). Calcium is a divalent cation that exists primarily in the bones; 99 percent of the total body calcium resides in the skeleton and teeth. However, of the remaining tissues, the brain contains the fourth largest amount. Calcium is an important ion for central nervous system functions since it stabilizes membranes by decreasing their permeability and also depresses neuromuscular excitability.

In the 1976 study at the Children's Brain Research Clinic in Washington, D.C., serum and 24-hour urinary calcium levels were determined on patients. There was no statistically significant difference between the serum or urine calciums in the autistic and control group (Table 8.2). The urinary levels showed a wide variation in range in both groups, although the pattern was more marked in the autistic patients. Of interest was the fact that 16 of the autistic patients in the study had urinary calcium levels below 0.7 mg/kg/24 hr., which is below two standard deviations as determined by the normal curve distribution based on the control children. These 16 children were also considered to have urinary levels below the normal range, because the lowest recorded level in the control group was 0.9 mg/kg/24 hr. The striking finding was that 22 percent of the autistic patients had hypocalcinuria by these criteria. Only one of these patients also had a serum level that was below the normal range.

At the time of the study, it was found that 10 percent of the patients had received a diagnosis of celiac disease from their pediatricians prior to entering the study. This included a number of the low calcium patients and, although later studies indicated this patient group did not have celiac disease (McCarthy and Coleman 1979), the finding of hypocalcinuria in about one out of five or six autistic patients has held up in patient testing in the succeeding years at the Children's Brain Research Clinic. As noted earlier, later studies have not indicated any evidence of a problem with serum levels of 1,25 dihydroxy vitamin D_3 in this patient population. Nor have calcitonin, parathormone or ionized calcium studies been revealing.

The Raiten and Massaro (in press) food intake study found no difference in calcium intake in autistic patients compared with controls. Shearer et al. (1982) also studied the nutritional intake of 12 children and 12 controls. Although they found that autistic children consumed most foods in the same proportion as normal children, they also found

TABLE 8.2. Calcium and Phosphorus Levels in Seventy-two Patients and Sixty-seven Controls. Serum and Urine Levels by Age. From 1976 Children's Brain Research Clinic Data.

	3–5 years		6–8 years		9–12 years		Over 13 years	
	Serum (mg%)	Urine (mg/kg/24 hr)	Serum (mg%)	Urine (mg/kg/24 hr)	Serum (mg%)	Urine (mg/kg/24 hr)	Serum (mg%)	Urine (mg/kg/24 hr)
Control calcium								
mean	9.3	2.3	9.2	2.1	9.3	1.9	9.4	1.6
range	8.8–10.0	1.6–2.9	8.4–10.3	1.8–3.0	8.8–10.3	1.1–3.1	8.4–10.5	0.9–2.9
Autistic calcium								
mean	10.2	1.7	9.5	1.9	9.4	2.6	9.3	1.7
range	9.7–11.1	0.3–7.0	8.9–10.9	0.5–6.7	8.1–10.3	0.1–4.8	8.9–10.5	0.0–4.2
Control inorganic phosphate								
mean	5.2	20.7	5.0	24.2	4.6	18.5	4.4	15.8
range	4.3–6.3	15.0–22.0	4.0–6.7	14.0–24.8	4.0–5.8	14.0–22.0	3.2–5.2	10.0–21.0
Autistic inorganic phosphate								
mean	5.3	21.2	4.8	21.2	5.1	22.5	4.3	15.5
range	4.8–6.0	9.1–40.4	3.7–6.6	10.4–42.0	4.2–6.0	10.6–41.6	3.3–5.6	4.9–23.2

that autistic children consume significantly lower amounts of calcium-containing foods compared with control children. They attributed this finding to the fact that autistic children consume significantly fewer servings from foods associated with milk than do control children. They pointed out that the amount of foods obtained from the milk group consumed by autistic children is more than one serving below the baseline recommendation for pre-adolescent children. Since the two food intake studies disagree about this point, it is possible that they were studying different populations.

Depression of calcium in the serum results in central nervous system signs. In newborns, neonatal tetany or seizure disorders are associated with hypocalcemia; and laryngospasm can be marked in patients with low levels of calcium in the serum. To our knowledge, autistic symptomology has not been recorded as a sign of hypocalcinemia.

Phosphorus.   In the 1976 Children's Brain Research Clinic study, inorganic phosphate was determined in both the serum and 24-hour urine in 72 patients and 67 controls. There is no statistically significant difference between the two groups. One patient had a high serum calcium of 10.9 mg.% and a low serum phosphate of 3.8 mg.%, but no known disease entity affecting calcium metabolism or kidney function could be identified in this child. In studies by Shearer et al. (1982) and Raiten and Massaro (in press) of nutrient intake, an adequate nutrient intake of phosphorus-containing foods in autistic patients was recorded even though their intake of calcium was depressed in the Shearer study.

Potassium.   Potassium levels have only been tested once in autistic patients. Saladino and Sankar (1973) found a depression of red blood cell potassium in patients compared with controls.

Lead.   In contrast to the other minerals discussed in this section, lead has no known enzymatic function in the human body. It is a contaminant. Lead levels 2,000 years ago in individuals were significantly lower than what is considered "normal" for an individual today. That lead has a well-known toxic effect on the central nervous system has been documented in many studies. Some patients with autistic syndromes suffer from pica, thus increasing the chance that they may ingest lead-contaminated objects.

There are three studies in the literature suggesting that the ingestion of or exposure to lead may have occurred in a pathological way in at least some autistic children. In 1976, Cohen et al. showed that blood lead levels in autistic children were significantly higher than those in their normal siblings or in non-autistic, psychotic youngsters (Cohen et al. 1976). Campbell et al. in 1980 reported that a large proportion of their autistic subjects also had blood lead levels that were elevated (over 35 ug/dl). Most significantly, they noted that intellectual functioning was negatively correlated with blood lead. In 1982, Cohen et al. conducted a screening for blood lead levels in the school for students with autism and atypical pervasive developmental disorders. They compared these children with 34 children having Tourette Syndrome and with 16 normal controls. In this study, there was no significant difference among the three groups, but 14 percent of the autistic and atypical pervasive developmental disorder group had lead levels greater than 26 ug/dl. None of the normal controls had levels this high and only 6 percent of the Tourette group had such levels. They concluded that, although this patient group as a whole does not differ statistically from controls and other psychiatric patient groups in blood lead levels, individuals within the autistic group run a risk of showing increased lead levels.

Copper.   Copper levels have been checked in autistic children in three studies. They were studied because of the observation that some symptoms in autistic children are suggestive of basal ganglia disease (the site in the brain which contains a significant amount of copper), and also because of its intricate relationship with zinc metabolism. In studies in the serum (Bakwin et al. 1961; Mahanand et al. 1976) and in plasma (Jackson and Garrod 1978) copper was found to be within the normal range in studies that compare autistic children with normal controls.

Zinc.   In the human brain, zinc is located primarily in grey matter, and the maximum zinc content is in the resistant sector and N-plate of Ammon's horn. Zinc deficiency results in the disorder, acrodermatitus enteropathica. In a 1976 paper, Moynahan observed that untreated children with this disorder display aberrant visual behavior and mood changes similar to those seen in autistic children. It has also been reported that acute zinc deficiency produces decreased emotional stability and difficulty with learning in rats (Caldwell et al. 1970).

In the Children's Brain Research Clinic Study of 1976, serum zinc levels were determined in 64 autistic patients and 69 control patients. The mean of the autistic patients was 171.05, while the control mean was 112.5. A comparison showed a significant difference with a p of

<.001 (Mahanad et al. 1976). This finding was quite unexpected because any zinc abnormality that theoretically could exist was thought to be a *low* rather than a *high* zinc level. For this reason, a study was repeated on 12 autistic patients and 12 age- and sex-matched controls. After both groups had spent a week on a carefully controlled low-zinc diet, in which the amount of zinc in the food was quantified, studies of blood, urine, and saliva in this second study showed no difference in the levels of zinc between patients and controls (Coleman et al. unpublished).

In 1978, Jackson and Garrod (1978) studied plasma zinc levels in 12 autistic children and an additional eight atypical autistic children and compared them with 30 normal children. They found no difference in their plasma zinc levels.

In view of the results in the second and third studies, it is unlikely that there is any significant involvement of zinc in the autistic syndrome as a whole.

Iron.   Although there are no published studies of iron metabolism per se in autistic children, evidence of anemia caused by iron deficiency is lacking in the clinical experience of many investigators working with these patients. Both the Shearer et al. (1982) and the Raiten and Massaro (in press) studies found adequate nutrient intake of iron in autistic children compared with controls.

CONCLUSION

Laboratory studies of patients with the autistic syndrome have several roles. One is the evaluation of the individual child in an attempt to determine biochemical abnormalities in that individual that might be helpful in diagnosis or treatment. Studies of large groups of patients also have several specific goals. One is to try to find specific subgroups within the autistic syndrome where more than one patient is found to have a laboratory abnormality which may or may not have relevance to a specific disease entity. Finally, laboratory studies in the autistic syndrome, attempting to delineate factors that may be involved in most or all autistic patients, may possibly point to a final common pathway that is affected in the variety of different disease entities showing autistic symptomology.

Many of the studies in this section were done in earlier years before it was clear that autism was a syndrome of multiple etiology, while others were looking for a limited or single pathogenesis. These studies have been useful since they have led us to our present knowledge of the subgroups of autistic patients as currently understood. But it is important to keep in mind that the autistic syndrome is a syndrome of multiple etiologies when reviewing the world literature concerning the biochemistry of the syndrome.

9   Endocrine and Immunological Studies

ENDOCRINE STUDIES

Endocrine studies have been conducted on groups of autistic children in two areas—those related to thyroid hormone and those related to steroid metabolism.

Since thyroid hormone is so critical in the programming of the developing nervous system and in the maintenance of central nervous system function in the perinatal and postnatal periods, it is a relevant area of investigation in a disease entity sometimes appearing at birth, and clearly affecting these critical developmental stages in virtually all patients. (For thyroid studies of parents of patients, see Chapter 7.)

The effects of thyroid hormone pervade the central nervous system. In addition to its effects on oxygen consumption and the uncoupling of oxidated phosphorylation, it has an even more dramatic effect on differentiation. Thyroid hormone functions in at least four basic ways during transcription and translation: (1) it affects RNA polymerase II, which assembles messenger RNA; (2) it affects tRNA sulfur transferase, which confers codon specificity on transfer RNA; (3) it affects the release of nascent polypeptide chains from ribosomes; and (4) it affects the activities of many enzymes, such as thymidine kinase, which assemble the nucleotides (Grave 1977). Also, rather than stimulating the initial release of encoded genetic information, thyroid hormone acts to control the rates of several critical enzymatic steps in the flow of that information from storage in DNA to expression in structural and enzymatic proteins.

Studies of thyroid function in autistic patients, however, have not tended to show much abnormality. In fact, a number of studies report that patients have been given thyroid hormone even though they were euthyroid.

When Sherwin et al. (1958) studied thyroid function in two autistic children and found them to be euthyroid, they nevertheless administered T3 to the children and reported an apparent clinical improvement. Subsequently, a British study reported diminished values in 45 out of 62 autistic children studied by T3 uptake (Khan 1970).

Following these early reports, the New York University group of investigators then published five studies in this area in the 1970s (Campbell et al. 1972b, Campbell et al. 1973, Campbell and Fish 1974, Campbell et al. 1978c, Campbell et al. 1978e). In the 1973 study, this group reported that triiodothyronine, administered to 14 psychotic (including autistic) and six severely disturbed but non-psychotic preschool children, resulted in improved social and stereotypic behavior. However, in a later 1978 study, Campbell et al., who used a careful placebo-controlled, double-blind, crossover methodology on 30 young, clinically euthyroid autistic children, were unable to support their previous findings of the beneficial effects, except in the case of a few symptoms. In this later study, they reported three children who improved by more than two standard deviations in bone age from retardation to normality by the end of the treatment.

In 1978, Abbassi et al. studied 13 autistic patients with T3, T4 and TSH levels; again, all patients were euthyroid. Two of the patients, however, had retarded bone ages and were treated with triiodothyronine for six months. Clinical signs of hyperthyroidism developed when T3 levels exceeded physiological concentrations in these patients.

In 1980, Cohen et al. studied 20 randomly-selected autistic children, compared with normal controls, for T4, TSH, total thyroxine binding capacity, present binding saturation, and estimated free thyroxine. They found no statistical difference between autistic and normal children in these parameters of thyroid function.

In summary, there is little evidence at this time, based either on baseline laboratory studies or on therapeutic trials, to indicate that thyroid hormone would be a successful therapeutic agent in the autistic syndromes.

Corticosteroids were studied in autistic children in two ways by Yamazaki et al. (1975). In human beings there is evidence to suggest that reactivity to pyrogen is established in the early months or years of life, while the circadian rhythm of plasma steroid hormones is established slightly later, four years of age being the outside limit. These two tests were performed on seven autistic children ranging from six to ten years of age. The authors report that reactivity for the most part was sufficient in the pyrogen test, although a normal circadian rhythm could scarcely be observed. Yamazaki et al. hypothesize that some functional change may exist in the cerebral hypothalamic system related to the mechanism of basal ACTH secretion in autistic children. This interesting observation needs further elucidation.

IMMUNOLOGICAL STUDIES

Among the etiologies of the autistic syndrome are several infectious diseases which can occur in utero (see chapter 14). Prenatal rubella, the best documented of these etiologies, can cause an altered immune response in a child owing to the prenatal viral insult (South and Alford 1973; Fuccillo et al. 1974).

In 1976, Stubbs checked rubella titers in 13 autistic children who had had a previous rubella vaccination. In contrast with the controls, five out of 13 of the autistic children had undetectable titers, in spite of the previous vaccination. Lack of antibody response to a previous vaccination is helpful in diagnosing in retrospect prenatal rubella (Cooper et al. 1971). In the same study, a rubella vaccine challenge did not differentiate autistic children from control subjects.

A year later, Stubbs et al. (1977) did a follow-up immunological study in 12 autistic children using phytohemagglutinin-P (PHA) to check T-cell stimulation and pokeweed mutogen (PWM) as a measure of B lymphocyte responsiveness. Results of the study were the first to suggest that autistic children may have a relative T-cell deficiency. Stubbs et al. raised the question as to whether autistic children might have a genetic predisposition to relative T-cell deficiency, or whether some viruses have a predilection for interfering with the thymus (which differentiates T-cells) but not a predilection for interfering with bone marrow or the bursa equivalent in humans (which differentiates B-cells). Regarding the possibility of genetic predisposition, he noted (Stubbs et al. 1982) that inherited enzyme deficiencies in purine nucleotide degradation have been associated with immune deficiencies (see chapter 15).

This study also raised a question about the possibility of autoimmune disease in some autistic patients. A common finding in immune systems of patients with autoimmune disease is a deficiency of one type of lymphocyte, termed 'suppressor T lymphocytes (Strelkauskas et al. 1978). A function of suppressor T lymphocytes is to maintain immune homeostasis by preventing immune responses against cell tissues. (For example, in the case of those suffering from multiple sclerosis, autoimmunity has been demonstrated against their own brain myelin protein of a type called basic protein.)

In 1982, Weizman et al. studied cell mediated immune response to human myelin basic protein by the macrophage migration inhibition factor test. They compared the results in 17 autistic patients with a control group of 11 patients suffering from other mental disorders. Of the 17 autistic patients, 13 demonstrated inhibition of macrophage migration, whereas none of the control group showed such a response. This study suggested that in the syndrome of autism there may exist a cell mediated immune response to brain tissue.

The first study that postulated a relationship between autism and autoimmune disease was done by Money et al. in 1971, using one family suffering from both syndromes. The authors postulated the formation of auto-antibodies against the central nervous system as a possible factor in autism. Raiten and Massaro (in press) also raised the possibility of auto-immune mechanisms when they unexpectedly found 12.5 percent of the mothers of autistics (whom they were evaluating for nutritional intake) were suffering from rheumatoid arthritis.

A study of shared HLA antigens between parents of autistics compared with parents of controls found that 75 percent of the parents of autistics shared at least one antigen (in contrast to 22 percent of the controls)(Stubbs et al. in press). Homozygosity at HLA sites may decrease the protection of the fetus from the mother's immune system.

Studies of possible autoimmunity and/or immune deficiency are areas where further research into the autistic syndromes is needed.

10   Electrophysiological Studies

One of the first tools used to look at autistic patients from a neurological point of view was the electroencephalogram. White et al. (1964), Lotter (1967), Creak and Pampiglione (1969), Gublay et al. (1970), and Kolvin et al. (1971) found that a sizable proportion of autistic patients had definite EEG abnormalities. Although a single case history of an adolescent with a persistent temporal lobe spike focus was mentioned by Rutter and Bartak (1971), most EEG abnormalities in this patient group are bilateral or have both diffuse and localized abnormalities (Tsai and Stewart 1982). No EEG pattern unique to autism has been found in any study. EEG abnormalities are most likely to be found in older patients who have developed seizure disorders; the majority of younger children have normal patterns.

BRAINSTEM AUDITORY EVOKED RESPONSE STUDIES

A significant literature exists regarding brainstem auditory evoked response studies in autistic patients. Auditory evoked potentials are specialized tests studying patterns on electroencephalic tracing that are caused (evoked) by some type of stimuli programmed to sound at planned intervals outside the patient's ear with the effect picked up on the tracing. Since 1975 there have been ten studies (Ornitz and Walter 1975, Student and Sohmer 1978, Ornitz et al. 1980, Rosenblum et al. 1980, Skoff et al. 1980, Novick et al. 1980, Fein et al. 1981, Tanguay et al. 1982, Taylor et al. 1982, Gillberg et al. 1983, Rumsey et al. in press).

Student and Sohmer (1978) were among the first to report a longer brainstem transmission time in a study that they did on 15 children with autistic traits compared with 12 normal children of similar age. Skoff et al. (1980) found that 56 percent of the autistic children had abnormal electrophysiological results on brainstem auditory evoked potential studies. They report that the most common BAEP abnormality was prolonged interpeak III to V latency on the left side. In the Fein et al. (1981) study of 16 autistic children, 9 of the 16 were found to have abnormal brainstem auditory evoked potentials. These authors suggested that social and attentional pathology could be specifically associated with the brainstem abnormality.

Taylor et al. (1982) studied 32 children and found that 11 had moderate hearing loss while 3 suffered from severe to profound hearing loss. Like many other examiners, they found that the I to III and I to V interwave latencies were significantly longer in the autistic children compared with the normal control children. The Tanguay et al. study (1982) also showed abnormalities—50 percent of a group of autistic children had at least one transmission time value that was greater than normal, primarily in the low intensity studies. Gillberg et al. (1983) showed a clearcut difference between pathological brainstem transmission times in one-third of the patients and normal transmission times in the other two-thirds. Perhaps the most interesting observation of that group is that seven out of eight of the children with abnormal brainstem auditory evoked potential studies also had concomitant clinical hypotonia.

In contrast to most of this literature, which suggested that at least one subgroup of autistic children appeared to have abnormalities in brainstem transmission, the paper by Rumsey et al. (in press) reports brainstem transmission times in a group of 25 patients, many of whom were adults. Only one of the 25 had a prolonged transmission time while four had shortened times.

These conflicting results come from very well-established, experienced laboratories; thus, it is likely, as is the case with so many of the results reported in this monograph, that different patient selection may underlie the differences. For example, some studies excluded patients with tuberous sclerosis; others included such patients. This is not to say that technical problems, such as the use of low and high intensity stimuli, could not account at least in part for the differences between research groups. But without homogeneous subgroups of the autistic syndrome, it is hard to compare studies.

If, in fact, there are significant subgroups of children who have brainstem dysfunction in auditory input, there are several possible interpretations of these data. One possibility, suggested by Ornitz, Ritvo, and others (Ornitz and Ritvo 1968a; Ornitz 1974; MacCulloch

& Williams 1971), is that the brainstem dysfunction leads to distortion of auditory input at higher levels, which may be one factor in cognitive and other defects. Another possible explanation is that the brainstem auditory evoked potential findings are incidental findings of a disease process which is affecting many parts of the brain, including the brainstem (see chapter 22).

CORTICAL EVOKED POTENTIAL STUDIES

Cortical evoked potentials, both auditory and visual, have been tested in autistic children in an effort to determine cortical functioning in children who often have profound handicaps in the areas under study. Ann Barnet (1979), in an excellent review of the subject, points out that the extraordinary difficulties in getting these children to cooperate with laboratory protocol has limited the possibilities of interpretation. However, it could be noted that stimulus-induced EEG change occurred in most autistic children under some of the experimental conditions used. When autistic children were compared with normal subjects, evoked potentials were not elicited as frequently (Walter et al. 1971; Lelord et al. 1973), or they were smaller in amplitude (Ornitz et al. 1972, 1974; Small 1971; Lelord et al. 1973), or they appeared only when stimuli were paired (Lelord et al. 1973). In a few patients, cortical auditory evoked potentials were absent, perhaps owing to peripheral factors. In general, small amplitude evoked potentials were observed in these series.

One of the most interesting uses of this technique was by Novick et al. (1979), where they recorded brain potentials associated with unexpected deletions of stimuli within regular trains of auditory or visual stimuli. In normal subjects, the deleted stimuli are associated with cortical potentials, the most prominent of which is a large positive deflection which reaches its peak 400 to 600 msec. after the omitted stimulus. These authors studied "missing stimulus potentials" (MSPs) in three adolescent males having a history of autistic traits and compared them with three age- and sex-matched normal children.

The normal controls showed a small, essentially constant standard deviation in the testing. By contrast, the MSPs were smaller or absent in the autistic subjects. It was particularly interesting that there was a smaller auditory than visual MSP in the autistic group. These authors put forth a theory related to the meaning of these potentials, indicating dysfunction within a system that includes posterior parietal cortex and its connections with the mesolimbic temporal cortex and hippocampus (see chapter 22). These results could be interpreted as evidence for a deficiency in information storage in the autistic boys in this study.

SLEEP STUDIES

Some autistic patients have a sleep disturbance, although many sleep a normal number of hours a night. The UCLA research group has addressed itself to the problem of sleep in autistic children and published a series of careful studies, evaluating normal REM and non-REM sleep cycle patterns.

In the earliest studies (Ornitz et al. 1965 and 1969), the overall REM/non-REM sleep cycle patterns appeared to be comparable to those of control children. However, when attention was directed to some of the phasic activities occurring during the REM portion of the cycle, this study showed that autistic children differed from age-matched, normal controls in several ways. Autistic children have failed to show a phasic inhibition of the auditory evoked response during the eye movement/burst phase of REM sleep (Ornitz et al. 1968). They have also shown significantly fewer single eye movements and a decreased percentage of time of eye movement/burst activity (Ornitz et al. 1969). In addition, autistic children have failed to react to vestibular stimulation with an increase in the duration and organization of eye movement/bursts (Ornitz et al. 1973a and 1973b). They reported that in autistic children the tonic aspects of REM sleep appeared to be within the normal range, while the phasic aspects were reported as abnormal compared with age- and sex-matched controls. This is in contrast, for example, with Down's syndrome patients, where it appears that there are marked deficiencies in the tonic aspects of REM sleep (Feinberg et al. 1969) while deficiencies in both tonic and phasic aspects of REM sleep can be found in a mixed group of mentally retarded individuals (Petre-Quadens and De Lee 1970).

Perhaps the most interesting finding of this research group was that autistic children have eye movement activity during REM sleep which resembles much younger, normal children. Ornitz et al. (1971) found them resembling patterns seen in six- to eight-month-olds, while Tanguay et al. (1976) found no significant differences between the pattern of autistic children and those of normal children under 18 months of age in both the tonic and phasic REM activity patterns.

EEG STUDIES AND CEREBRAL LATERALIZATION

In 1975, Small suggested that a failure of cerebral lateralization might underlie the autistic syndrome because she found that normal children differ from autistics in that they have higher EEG voltages over the left hemisphere than over the right during a standard electroencephalogram.

Auditory evoked responses have also been used to compare right/ left differences in autistics. Tanguay (1976) found no consistent hemispheric differences in autism compared with the usual larger evoked response seen over the right hemisphere in REM sleep in normal children.

Ogawa et al. (1982) studied the EEG in 21 right-handed autistic children, compared with 28 normal children in the same age range. The children were studied during stage two sleep and, by a process called autoregressive analysis and component analysis, the authors determined that there was significant hemispheric lateralization in the EEG in normal children, but not in the autistic children. Random click and random light stimulation suggested to the authors of this paper that autistic children were less responsive to external stimuli.

In 1982, Tsai and Stewart decided to study the correlation between handedness and EEG findings in autistic patients. Out of 40 children, 24 had normal EEGs and 16 had unusual ones. Of the children with the unusual EEGs, 50 percent had bilateral diffuse records with no evidence of focalization, while 38 percent had both diffuse and localized abnormalities and 12 percent had multiple foci. The authors report that they did not find any EEG pattern unique to autism in the study, but noted that the finding of bilateral abnormalities in a number of the patients adds weight to the idea that autistic syndrome results from dysfunction in both sides of the brain. They were unable to discern any relationship between handedness and the EEG patterns.

COMMENT

Neurophysiological studies in autistic patients raise more questions than they answer. Although the REM sleep studies and studies of lateralization can be interpreted as suggestive of immaturity of the brain, the cortical auditory evoked studies with small amplitudes do not support such an interpretation.

11   Studies Based on Brain Imaging

Studies of the brain using imaging methods such as pneumoen-cephalograms and computerized axial tomography have been performed in autistic patients by a number of research groups in an effort to delineate any structural evidence of brain damage. As might be expected in the study of a syndrome of multiple etiologies, these surveys have shown no consistent pattern, no consistent evidence of any particular type of lesion, and no particular location of the lesion. In fact, the literature even contradicts itself as to whether the brains of autistic children are more or less asymmetrical than the brains of normal controls. The heterogeneity of autistics is particularly well pointed up by these studies.

In the older literature, Aarkrog (1968) studied 46 children with infantile autism or "borderline autism" and found that 54 percent had abnormalities that could be detected by pneumoencephalogram. It should be noted, however, that as a technique pneumoencephalography, on the whole, yields more pathological results with regard to the widening of the ventricles than does computer tomography (CT scan), which does not disturb the anatomical state of the brain by its methodology.

In 1975, Hauser et al. reported on the results of pneumoencephalographic studies of 18 developmentally disabled children who had autistic symptoms. The pneumoencephalograms showed enlargement of the left ventricular system and especially of the left temporal horns in 13 cases, and isolated widening limited to the left temporal horn only in two other cases. There was no association between the severity of the clinically assessed symptoms and the degree to which the left temporal horns were enlarged, or between intelligence and the severity of pneumoencephalographic findings. In 1981, DeLong et al. discussed these patients in greater detail, and pointed out that five had definite focal findings on neurological examination. This study probably included a specific cohort of children, some of whom may have had a reversible encephalopathy syndrome described by DeLong et al. (1981). Thus, there may be more uniformity in their findings than has been found in other studies.

A review of PEG studies in the medical literature (Melchior et al. 1965, Boesen and Aarkrog 1967, Schönfelder 1964) discloses that when abnormalities are reported, mild or moderate ventricular dilatation appears as the most common finding.

In recent years, computerized tomography has been developed and there are now eight studies available describing the results of CT scans in the selected group of autistic patients. The first study by Hier et al. (1979) evaluated 16 autistic patients and compared them with many retarded and neurological patients. Although none of the patients had evidence of focal or diffuse brain injury, the authors reported that left/right morphologic asymmetry of the parietal occipital region was found in 57 percent of the autistic patients whose right parietal occipital region was wider than the left. Although such asymmetry is seen in up to 25 percent of other neurological patients, the higher figure of 57 percent suggested that the reversal of the asymmetry may have some significance for autism.

The second published study (Damasio et al. 1980) looked at 17 patients with autistic behavior, but only showed the reverse asymmetry in 18 percent of these patients. In the Damasio study, specific brain lesions were found, such as hydrocephalus and right frontal lobe lesions. Moreover, Damasio et al. reported that 29 percent (or five of their patients) had evidence of bilateral ventricular enlargement.

Caparulo et al. 1981, did a careful CT study of 22 autistic males. They reported that nine percent were markedly abnormal (occipital horn dilatation and left ventricular enlargement). Another nine percent were mildly abnormal. In most patients they found no distinct abnormality. They reported mild asymmetries involving increased size of the left hemisphere and the left ventricular system in all patients studied. These patients included not only the autistic patients, but also a group having pervasive developmental disorders, developmental language disorders, severe attentional deficit syndromes, and the Tourette syndrome.

In 1982, Campbell et al. did a larger study of 45 carefully diagnosed, and clinically homogeneous autistic children. They compared them with hospitalized controls who had seizures, headaches, tumors and trauma, but normal IQs. These autistic patients were selected to be as free as possible from primary neurological abnormalities. In this group of patients they found that 11 out of 45 (or 24 percent) had mild or moderately prominent enlargement of the ventricular system, and categorized these patients as a subgroup of autism. This 24 percent roughly accords with the 29 percent found by Damasio et al. to have bilateral ventricular enlargement. One of the first autistic patients ever to be examined neurologically, and described in the early literature, had ventricular enlargement (Schain and Freedman 1961). It is important to remember, however, that nonspecific bilateral ventricular enlargement is also found in many other central nervous system syndromes of children.

In 1982 and 1983, Tsai et al. published a two-part study of 18 autistic children compared with controls studied for headache and seizures, and linear skull fractures. They excluded from their study left-handed autistics and controls. None of the scans of the autistic patients showed evidence of focal or diffuse brain pathology. This study looked closely at the issue of cerebral asymmetries, and found that the CT pattern of cerebral asymmetries in autistic children was the same as observed in neurological patients. One of the striking findings of the study was that the brains of these autistic patients appeared, if anything, to be more symmetric than those of the normal controls. A similar lack of the usual percentage of left parieto-occipital preponderance has also been reported in dyslexics (Haslam et al. 1981).

Gillberg and Svendsen (1983) studied 21 autistic patients. In their group they found 26 percent who had gross abnormalities in the brain, such as a left parietal occipital porencephaly in one patient. Other abnormalities they described were a loss of substance near the right lateral geniculate body, a conspicuous widening of the left frontal horn of the ventricular system, and a right parietal low attenuation, possibly indicative of the residual encephalitis. They also had three boys with widening of the ventricular system. In this study, the autistic patients did not appear to have unusual brain asymmetry, although in cases of other childhood psychoses, such asymmetry was common.

Rosenbloom et al. (1984) used CT scanning for special studies of linear and volumetric measurements of ventricles, subarachnoid cisterns, and cranial size. The autistic population was carefully preselected, by omitting those with neurological signs or symptoms. These studies confirmed that a small proportion of autistic children do have ventricular enlargement but otherwise do not reveal any consistent differences when compared with controls. The authors concluded that the structural substrate in autism is a heterogenous one.

In 1984, a special study was performed using CT scans on autistic patients who had borderline or normal intelligence. All retarded autistics were omitted (Prior et al. 1984). Although it was a relatively small study limited to nine boys, and although all scans were judged normal with no evidence of unusual asymmetry, the authors felt nevertheless that the study was a contribution to the concept of homogeneity of populations studied among the autistic syndromes. By eliminating retarded autistics, they believed that they might have identified a different subgroup from previous CT studies in autism. Thus, they raise the question of a relationship to retardation in previous reports of abnormal CT scans in autism.

One thing is clear: there is great diversity in the findings of CT scans in autistic patients. Originally it was hoped that the use of the CT scan and other methodologies would help decide if there were any specific locations in the central nervous system more likely to be responsible for autistic symptomology. The inconsistent results to date have dashed the hopes, thus far, in this attempt.

Recently, positron emission tomography (PET) studies of the rate of cerebral metabolism have been performed on a few autistic adults. These studies indicate no unusual evidence of asymmetry in uptake of the radioactive traces on both sides of the brain. There was a finding of hypermetabolism, or an increase in the rate of cerebral metabolism, compared with controls (Rapoport et al. 1983), a finding also noted in other syndromes with mental retardation, such as Down's syndrome. In the autistic subjects, metabolism in all lobes on the left side of the brain was higher than on the right, and the frontal and parietal lobes had lower metabolism than the mean values for the brain as a whole.

In summary, two abnormalities have been reported in more than one study of autistic patients. One is evidence of generalized ventricular dilatation, either mild or moderate, reported in a number of patients in the literature. The other finding, more difficult to replicate, is a tendency among a small subgroup of patients to have predominantly left-sided ventricular dilatation or evidence of left-sided lesions.

12   Neuropathological Studies

Autopsy literature on autism is very fragmentary. There are a number of problems. Even when there are adequate pathological studies, the case histories often are incomplete. The age of onset is often after 30 months. Laboratory tests performed during life sometimes appear sketchy. Pathological studies are uneven in their thoroughness. The problems in understanding this syndrome during the forty-year history since autism was identified are particularly exemplified by a review of the meager pathological studies that have been published.

One example of the early literature is the Ross case (Ross 1959). Called "An Autistic Child," this paper reports on a girl who had neonatal trouble with feeding, an odd, uncoordinated walk, regurgitated after meals by two years of age, and developed a major psychiatric syndrome at four years of age after an infection requiring hospitalization. The child then slowly deteriorated. She showed increasing depersonalization, a lack of response to affection, jerky movements and ritualistic attachment to a doll. She began talking to herself. She was then placed in a special school for retarded children and received psychotherapy three times a week. Most of her physicians believed that her mother's rejection caused the child's problems. When the girl died at 11 years of age, a diffuse encephalopathy was discovered, including cortical atrophy, diffuse gliosis of white matter, and lesions in the hypothalamus, mammillary bodies, hypophyseal eminence, reticular formation, anterior nuclei of the thalamus and cerebellum. There was relative sparing of the hippocampal zones of the temporal lobes.

In 1968, a brain biopsy of the right frontal lobe of an autistic patient showed "slight thickening of the arterioles, slight connective tissue increase of the leptomeninges, and some cell increase" (Aarkrog 1968).

In 1976, Darby attempted to search the literature and find all possible neuropathological cases that could be related to autism. Many of the cases that he published showed onset after 30 months of age and the information in most cases was incomplete. However, among his cases some probably would meet modern criteria. In one case published by Yakovlev et al. (1948), the neuropathological data were published by Benda and Melchior (1959). The pathology showed severe atrophy in the brain, in spite of normal weight, and chronic, severe degeneration of the Nissl substance and fibrous meninges. The authors suggest that some type of sub-acute encephalitic process had taken place in this child. In another case described by Yakovlev et al. (1948), which could be interpreted as an autistic child, there was evidence of areas of cell devastation, especially in the intra-granular layers. However, the finding was non-specific. In an unpublished DeMyer case reported by Darby, a microcephalic child with autistic features had a brain biopsy which indicated non-specific histologic and ultrastructural abnormalities.

In recent years, there have been a few thorough pathological studies performed. In 1980, Williams et al. did a careful neuropathological examination of the cortex of four individuals who exhibited prominent autistic symptoms throughout life. They studied the hippocampus, parahippocampal gyrus, thalamus, hypothalamus, striatum and midbrain tectum. The brainstem was not examined. In two of the cases, minor abnormalities were found after extensive study.

One of these patients had phenylketonuria that had been diagnosed during life, and this patient and one other appeared to have some diminution in dendritic caliber and spine density of layer V pyramidal neurons of the mid-frontal gyrus. The other patient was a severely retarded individual who did not walk until two years of age, then began grand mal seizures at five years of age. (This boy also had a younger sister who was mentally retarded, mute, socially isolated, and had a refractory seizure disorder.) The findings in both these autistic patients were quite subtle and limited to dendritic caliber and spine density. The pyramidal neurons from layer V were oriented normally and had richly branched dendritic arbors in these patients. The development of dendritic spines begins at the thirtieth gestational week and goes on until the age of one year or older.

The other two cases (one male and one female) described by Williams et al. had normal motor milestones but many classic autistic symptoms. Detailed neuropathological examination, including analysis of cortical neurons impregnated with the rapid Golgi method and EM analysis, failed to reveal any abnormalities in these two cases.

In 1984, a very detailed autopsy was performed on the brain of an autistic 29-year-old man who died by drowning. As a child, he displayed the familiar clinical criteria seen in autistic children. At four years of age he began intensive individual psychotherapy and attended a special therapeutic nursery school, but it resulted in no appreciable progress. There was no available workup regarding a specific etiology; he was not known to have been tested for PKU or other subgroups of the autistic syndrome. Language never progressed beyond two-word phrases. He began seizures at 21 years of age and took anti-convulsants until his death at 29. More to the point regarding his autopsy findings, he was treated with psychotropic drugs from adolescence because of self-abuse and temper outbursts. These included chlorpromazine, trifluoperazine, diazepam and up to 300mg. daily of thioridazine as an adult (Bauman and Kemper, in press).

The serial sections of the brain were compared with that of an age- and sex-matched control. The autistic brain showed no abnormality of gyral configuration or myelination, and no evidence of significant gliosis. However, compared with the control, the autistic brain showed increased cell packing density and reduced cell size in the hippocampal complex, the entorhinal cortex, the selected nuclei of the amygdala, the mammillary body and septal nuclei which project to the hippocampus. In addition, loss of Purkinje cells was seen in the neocerebellum with related parts of the inferior olive showing abnormally small, pale neurons rather than the expected retrograde cell loss. Also, the emboliform, globose and fastigial nuclei showed small neurons which were reduced in number. This patient showed lesions in the forebrain (in areas related to memory) and in the cerebellum. Another interesting finding was that in the autistic brain there was a clear zone, deep to the superficial layer, which was not present in the control. This clear zone, generally referred to as the lamina desicans, normally appears in the second trimester of fetal life, but disappears by 15 months of age.

This study is of particular interest because of the care with which it was performed, because of the attempt to match the subject against a normal control, and because it echoes an older paper by Schain and Yannet (1960) which reported decreased cells in the hippocampal formation.

In summary, in evaluating all neuropathological studies, we must remember that autism is a syndrome of many etiologies. Careful laboratory studies during life, when combined with detailed autopsy examinations, should eventually lead to a scientific sorting-out of this syndrome into specific disease entities. Studies of non-retarded autistics may be especially illuminating.

Part III

Disease Entities That Have a Subgroup with the Autistic Syndrome

13   Genetic Disorders

There is now abundant evidence that a number of well-defined disease entities have a subgroup with the autistic syndrome. Kanner and others after him have argued for the distinction of autism with and without associated major signs of "organic involvement." The rationale for such a distinction has been the aim to find a specific etiological/pathogenetic mechanism in the classical variety of autism (corresponding to the idiopathic "Kanner syndrome"). However, such a standpoint now seems obsolete in the face of the ever-accumulating evidence that autism with and without "neurological disorders" does not differ with regard to behavioral symptomatology. Autism *is* a behavioral syndrome, and should be analyzed from this perspective. Twenty years ago, autism associated with clear organic impairment seemed rare. Today, with advances in epidemiological research and new methods of examining the nervous system, autism, more often than not, is shown to run parallel to brain dysfunction. The proportion of "non-organic" cases is rapidly diminishing as scientific progress and follow-up studies are made. Eventually, we may have a situation, in which all—or almost all—cases of autism have been demonstrated to have an associated biological disorder.

In this chapter, we focus on some of the genetic disorders which have been documented to be linked with autism. There are a number of such disorders, usually associated with variations of one and the same phenotype, in which autistic symptoms occur in a frequency surpassing that of mere chance.

Some of the genetic disorders possibly or definitely associated with autism are tuberous sclerosis, neurofibromatosis, and the Martin-Bell (fragile-X) syndrome. There is also evidence pointing toward an autosomal recessive group and studies linking certain chromosomal syndromes with autism. In the following, these disorders will be dealt with in turn.

Tuberous Sclerosis

Valente (1971) was the first to describe the association between autism and tuberous sclerosis, a neurocutaneous disorder, usually displaying an autosomal dominant mode of inheritance. Several years later, Lotter (1974) reported that indications of tuberous sclerosis might eventually develop in autism, even among children who had shown no major signs or family history of this disorder. In a continuing study of autism in the Göteborg region in Sweden, one of the authors (CG) has encountered five cases of tuberous sclerosis among 108 individuals with typical infantile autism. These five also had moderate or severe mental retardation and fits (infantile spasms, grand mal and psychomotor epilepsy).

In a follow-up study of 214 children with infantile spasms, Riikonen and Amnell (1981) found that 25 percent of the autistic children with normal levels of motor activity who had experienced infantile spasms also suffered from tuberous sclerosis. This figure should be compared with eight percent in the autism–infantile spasms group as a whole (regardless of motor activity level) and three percent among infantile spasms cases without major psychiatric sequelae at follow-up.

All these studies agree that tuberous sclerosis, which occurs in the general population in a frequency of 1/20,000 to 1/50,000 (Menkes 1974; Kirman 1977), is definitely correlated with autism in a small, but significant, percentage of cases.

It is interesting that Hunt (1983) found that out of 75 children over the age of two suffering from tuberous sclerosis, 61 percent had no meaningful speech. A majority of these had severe behavioral problems, characterized by that author as "psychotic." No detailed case description pertaining to the diagnosis of autism is given in the paper, but it seems likely that a number of children were indeed autistic. All those without speech had experienced infantile spasms. This combination of autism and infantile spasms has been well described (see above, and chapter 4).

Tuberous sclerosis in autism provides a striking illustration of the misconceptions of those who make claims for a subdivision of autism into organic and non-organic cases (e.g. Fish and Ritvo 1979). In the majority of tuberous sclerosis–autism cases, there is no early indication of tuberous sclerosis at the time when autism is diagnosed. In four of the five cases seen by one of the authors, there were no signs of the somatic genetic disorder before age five, by which time all had received their psychiatric diagnosis.

Neurofibromatosis

Tuberous sclerosis belongs in the comprehensive category of "phakomatoses." Neurofibromatosis is another neurocutaneous genetic disorder often grouped in that same general category. It appears to be more common than tuberous sclerosis, occurring in classic form in as many as 1/2,000 cases (Samuelsson 1981). The genetic mode of transmission is usually autosomal dominant.

Neurofibromatosis has not previously been described in association with autism. However, in 1984, Gillberg and Forsell published case reports on three psychotic children (two of whom were classic Kanner autists) from a total population screening who showed clear-cut evidence of neurofibromatosis. It was calculated that there was at least a 100-fold increase of autism among those suffering from neurofibromatosis as among the general population.

Although there are to date no other systematic studies to corroborate the suggestion made by the Swedish authors, the concurrence of autism and neurofibromatosis in two out of 26 cases is impressive and favors a causal-pathogenetic link. Clinical experience by other authors (e.g. Coleman 1984, unpublished data) indicates that the simultaneous appearance of the two disorders is certainly more common than suggested by any chance occurrence.

The Fragile-X Syndrome (the Martin-Bell Syndrome)

Lubs (1969) was possibly the first to describe this familial syndrome of mental retardation found in males, and characterized by hypertrophy of secondary sex characteristics (after puberty), large ears, and minor malformations of the hands and feet. Several authors (see Gillberg and Wahlström 1984 for a review) in the late 1970s testified to its concurrence with a fragile site on the long arm of the X chromosome at the location of q27. The fragile-X (q27) chromosome abnormality has since (Blomquist et al. 1982, 1983) been shown to account for five to seven percent of all cases of mental retardation (see Figures 13.1 and 13.2).

Brøndum-Nielsen (1983) found psychiatric (mostly psychotic) behavior disturbance in a majority of cases with the syndrome, now

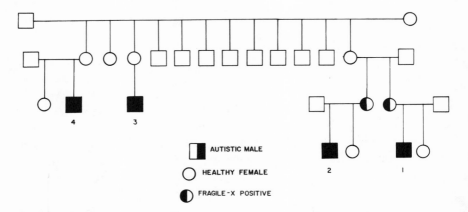

FIGURE 13.1. Family with several autistic fragile-X positive males. Case 1 diagnosed at age eleven as suffering from typical Kanner autism and mild mental retardation. Chromosome culture revealed 20 percent fragile-X positive cells. His maternal first cousin was diagnosed as suffering from infantile autism and mental retardation at age 2 (case 2), without knowledge of the cousin's diagnosis. Chromosome culture showed 2 percent fragile-X positive cells. Both mothers of these cousins were fragile-X positive. Two male first cousins of the mothers were fragile-X positive, were mildly to moderately retarded, and at the ages of 39 and 45 respectively showed marked autistic features (cases 3 and 4).

commonly referred to as the Martin-Bell syndrome, and in 1982 Brown and co-workers and Meryash and collaborators reported on the concurrence of infantile autism and the fragile-X syndrome.

Watson and co-workers (1984) recently reported that in a training school population of 76 autistic or autistic-like males, 5.3 percent had the fragile-X chromosome abnormality. Although the authors claim that DSM-III criteria for infantile autism were used, they go on to say that 40 of their 76 cases suffered from "infantile autism *or* [our italics] severe mental retardation with clear 'autistic features.'" Clearly this raises considerable doubt as to the validity of the diagnostic criteria used. Furthermore, the age range in their sample spanned five to 46 years, and when we consider the decreasing demonstrability of the fragile-X chromosome abnormality with increasing age, we must regard their reported finding with considerable caution.

Even more recently, Gillberg and Wahlström (1984), in a total population study of strictly defined infantile autism, found the fragile-X (q27) abnormality in 20 percent of the autistic boys (ranging in age

FIGURE 13.2. Eight-year-old child with the fragile-X syndrome. The boy has many autistic features, is a "child gourmet" good at jigsaw puzzles, a toe-walker and holds his ears (the auricles are 97 percent in the presence of overall 50th percentile milestones).

from two to 20 years), but in none of the boys with other kinds of childhood psychosis. Gillberg (1983a) has also described a set of identical triplets with infantile autism and mental retardation. The population study indicated that the concurrence of autism and the X chromosome abnormality is much higher than accounted for by the often concomitant mental retardation. In a Swedish multicenter study of 83 autistic male children (Blomquist et al. 1984), most of whom participated in population screening studies and were diagnosed in accordance with Rutter's criteria, 16 percent showed the fragile-X (q27) abnormality. Levitas and co-workers (1983) have suggested that a majority of patients with the fragile-X syndrome exhibit marked autistic features.

The bulk of the available evidence suggests that the fragile-X chromosome abnormality is responsible for an important minority of male autism cases, and that it is associated with autistic features more often than not.

It is further hypothesized, in agreement with Brøndum-Nielsen (1983) and Jörgensen et al. (1984), that the fragile-X chromosome abnormality renders the child susceptible to cognitive dysfunction which, in turn, provides the epigenetic mold for developing autism.

In the study by Gillberg and Wahlström (1984), fragile-X-associated autism was correlated with psychomotor epilepsy and brainstem dysfunction (with its concomitant hypotonia). This possibility of a specific connection of this kind is currently being investigated in a large-scale study of autism–fragile-X in Göteborg, Sweden.

We could only demonstrate the fragile-X (q27) abnormality in three of the examined mothers of five families containing at least one boy with autism–fragile-X. Of these three mothers, two each had two affected sons. The remaining two mothers showed no evidence of chromosomal damage in folic-acid deficient culture. This is not to say that they are free of chromosome abnormalities. It is well established that the demonstrability of the fragile-X abnormality decreases with the increasing age of the person being examined. With further "stress" in the culture (for example, added methotrexate), it is possible that chromosomal cultures would have disclosed a fragile site on one of the X chromosomes of the mother, too. However, it is also quite possible that there do exist cases with new mutations. Future studies will have to focus on detailed family pedigrees and more "stressing" chromosomal cultures in order to establish the true frequency of heritable Martin-Bell–autism cases.

The frequency of the fragile-X (q27) abnormality in the general population is not definitely known. However, Sutherland (1982), in a survey of 1049 healthy unselected newborns, found no case of this chromosome marker. A chromosomal culture in folic acid deficient medium is therefore called for in all new male cases of childhood psychosis.

Several placebo–folic acid, double-blind, crossover studies are currently in progress. A report of two brothers with autism and the fragile-X abnormality (Gilberg, unpublished data; see also Levitas et al. 1983) showed a decrease in the frequency of cells affected by the chromosome abnormality and simultaneous improvement in mental symptoms. Preliminary results from a somewhat larger study of the effect of folic acid in Martin-Bell–autistic boys point in the same direction (Gillberg et al. 1984b). In this study, folic acid was administered orally three times a day with a dosage of 0.5 mg/kg bodyweight per day. No obvious adverse effects have yet been noted. However, it is still too early to evaluate the importance of this possible pharmacological treatment method in a subgroup of autistic boys.

Other Chromosomal Syndromes

Supernumerary Sex Chromosomes. The addition of an extra sex chromosome in the human karyotype is often associated with specific speech-language difficulties (Guichano et al. 1982). A speech-language deficit might be the sine qua non in autism though not in itself a sufficient cause (Rutter 1983).

The XYY Syndrome. This has long been considered relatively harmless in respect to human psychiatric development. However, there is now good evidence that, apart from the fact that a small minority of the cases with this karyotype develop into antisocial adults, speech-language disorders in childhood are the rule rather than the exception (Guichano et al. 1982, Bender et al. 1983). Moreover, autism has been described in a number of cases in association with the XYY syndrome (Forsius et al. 1970; Nielsen et al. 1973; Gillberg et al. 1984c, Gillberg and Wahlström 1984) in such a way that pure coincidence is unlikely to be a plausible explanation.

In a Swedish population study of chromosomes in early childhood psychosis (Gillberg and Wahlström 1984) three out of 55 boys (five percent) showed either the complete XYY syndrome or mosaicism involving a small number of cell populations containing an extra Y chromosome. Two of these boys had classic autism, and the third had Asperger's syndrome. Again, in these cases, the most probable explanation for the link between the autism-sex chromosome abnormality is a common speech-language disorder. In combination with pre-, peri- or postnatal brain damage, the child already vulnerable to speech-language problems because of the XYY abnormality may develop autism.

In addition to these examples of the XYY syndrome, one case of infantile psychosis and the XXX-syndrome has been reported in the literature (Wolraich et al. 1970).

Other Gonosomal Abnormalities

Judd and Mandell (1968) and Gillberg and Wahlström (1984) have commented on the high frequency of long Y chromosomes in autistic boys. Fragile sites on the p-arm of the X chromosomes have also been found in autistic boys and girls (Gillberg and Wahlström 1984), but in view of non-existent controls, the importance of these results remain quite obscure. However, taken with the other data implicating sex chromosome abnormalities in autism, the results may prove to be interesting. Lorna Wing (1981a) has put forward a theory linking autism with normally occurring sex differences. Autism might, in her view, be seen as a pathological exaggeration of normal male features. The findings in the sphere of sex chromosomes in autism so far are almost totally consistent in that they show a relative "decrease" in the influence of the female chromosomes, either through defects (fragile-X (q27), fragile-X (p22)), or through an "increase" in the influence of the Y chromosome(s) (XYY syndrome, long Y chromosomes).

Autosomal Chromosome Abnormalities

There is as yet no convincing evidence for any link between autism and major autosomal chromosome aberrations. Down's syndrome (trisomy 21) has been reported by some authors (Knobloch and Pasamanick 1975; Campbell et al. 1978b; Wakabayashi 1979; Gillberg and Wahlström 1984) to have occurred in connection with autism, but, in at least some of these cases, there have been signs of added brain damage (such as regression of motor skills and cerebral palsy) which might have accounted for the development of autism. Three cases of trisomy 22 (Turner and Jennings 1961; Biesele and Schmid 1962) and childhood psychosis have also been described, but the importance of these findings remain unclear at the moment.

In the Swedish population study referred to above, a rather high frequency (17 percent) of the autistic children (both boys and girls) had fragile sites on the sixteenth chromosome at the q23 location. Two boys with both autism and this chromosome abnormality were paternal first cousins. These findings might indicate the existence of another group among the autistic syndromes, namely, the fragile (16) (q23)–autism syndrome (Gillberg and Wahlström 1984). However, the frequency of fragile sites on this chromosome in the general population remains to be established before any definite conclusions can be drawn.

14   Infectious Diseases

One of the questions that has been raised about autism is the possibility of an infectious etiology to the syndrome. Could infection of the central nervous system cause autistic symptoms? The possibility of prenatal infection has to be considered when studying a syndrome with symptoms sometimes already present by the time of birth. A study of the monthly distribution of births of autistic children has disclosed a statistically significant increase (Bartlick 1981) in the months of March and August, a finding compatible with, but certainly not establishing, possible infectious causes.

In the mental retardation syndromes, both prenatal and postnatal infections are known to be responsible for some of the most severely damaging brain syndromes. In one study, Rostafinski (1964) reported that nine percent of mentally institutionalized children have either a prenatal or postnatal encephalopathy owing to an infectious process. An examination of this question regarding autistic patients will be divided into two different time periods in the life of a child: before birth and during infancy. Gestational infections occur when the virus or the infectious agent travels through the mother's bloodstream to the placenta, and then on to the fetus. Since the active transport system into the brain (the "blood/brain barrier") has not yet developed in the fetus, the virus enters the brain and causes damage that does not occur when the same virus passes through the bloodstream of an adult whose brain does have the protective barrier. Children with congenital infections may continue to excrete virus in the urine after they are born, sometimes up to 18 months of age (Blattner 1966).

When we use the term "prenatal damage," it is important to remember that there may be continuing damage after birth owing to the chronic and persistent nature of many of these infections. The insidiousness of some viral infections is caused by the fragility and vulnerability of fetal tissues. Often the damage done to the fetus bears no relation to the severity of the disease in the mother, and sometimes a pregnant woman who has no obvious infection at all may still give birth to a child damaged by one of these viruses (Avery et al. 1965).

The central nervous system is not fully developed at birth. Because of the immaturity of the brain, even after birth infants are at special risk for viral damage to the central nervous system in a way that adults are not. For example, a study of the long-term effects of enterovirus infections of the brain in children affected between birth and two-and-a-half years of age was done by Sells et al. (1975). This group found that when compared with controls matched in age, sex and social class, the children who had sustained infections during the first year of life had significantly lower IQ scores and lower scores on most measures of language comprehension, expression, and articulation. However, there was no difference between patients and controls in children past 12 months of age, suggesting that the first year of life is the time of greatest vulnerability of the brain.

To study the possibility of an infectious etiology in autism, in 1979 Deykin and MacMahon did a retrospective epidemiological study of 163 cases of autism and 355 unaffected siblings, using parent interviews and medical records. The number of cases where an infectious etiology could be established was small, indicating that the viruses studied were unlikely to have played a major role in any substantial proportion of the autistic patients. However, they did note in children whom they indentified as "partially autistic" (that is, not having the full syndrome) that there was a statistically significant difference between cases and sibling controls in household exposure or clinical illness of the mother with prenatal rubella. In the fully autistic children, there was an increased frequency of combined maternal illnesses (of rubella and mumps) and household exposure for cases, relative to their sibling controls. They also noted that prenatal maternal influenza was four times as common among fully autistic children as among their siblings. In the postnatal period, the exposure (either household exposure or the infant's clinical illness) to mumps was seen with increased frequency in fully autistic patients.

In 1976, as part of the Children's Brain Research Clinic study of 78 autistic patients and controls, cultures were collected for the presence of active cytomegalovirus and rubella virus in both autistic and control groups, most of them well beyond the age of three years (Peterson and

Torrey 1976). The study yielded negative results, which was not unexpected in view of the mean age of the children, since continued excretion of the virus is unusual in later childhood. In serum antibody titers, there was no difference between patients and controls regarding cytomegalovirus, rubella, and rubeola. In the case of toxoplasmosis, six autistic children were positive, while only two control children were positive. However, the mothers of all six children were studied and were found to be negative, ruling out the possibility of congenital toxoplasmosis infection.

The only possibly significant finding of the viral antibody screen was the herpes virus result. In the case of HSV-1 (oral herpes), antibodies were positive in 25 percent of the autistic children compared with 13 percent of the control children. This may be coincidental, and although it is impossible to determine its relevance, it is interesting in the light of reports that show an increased incidence of HSV-1 antibodies in adult psychiatric populations compared with controls (Halonen et al. 1974). Two autistic males, ages four and eight, were positive for herpes, type 2 (HSV-2) antibodies. This type of herpes (genital) has been thought to be transmitted primarily be genital contact after puberty. In the case of these two patients, the mothers were screened and both were positive, making it possible, but not proving, that these children could have had in utero herpes encephalitis infections (Peterson and Torrey 1976).

The same group studied serum immunoglobulins IGG, IGM, and IGA and found no difference between the control children and the autistic children. (In fact, the control children appeared to have more abnormalities than the autistic.) Young et al. (1977) also studied immunoglobulins in the cerebral spinal fluid of five autistic children and found no increases.

The results of these studies, in addition to other cases reported in the literature, are seen in Table 14.1.

At this time, it is difficult to be sure in any individual case whether the autistic symptomology was caused by exposure to viruses. However, in the case of rubella encephalopathy, the connection has been more firmly established by a number of case reports. With respect to other viruses, further study is needed to delineate the relevance to the autistic syndrome.

Bacterial infections, such as meningitis, are rare in histories of autistic patients, although an occasional case is reported in the literature (Knobloch and Pasamanick 1975). Judging from the information we

TABLE 14.1. Children with Autistic Symptoms Exposed to Viral Protozoal or Spirochaetal Infection. Review of Published Literature.

Prenatal*	Number of cases	Authors
Rubella	1	Rimland 1964
	8	Desmond et al. 1967
	1	Freedman et al. 1970
	18	Chess et al. 1971
	4 (late onset)	Chess 1977
	2	Deykin & MacMahon 1979
CID	1	Stubbs 1978
	1	Markowitz 1983
	2	Stubbs et al. 1984
Toxoplasmosis	1	Rutter & Bartak 1971
Syphilis	1	Rutter & Bartak 1971
	1	Knobloch & Pasamanick 1975
Varicella	1	Knobloch & Pasamanick 1975
Rubeola	1	Deykin & MacMahon 1979
Postnatal*		
Herpes	1	Delong et al. 1981
	1	Gillberg 1985
Mumps	8	Deykin & MacMahon 1979

*Table limited to exposure (gestational or postnatal) by documented infection. Household exposure cases not included.

have in general about autism, we might conclude that meningitis should cause autistic-like symptoms if it resulted in the blockage of cerebrospinal fluid with resultant mild or moderate hydrocephalus.

Regarding fungus infections, there is only anecdotal literature suggesting that such infections conceivably could be a factor, possibly in the postnatal period.

A review of the literature by etiologic agent follows.

RUBELLA

Rubella is a virus that causes epidemics. Since the program of rubella inoculation was initiated in the United States in 1968, these periodic epidemics have stopped and the incidence of rubella pathology in children has now decreased dramatically.

One of the last documented epidemics occurred in 1964. It has been estimated that at least 20,000 children in the United States alone were born damaged as a result of the 1964 rubella epidemic. At New York University Medical Center, a rubella birth defect evaluation project was established in which 243 children were studied. Chess et al. (1971) undertook a psychiatric study of these patients and found that 118 of them had no psychiatric disorder. In the remainder of the patients, they identified 18—ten who had, in their opinion, an autistic syndrome and eight who had a partial syndrome of autism. They pointed out that none of those affected by rubella gave evidence of any other type of psychosis or childhood schizophrenia syndrome.

An early mention of rubella autism in the literature was a case treated in the Netherlands by Dr. Van Krevland, and mentioned by Rimland (1964). In 1967, Desmond et al., in studying a series of patients at Baylor University, noted that out of 64 children surviving congenital rubella eight appeared autistic, isolated, and out of communication with the environment. Freedman et al. in 1970 also described one case.

In the monograph by Chess et al. (1971), an analysis was made of the auditory and visual problems in the rubella infants with autism compared with those without the behavioral syndrome. Among her group, one of the autistic patients had combined auditory and visual loss, seven had an auditory loss and a retardation syndrome, and nine had an auditory and visual loss and a retardation syndrome. Thus, 17 out of 18 of the autistic patients had some sensory impairment. However, it is important to note that 76 of the rubella children who had no autistic disorder also fell into one of those three categories, showing that the presence of a sensory and cognitive defect does not in itself account for the number of rubella children who fulfill the criteria for autism. These authors also noted that the degree of the sensory or cognitive defect was not correlated in any way with the presence or absence of autism, so that a severely hearing-impaired rubella baby might have no autistic component at all, while a mildly retarded child with a moderate hearing loss could have a severe autistic syndrome.

In 1977, Chess published a follow-up longitudinal study of the children with congenital rubella. Four *new* cases, one of the full and three of the partial autistic syndrome, were identified on follow-up. Most interestingly, she reports that of the original 18 cases, six had recovered and one had improved with respect to autistic symptomology. Evaluation of the data indicated that the lack of improvement or worsening of psychiatric status in cases of autism tended to be associated with a more severe degree of mental retardation initially than in those cases in which there was recovery or improvement.

The interesting finding in this 1977 paper was the presence of the autistic symptoms in the four patients at school age (seven years of age), although four years earlier none of them had behaved in a manner which fulfilled the criteria for either full or partial autism. Thus, in those rare cases with autistic symptomology developing *after 30 months of age*, the underlying presence of congenital rubella syndrome should be considered in the differential diagnosis.

In the Chess study, none of the rubella children who had full hearing showed autism. Thus, in an autistic child with intact hearing, the possibility of congenital rubella is much less likely. However, the study showed that a hearing defect alone was unimportant with respect to rubella autism. The autistic syndrome was most common when a hearing defect was associated with mental retardation, but interestingly, in this study a visual defect did not add to the risk of autism. It is of note that five out of nine autistic children with severe or profound deafness were in the group that recovered from autism.

With the new preventive approach of rubella inoculations, it is hoped that this form of autism will become a disease entity of the past.

CYTOMEGALOVIRUS

It is less clearly established that cytomegalovirus infection could be an etiological agent in the autistic syndromes. However, there are some suggestive data in the literature. A group from the Oregon School of Medicine (Stubbs et al. 1984) have reported several cases and state that they think the congenital infection might well be related to the autistic symptoms. In fact, in one of the cases, a treatment with transfer factor immunotherapy was tried for the congenital cytomegalovirus infection, and some possible good results, such as marked decrease in spasticity and increased eye contact, were reported (Stubbs et al. 1980). However, it should be noted that the cytomegalovirus is a very common virus; between 0.5 and 1 percent of newborns have a congenital infection (Walker and Tobin 1970, Starr et al. 1970, Elek and Stern 1974). Thus, it is necessary to consider the possibility that the CID infection could have been an incidental finding in the cases that have been reported.

OTHER PRENATAL VIRAL INFECTIONS

Adequate documentation of a significant number of cases with other prenatal viral infections has not been established. It is important to point out again that when the term "prenatal infection" is used (because of the presumed time of the onset of the infection) it does not mean that the infection did not continue into the postnatal period with the shedding of viruses in some cases for months after birth.

As can be seen from Table 14.1, there are a few cases of other viruses reported in prenatal gestational exposures. Although rarer than CID, there are quite a number of cases of congenital toxoplasmosis, syphilis, varicella, and rubeola reported in the medical literature. Autistic symptoms have not been described in most patients. Thus, this infection could be coincidence in the patients listed in Table 14.1 in view of the rarity, at least to date, of autism compared with the more classical clinical pictures described in each of these virus syndromes.

However, since relatively few autistic patients to date have received complete medical workups, it is premature to rule out any virus at this time as a factor, and further investigations are indicated.

POSTNATAL INFECTIONS

Can an infection after birth cause an autistic syndrome? An important contribution to our understanding of this possibility was made by DeLong et al. (1981) when they published a paper entitled "An Acquired Reversible Autistic Syndrome in Acute Encephalopathic Illness in Children." In this paper they identified three cases with striking autistic features that had developed in previously normal children in the course of an acute encephalopathic illness in which clinical evidence was compatible with the involvement of function ascribed to a temporal lobe location. In two of the children, the specific etiology was not identified and the children eventually made a complete recovery. In the third, herpes simplex infection was confirmed, and extensive left temporal lobe necrosis was found on CT scans. Herpes, a term used in medicine for at least 25 centuries since Hippocrates, refers to a group of viruses which share a number of distinguishing features. In the patient described by DeLong et al., a herpes simplex encephalitis was documented by a rise in serum titers. Herpes simplex has a predilection for infecting the temporal lobe area of the brain. The interesting fact about these three cases is that the behavioral syndrome was acquired at a clearly definable time in the context of an acute encephalopathic illness and then was reversible. DeLong et al. pointed out that the post-encephalitic syndrome in these patients resembled the adult Kluver-Bucy syndrome of bilateral medial temporal lobe dysfunction after surgical ablation. The syndrome in adults includes

> an incapacity for adaptive social behavior and a loss of recognition of the significance of persons and events. Such patients show an empty blandness and absence of emotion or concerns for family or other persons and pursue no sustained purposeful activity. (Terzian and Delleore 1955)

Gillberg (1985) has described a 14-year-old girl who, after quite normal development, was suddenly taken ill with herpes encephalopathy, and after three weeks showed (and still shows, ten years later) many of the classic symptoms of autism.

Deykin and MacMahon (1979), in their epidemiological study of autistic children described eight who had a postnatal mumps infection. This is of interest in view of the work with animals showing that mumps sometimes causes a blockage of cerebrospinal fluid and the development of a partial hydrocephalic syndrome.

Other infectious agents, such as bacteria and fungi, have very little documentation as etiological agents in autistic patients. With regard to bacteria, Knobloch and Pasamanick (1975) described an autistic patient who had a hydrocephalic picture secondary to meningitis. Since mild or moderate hydrocephalus has been described in a few autistic patients (see chapter 17), this may be one mechanism by which infectious agents could cause pressure changes in the brain that eventually are found in conjunction with autistic symptoms.

The possibility of fungus infections as an etiological agent in autism has been raised by William Crook in his book, The Yeast Connection (1983). Chronic infection with candida albicans can be a sign of impaired immunity, a problem under discussion in autism (see chapter 9). Only anecdotal material exists at this time on the possibility that candida causes autistic symptoms (Crook 1983, D.G. Campbell 1983).

In summary, evidence in a few patients suggests that infectious agents both in the prenatal and postnatal period may be a factor in the development of autistic symptoms. The mechanism appears to be a direct toxic effect on brain cells (encephalitis), but there is a second possibility of indirect damage resulting from altered pressure relationships within the brain (mild hydrocephalus).

15   Birth Injury

The question of birth injury as a cause of autism is one of the most difficult topics to discuss. A brief look at the literature regarding mental retardation and cerebral palsy, both of which are more common and better studied syndromes, indicates the difficulty of establishing that particular etiology in any individual case.

Presumably birth injury involves either hypoxic or ischemic injuries during birth or intracranial hemorrhage during the birth process. Hypoxia, or hypoxemia, refers to a diminished amount of oxygen in the blood supply, and ischemia refers to a diminished amount of blood suffusing the brain tissue. This combination of circumstances can then result in intrauterine asphyxia or acidotic hypoxia.

Four types of intracranial hemorrhage have been described that can be detected clinically in preterm and fullterm newborns. Subdural hemorrhage, a traumatic lesion, can result from the rupture of superficial cerebral veins or from the laceration of the falx or the tentorium, thereby injuring the sinus or venous system of the brain. In modern medical centers, clinically important subdural hematomas are unusual. A second type of intracranial hemorrhage is the primary sub-arachnoid hemorrhage, which is more frequent and is caused by venous bleeding. A third type in the cerebellum (or intracerebellar hemorrhage), is seen mostly in small, premature infants and may be secondary to bleeding elsewhere in the brain. Finally, periventricular hemorrhage is seen in almost 50 percent of all infants weighing less than 1500 grams. A review of the literature on this subject is found in the work by Volpe (1981).

One of the major problems with birth injury is the identification of the origin of the central nervous system lesions. According to Towbin (1969), careful pathological studies suggest that a major portion of central nervous system lesions appearing at birth in full term infants are caused by processes of prenatal origin that have occurred well in advance of labor. Such a full term infant, or any very premature baby, enters the birth process already at risk (Coleman 1981).

Thus, when we discuss birth injury as an etiological factor in autism in a syndrome where very few autopsies and a paucity of adequate epidemiological studies are available, it is only for the purpose of raising questions about this possible diagnosis.

Studies of perinatal complications in autistic children are circumscribed by the same problems as all other studies reviewed in this monograph. Cases of autism have often been mixed up with infant psychoses, childhood schizophrenia and other diagnostic entities in past studies. In the study by Taft and Goldfarb (1964), childhood psychotics were compared with siblings and normal controls and found to have a significantly higher occurrence of pre- or perinatal complications. The same pattern of increased perinatal complications compared either with siblings or normal controls was also found in the studies of Whittam et al. (1966), Lobascher et al. (1970), Kolvin (1971), and Rutt and Offord (1971). All these early studies suggested that perinatal complications could have been a factor in some cases of infantile psychoses.

More recently, Campbell et al. (1978b) published a perinatal profile of 105 autistic children. The authors carefully report that "Children with identifiable causes of autism are excluded from the study." In other words, they had a preselected population according to their own diagnostic criteria. Even so, in this study, Apgar scores were less than eight at one minute in 16.2 percent of the males and 14.3 percent of the females. Infant weights ranged from normal values to as low as 1.33 kg., suggesting that the sample included some preterm or small-for-dates infants. Pre-eclampsia was present in 3.8 percent of the cases, and maternal hypertension in 6.7 percent. Clearly some of these children met the criteria for being at risk even prior to the birth process.

In 1980, Deykin and MacMahon investigated the prenatal, delivery, and neonatal histories of 145 autistic children matched with 330 unaffected siblings. Obstetrical records which had been made prior to diagnosis of autism indicate that the autistic children were more likely than their siblings to have experienced at least one untoward event during gestation and delivery. Similarly, the autistic children showed an increased risk of neonatal complications. In this study, eight complications of delivery were investigated: (1) emergency Cesarean section,

(2) vaginal delivery aided by forceps, (3) malposition of the fetus, (4) cord problems (which included both prolapse of the cord and wrapping of the cord around the child's neck), (5) hemorrhage during delivery, (6) unduly long labor (first stage lasting more than 12 hours), (7) precipitate labor (labor lasting one hour or less), and (8) maternal weight gain of less than 4.5 kg. or more than 13.6 kg. All eight events were more common in the delivery of autistic children. The individual frequency of unfavorable events, however, was relatively low for both the autistic children and their siblings; and the difference between the two was statistically significant only when all complications were grouped together. In this study, there was a statistically significant excess of firstborn and a deficit of second born among autistic children.

Gillberg and Gillberg (1983) applied the Prechtl (1980) optimality score (adapted to Swedish obstetrical and neonatal records) to a group of 25 autistic children, and compared them with the same-sex controls born about the same time in the same obstetric department. In this study, autistic children showed statistically significantly increased scores for reduced optimality, although individual items in the perinatal period were not statistically significant, except for lower gestational age. The greatest rate of reduced optimality was in the prenatal rather than in the perinatal period.

While on the subject of birth injury, one theory regarding anatomical location of autistic symptomology is that injury to the thalamus has occurred owing to vascular damage in the birth process. The thalamus is a nuclear mass in the central nervous system that, when damaged, can cause excruciating pain. A lesion here, particularly at the level of the inter-laminar nuclei, is known to cause pain called causalgia in adults. A characteristic of this disease process in the lateral or central thalamus is occasional, sudden, unexplained attacks of pain. The thalamic blood supply comes primarily from the posterior cerebral artery and, in part, from the posterior communicating artery, feeding from the basalar artery. These arteries branch off at the base of the brain and because of their position are particularly vulnerable to damage during the birth process. Damage to the thalamus at birth conceivably could account for some autistic symptoms, such as the early age of onset, the unexplained rages, the auditory problems (the medial geniculate), and the visual problems (lateral geniculate). Perceptual integration is one of the primary jobs of the thalamus. However, of the few recent autopsies available in autism, none has shown thalamic damage. (For further discussion, see chapters 12 and 22.)

In summary, although epidemiological studies show some evidence of overall increased perinatal risk in autistic patients, at the present level of knowledge there is very little hard evidence to indicate that birth injury per se is a factor in any significant number of patients with the autistic syndrome.

16   Metabolic Diseases

The possibility that various metabolic diseases might underlie autistic symptomology has been raised ever since it was discovered that some of the children with phenylketonuria were mistaken for Kanner autistics (Friedman 1969). This section discusses our current understanding of the question, which means outlining research questions rather than listing clear answers. However, in spite of the newness of the field and the relatively few investigators, some significant progress has been made.

PHENYLKETONURIA

The first step in the metabolic pathway that produces catecholamines is the change of the amino acid, phenylalanine, to the amino acid, tyrosine, by the enzyme phenylalanine-4-hydroxylase (see Figure 8.2). In 1934, Folling identified excessive phenylpyruvic acid in the urine of a group of retarded patients, and it is now understood that a block of phenylalanine-4-hydroxylase results in a back-up with minor metabolites, such as phenylpyruvic acid, spilling over into the urine (Figure 16.1). In 1937, Penrose and Quastel suggested for this condition the name phenylketonuria (PKU) which has remained in common usage.

Jervis was the first to demonstrate that the liver of these patients was deficient in the ability to convert phenylalanine to tyrosine (Jervis 1953). That same year, a dietary therapy was developed by Bickel, Gerrard and Hickman (1953). The diet consisted of a special formula for the babies containing a very low amount of phenylalanine, which would prevent a back-up of unused phenylalanine in the child and thus its conversion into minor metabolites which would interfere with the function of neighboring metabolic pathways.

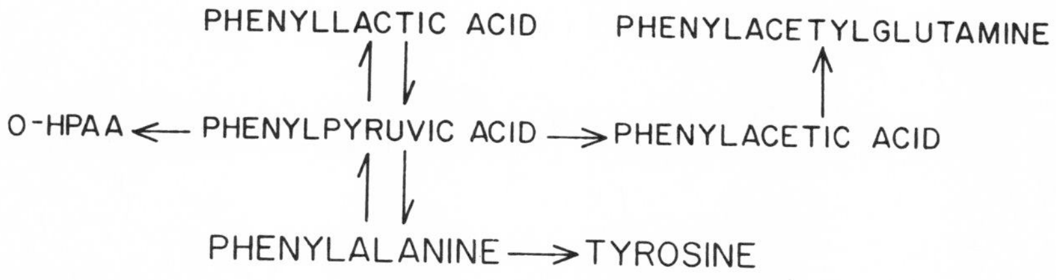

PHENYLLACTIC ACID   PHENYLACETYLGLUTAMINE

O-HPAA ←— PHENYLPYRUVIC ACID —→ PHENYLACETIC ACID

PHENYLALANINE —→ TYROSINE

FIGURE 16.1. Minor metabolites seen in phenylketonuria.

The failure of phenylalanine hydroxylase to work as it should can be caused by several different factors. Either the enzyme itself can be diminished, or co-factors such as biopterin or dihydropteridine reductase (see Figure 16.2) can be diminished, making the enzyme, even if it is present in normal amounts, nonfunctional.

Patients with classic PKU (genetic diminution of phenylalanine-4-hydroxylase) usually have few or no symptoms in the neonatal period. Although they are reportedly normal at birth, there is some dispute in the literature as to whether they have lower live-birth rates and a higher

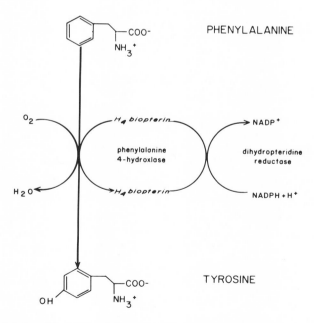

FIGURE 16.2. The phenylalanine hydroxylase complex.

frequency of perinatal difficulties (Partington 1961; Rothman and Pueschel 1976). Sometimes neonatal nurses have noted a musty odor resulting from increased phenylacetic acid excretion. Increased frequency of vomiting occasionally results in surgery for suspected pyloric stenosis. Eczema also occurs soon after birth in a small percentage of patients. But usually there is no evidence that alerts the medical staff to the presence of the serious disease about to engulf the infant.

Phenylalanine-4-hydroxylase is a hepatic enzyme and not present in serum or fibroblast cells, so for many years there was no available methodology for prenatal diagnosis of this hereditary disorder. However, the recent cloning of the gene by Woo et al. (1983) now makes the feasibility of prenatal diagnosis possible for patients with the classic form of phenylketonuria. Identification of carriers of this abnormal phenylalanine hydroxylase locus in the human genome is also now possible (Woo et al. 1983).

The successful treatment of phenylketonuria in a living infant depends upon early identification of the abnormality. Since it is virtually impossible to detect it by clinical examination of a young infant, newborn screening laboratories exist around the world for the purpose of testing every baby for this inborn error of metabolism. If patients are not started on treatment in the early weeks of life, the central nervous system starts to deteriorate, which results in delayed psychomotor development and a loss of approximately 50 IQ points during the first year of life. This program of early detection of PKU in infants was begun by Dr. Robert Guthrie of Buffalo, New York in 1961 (*Profiles in Preventive Medicine* 1983).

One of the problems in PKU screening is the age at which it can be most effectively done. During gestation, the mother's liver effectively hydroxylizes the phenylalanine to tyrosine, so it is not until the baby is born and is attempting to handle amino acids on its own that the rise in the level of phenylalanine begins. Thus, using present screening cutoff levels of serum (phenylalanine levels of 4 mg.%), approximately one-third of the patients with PKU will be missed by samples taken in the first 12 hours of life, and nearly 10 percent will be missed by samples taken during the second 12 hours of life (McCabe et al. 1983). Since many newborns leave the hospital within 24 hours of birth, a percentage of these infants will not be effectively screened for PKU. Infants can also be missed even with a longer hospital stay if the staff neglects to get a specimen from a particular newborn; in fact, one survey found that as many as 20 percent of liveborn infants in the United States may not even receive an initial neonatal screening test (Sepe et al. 1979). In some states, a second screen is done a week or two later in an attempt to catch infants who may have been missed in the first screening (Holtzman et al. 1981). Infants can be missed because of errors in processing the blood specimens in these endlessly repetitive procedures that screen many thousands of newborns annually (*Report of the New England Screening Program* 1982).

But if patients with phenylketonuria are *not* started on treatment in the early weeks of life, they begin a deteriorating course which can result in microcephaly, severe retardation, a multitude of neurological signs, and a behavioral disorder. In a few PKU cases, this behavioral disorder has a number of the components belonging to the autistic syndrome. In 1969, Friedman wrote an excellent paper pointing out that 50 patients had been called autistic who, in fact, actually had phenylketonuria. Fourteen cases of autistic symptoms in children with PKU were reported by Knobloch and Pasamanick in 1975. Also in 1975, Bliumina reported a child with autistic-like symptoms and phenylketonuria. In 1980, while screening 65 children with autism and atypical childhood psychosis, Lowe et al. (1980) from the Yale University School of Medicine found three chldren with phenylketonuria. One child, aged two years, had been tested for PKU in the neonatal period and had been reported as negative. The second, aged seven months, had not been screened at all as a newborn. The third child, aged four years, had been born in a state that did not require testing.

This type of autistic child could potentially have been spared if effective screening programs were available everywhere in the world. If PKU therapy is started under three months of age, the PKU Collaborative Study results indicate that the mean IQ can be in the normal range and behavior can be normal (Dobson et al. 1977).

There is a sizable animal literature which has investigated the effects of high levels of phenylalanine (or hyperphenylalaninemia) on the brains of suckling rats (Chase and O'Brien 1970; Prensky et al. 1971). In these patients no organ other than the brain is affected to such an extent. One of the areas affected specifically by experimental hyperphenylalaninemia is the cerebellum (Huether et al. 1983). Loo et al. (1977) reported that the minor phenylalanine metabolite, phenylacetic acid, appeared to be the most potent agent interfering with myelinization in the brain. In one experimental mode, the excess phenylalanine itself had an effect on cell metabolism, primarily protein synthesis (see for a review Hughes and Johnson 1978). The disturbed sequential timing of neurodevelopmental events leading to reduced connectivity, false contacts, degeneration of cells or processes, and other structural abnormalities in nerve cell development may also be responsible for the severe problems seen in PKU patients. In the one autopsy available on an autistic patient with documented phenylketonuria, the only gross abnormality found was in the diminution of the dendritic spines (see chapter 12).

Several different treatments are available for patients with phenylketonuria, depending upon the factor that has depressed phenylalanine hydroxylase function. Because of the genetic and phenotypic heterogeneity, the treatment of the disease depends upon the specific type of metabolic error. The majority of patients who have classic phenylketonuria, or severe phenylalanine-4-hydroxylase deficiency, receive a diet low in phenylalanine as treatment. There also is available a dietary formula which is totally free of phenylalanine, but in the past this has been used only with PKU children past infancy. More recently, the use of the phenylalanine-free formula, combined with some breast feeding and other foods containing small amounts of phenylalanine, has been introduced as an alternative therapeutic regimen for such patients (Flannery et al. 1983). The standard dietary treatment in newborns is complicated in the sense that excessive levels may result in irreversible damage to the central nervous system while insufficient levels may retard growth or even be life-threatening. However, the success of early diagnosis and early treatment if properly administered is now well documented (Berry et al. 1979). Patients receive the diet for different lengths of times, but most clinics in the past have discontinued it somewhere between the ages of 9 to 12 years, and the children appear to tolerate it fairly well (Schuett et al. 1980). Recently, it has been suggested that the diet should be continued longer.

The first case of a special type of PKU or hyperphenylalaninemia caused by the lack of a component of the phenylalanine hydroxylating system other than the enzyme, phenylalanine hydroxylase itself, was reported in 1975 when it was shown that a child, with a type of PKU that did not respond to phenylalanine restriction, lacked dihydropteridine reductase in biopsy samples of the liver and brain and in fibroblasts cultured from the skin (Kaufman et al. 1975). The therapy for this variant form of PKU involves some restriction of phenylalanine intake, combined with administration of the precursors of catecholamines and serotonin, L-DOPA and 5-hydroxytryptophan (Butler et al. 1978).

They are usually given with an inhibitor of peripheral aromatic amino acid decarboxylase to enhance the entrance of the amino acids into the brain.

Another variant form of PKU is the type in which both phenylalanine hydroxylase and dihydropteridine reductase levels are normal but total biopterin levels in liver, blood and urine are low (Bartholome et al. 1977; Milstein et al. 1977). Since these patients have a block in the metabolic pathway for tetrahydrobiopterin (BH_4), their therapy (which is still under research investigation) includes the administration of BH_4 or its synthetic analog, 6-methyltetrahydropterin ($6MPH_4$) (Kaufman et al. 1983).

To the clinician finding the diagnosis of phenylketonuria in an older autistic child, the question arises, "Is there any value in starting treatment past early infancy?" In the medical literature, L-DOPA has been used to treat the extrapyramidal manifestations of these children (Macleod et al. 1983). There is relatively little experience with starting the diet at later ages. A few studies (Lewis 1959; Gruter 1963; Lowe et al. 1980) do however suggest that dietary treatment of the disorder can prevent further progression of the disability and might even have some behavioral benefit in the child. This question needs evaluation by a larger series before the value of late onset dietary treatment in PKU in autistic patients can be ascertained.

OTHER AMINOACIDOPATHIES

Phenylketonuria is the only inborn error of amino acid metabolism that has been established to produce a significant number of patients with the autistic syndrome. In contrast to the studies on mental retardation syndromes which rapidly yielded a number of amino acidopathies when these patient groups began to be tested, there is very little literature suggesting a correlation between the inborn errors of metabolism of amino acids and the autistic syndromes. Histidinemia has been reported (Rutter and Bartak 1971), but elevation of that amino acid is no longer thought to be toxic to the central nervous system (Levy et al. 1974; Kotsopoulos and Kutty 1979). However, since relatively few autistic patients have had adequate medical workups, the possibility of other amino acidopathies underlying autistic symptoms remains an open question at this time.

PURINE AUTISM

There are now a number of cases cited in the medical literature of patients who have autistic symptomology and evidence of an error in purine metabolism. Perhaps it is not surprising since the purine errors documented to date often have a behavioral or psychiatric component (Table 16.1). In some of the earlier patients described, autism was merely one feature of a much more complex syndrome, such as spasticity or deafness, but more recently purine dysfunction has been found in the more classically autistic patients.

In 1968, Hooft et al. reported a child with increased excretion of uric acid of 35 to 45 mg/kg daily. The patient, who had spasticity and choreathetosis, was also described as self-mutilating and in her case "social contact was practically absent" (Hooft et al. 1968).

In 1969, Nyhan et al. described a three-year-old boy with unusual autistic behavior, failure to cry with tears, absence of speech, hypoplastic discolored teeth and persistently pink urine. The description was of a boy "very disturbed and autistic who seemed to be totally oblivious to the people around him." Later studies also indicated deafness in this child. The research team documented an increased synthesis of purines de novo by the rate of conversion of glycine to uric acid that was seven times that of a control patient. In this first study of the patient, the activity of the enzyme, hypoxanthine guanine phosphoribosyl transferase (HGPT), was normal, although that of adenine phosphoribosyl transferase (APT) was increased (Nyhan et al. 1969). In 1980, Becker et al. demonstrated that the excessive rate of uric acid synthesis in this child might be explained by an increase in the purine enzyme, phosphoribosyl-pyrophosphate synthetase (PRPP synthetase) in his fibroblasts (Becker et al. 1980) (see Figure 16.3).

In 1974, a large research project was conducted at Children's Brain Research Clinic of Washington, D.C. on 69 patients who met the Clinic's criteria of autism (Coleman et al. 1976a). Controls were age- and sex-matched with the autistic patients. The median age was nine years and the ratio of males to females was 4.6:1. The patients and controls had many studies performed including serum and 24-hour urine studies of uric acid (uricase method). In this study, no statistical difference was found when comparing the serum levels of the patients and the controls, and no single serum level was high enough for a definite diagnosis of hyperuricemia. Two young patients did have borderline serum levels between seven and eight mg.%. However, 15 out of

TABLE 16.1. Patient Groups from the Literature with Purine Overproduction and Central Nervous System Symptoms.

First report	Central nervous system signs				Enzyme abnormality
	Psychiatric symptoms		Mental retardation	Neurological symptoms	
	Self-mutilation	Other			
Lesch & Nyhan, 1964	Severe	Aggressive	Usually severe	Chorea, athetosis, spasticity, seizures (rare)	HPRT
Sorensen & Benke, 1967	self-induced alopecia	Antisocial behavior		Chorea	
Hooft, et al. 1968	Mild	Autistic	Severe	Chorea, Athetosis, spasticity	
Nyhan et al. 1969		Autistic Deaf	Moderate		PRPP synthetase
Rosenberg et al. 1970		Deaf		Ataxia, Spasticity	

TABLE 16.1 (continued)

	Central nervous system signs				
	Psychiatric symptoms		Mental retardation	Neurological symptoms	Enzyme abnormality
First report	Self-mutilation	Other			
Coleman et al. 1974		Social immaturity	Pseudo-retardation	Ataxia, Seizures	
Coleman, 1974	Mild	Psychotic	Moderate		
Coleman et al. 1976a	Mild	Autistic	Borderline to severe	Toe-walking	(one possibility) Inosinate dehydrogenase
Stoop et al. 1977				Tetraparesis, tremor, ataxia	PNP
Duran, 1978				Tetraparesis (cranial dysmorphism)	Xanthine Oxidase (sulfite oxidase)
Jaeken and van den Berghe, 1984	Mild	Autistic	Severe	Hypotonia	Adenylosuccinase

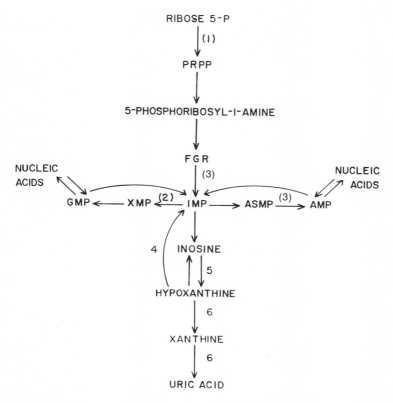

FIGURE 16.3. Schematic drawing of the purine pathways in humans to demonstrate enzymes which have been found to be abnormal in patients with central nervous system dysfunction. Three of the enzymes (1, 2, and 3) have been found in abnormal levels in autistic children. The enzymes are (1) 5-phosphoribosyl-1-pyrophosphate (PRPP synthetase), (2) inosinate dehydrogenase, (3) adenylosuccinase (adenylosuccinate lyase), (4) hypoxanthine guanine phosphoribosyltransferase (HPRT), (5) purine nucleoside phosphorylase (PNP), and (6) xanthine oxidase. See Table 16.1 for further details of clinical symptoms.

the 69 patients tested (22 percent) had uric acid levels in the urine more than two standard deviations above the top of the control range, or 14 mg/kg/24 hr. (Coleman et al. 1976a) (Table 16.2). In contrast, only two (3 percent) of the control children had urinary values above two standard deviations. Gruber et al. have demonstrated that two of these patients had abnormal levels of inosinate dehydrogenase in their lymphoblasts (Gruber et al., in preparation) (Figure 16.3).

TABLE 16.2. Urinary Uric Acid Levels in Autistic Patients (Values in mg/kg/24 Hours). From 1976 Children's Brain Research Clinic Data.

Age group	N	Mean for control group	Mean for autistic group as a whole	Autistic values above two standard deviations of control mean		Percentage of age group
				Actual individual values		
				mean		
3–5	12	6.4	12.3	19.1	16.4	30%
					18.1	
					20.3	
					21.5	
6–8	16	7.3	11.4	19.4	14.7	25%
					20.1	
					20.6.	
					22.0	
9–12	24	7.8	12.2	20.7	16.0	25%
					16.8	
					18.4	
					19.1	
					24.1	
					30.0	
Over 13 years	17	7.1	8.3	16.9	16.9	6%

Stubbs et al. (1982) assayed 18 unselected autistic subjects for six purine enzymes. The patients had not had previous evaluations of uric acid in serum or urine. They studied adenosine deaminase, nucleotide phosphorylase, hypoguanine phosphoribosyltransferase, adenine phosphoribosyltransferase, ecto-5-nucleotidase, and adenosine kinase in blood specimens. The autistic children were compared with normal children, retarded children and cerebral palsied children. The authors point out that there was much overlap of purine enzyme values between the experimental and control subjects and they interpreted that to mean they were dealing with a heterogeneous population.

Decreased levels of adenosine deaminase were found at a level of significance of <0.02. Hereditary absence of adenosine deaminase activity is known to cause severe combined immune deficiency in children. Thus, the possible relationship between purine metabolism and immune defects in autistic children is an area that needs extensive investigation (Mills et al. 1982) (see chapter 9).

Lis et al. (1976), studying a few autistic children by chromatographic methods, found low uric acid levels combined with high hypoxanthine levels in the urine of some of these patients.

Many studies of purine metabolism in children are based on 24-hour urine specimens instead of on serum levels as is done in adults. Lesch and Nyhan (1964) emphasized the rarity in children of elevated uric acid in the serum in most disease entities. Boss and Seegmiller (1982) noted that there is a chance of missing the diagnosis if one relies on a blood test rather than on a 24-hour urine sample in many of the purine syndromes seen in children. However, it is possible to find an elevated level of serum uric acid after a very stressful episode. In the Nyhan autistic patient, at four months of age a serum level of 23.5 mg.% occurred post-operatively after correction for hypo-spadius. However, this is the exception to the rule, and in general, uric acid in autistic patients, as in other children, should be measured by 24-hour urines rather than serum in children with normal renal functions. Another factor that can alert the clinician to the possibility of a purine syndrome is the presence of uric acid crystals in the urine, seen under the microscope, or a report that the urine appears to have a pink color or a pink sediment. Both Hooft et al. 1968 and Nyhan et al. 1969 reported a pinkish color to the urine of their patients. Since an error in purines can also be associated with seizures (Coleman et al. 1974), this is a laboratory test that should be investigated in an autistic patient who develops seizures (Figure 16.4).

The value of studying uric acid levels in the urine may be greater prior to the onset of puberty. In the 1976 study of the Children's Brain Research Clinic, 14 out of the 15 patients with hyperuricosuria were 12 years of age or under (see Table 16.2). This phenomenon (of diminution of the levels of hyperuricosuria past puberty) has been noted in other autistic patients at the clinic since the publication of the 1976 book. A similar observation has been noted in other purine syndromes of childhood, such as the seizure or childhood schizophrenia syndromes (Coleman 1974).

It is important to note that the finding of hyperuricosuria in an autistic patient does not establish the fact that this particular patient's autism is necessarily related to this biological finding. First of all, a certain percentage of children who are otherwise normal have hyperuri-

FIGURE 16.4. Five-year-old girl with purine autism. Height is only milestone below third percentile. Child was echolalic, irritable, bit her parents' arms, and toe-walked. Seizure disorder started at four years and four months of age.

cosuria (Coleman et al. 1976a). Thus, in any given child it may be an incidental finding.

Also, it is important to establish the cause of hyperuricosuria in any individual autistic patient. Elevated uric acid levels per se are not pathognomonic of a purine disorder.

Purine compounds are essential constituents of all living cells. They include (1) *free bases*, mainly adenine, guanine and hypoxanthine; (2) *nucleosides*, such as adenosine, guanosine, inosine and their deoxy derivatives, in which the free bases are combined with the pentose sugars, ribose or deoxyribose; and (3) *nucleotides*, that in addition contain phosphate to form adenosine monophosphate (AMP), guanosine monophosphate (GMP) via inosine monophosphate (IMP). The nucleotides constitute most of the intracellular purines.

To date, there are three enzymes of the purine pathway which have been found in non-physiological levels in patients who have autistic symptomology. The location of these two enzymes in the purine pathway can be seen in Figure 16.3. One is PRPP synthetase, an important early rate-limiting enzyme in the pathway, which was found in abnormal levels in the original Nyhan et al. (1969) case by Becker et al. (1980). PRPP is a sugar phosphate which is synthesized from ATP and ribose-5-phosphate. In a reaction requiring magnesium and inorganic phosphate, catalyzed by PRPP synthetase, the PRPP formed is a substrate in the first and probably rate-limiting state of purine synthesis de novo. In addition, PRPP is a substrate in the purine phosphoribosyl transferase reaction which constitutes a pathway for the salvage of purine bases. The second enzyme, inosinate dehydrogenase, has been found to be abnormal in several patients with classic autism (Gruber et al. in preparation), and is an important enzyme in the purine interconversion pathway. Inhibition of the inosinate branchpoint enzymes results in purine overproduction. However, at this time, it is not clear whether the abnormal level of the enzyme is a primary abnormality or a secondary compensation to another, as yet unidentified, enzyme abnormality in this patient group. Two siblings whose grandparents were first cousins and another autistic child have been found deficient in the third enzyme, adenylosuccinase (adenylosuccinate lyase) (Jaeken and van den Berghe, 1984).

Since identification of these enzymes is an elaborate procedure only possible in a few research laboratories in the world, this should be a last step in the evaluation of an autistic patient with hyperuricosuria. First, the differential diagnosis of other causes of hyperuricosuria should be worked through to make sure the patient does not have one of these other etiologies. There are many disease entities in children that cause increased excretion of uric acid. These include Hand-Schuler-Christian disease (Haslam and Clark 1971); Franconi's syndrome, both the hereditary variety and the acquired type (Fulop and Drapkin 1965); type 1 glycogen storage disease (absence of glucose-6-phosphatase) (Seegmiller 1967); homozygous hemoglobin C disease (Addae and Konotey-Ahulu 1971); hypo- and hyperthyroidism; hypo- and hyperparathyroidism; psoriasis; sarcoidosis; pernicious anemia; lymphomas and leukemias; primary and secondary polycythemia; sometimes hypertension; sickle cell anemia; Walstrom's hypoprothinemia; non-

tropical sprue; hereditary fructose intolerance; and idiopathic hypocalcinuria (Seegmiller 1967). Hyperuricemia is also sometimes seen in
association with a debilitating illness (Van Peenen 1973). There are also
isolated defects of tubular urate reabsorption in the tubular mechanism
for urate secretion in a few families.

It is clear that many of the diseases on the differential diagnosis
can be ruled out on clinical grounds without additional laboratory
testing. It is important to remember that since autism is a syndrome
of multiple etiologies, even purine autism is not a pure subgroup,
but occasionally has patients who have other disease entities along
with hyperuricosuria.

In the evaluation of patients past puberty, both serum and 24-hour
urinary uric acid specimens should be taken as a screening measure. To
confirm the hyperuricosuria, it is best to do a uric acid clearance study
(including creatinine, calcium, phosphorus, sodium and potassium),
which will then establish that kidney function is relatively intact with
metabolic over-production of uric acid, the most likely diagnosis except
in those rare cases of isolated renal tubular defects.

There is no published literature to date on the treatment for purine
autism which uses double-blind and crossover techniques. It is difficult
to get obsessive autistic children to accept a diet change, and once that is
accomplished, parents of autistic children are quite reluctant to try
crossover techniques. In the Hooft et al. (1968) case, a low purine diet
was said to result in "an undeniable improvement in the child's condition" and "whereas she had previously taken no interest in the outside
world, she now even smiled at her parents." A diet for purine autism
can be found in Appendix IV-B of *The Autistic Syndromes* (Coleman et
al. 1976). In cases where diet does not correct the biochemical abnormality, allopurinol (a xanthine oxidase inhibitor) can be effective in
lowering the uric acid levels in the urine. The correlation of these
treatments with clinical phenomena, however, has not yet been scientifically documented, so the value of the diet still remains a question for
research.

HYPERLACTATEMIA AND AUTISM

Lactic acidosis or hyperlactatemia without acidosis indicates some
abnormality in the utilization of sugar, which increases the rate of
lactate production relative to the rate of lactate utilization. Often the

primary abnormality is in the rate of oxidation of glucose, and the increase in lactate production is by analogy of the Pasteur effect. Sometimes the lactic acidosis appears to be caused by a decrease in the rate of lactate utilization in gluconeogenesis.

Thus, hyperlactatemia is not a specific biochemical abnormality in itself, but is rather an indication that a particular patient may have had an inborn error of metabolism in the family of disorders of carbohydrate metabolism.

Four patients have been described who have the co-existing syndromes of autism and lactic acidosis (Coleman and Blass 1985). Three of the patients described are males, and in those cases motor milestones were within the normal range. The female patient, however, was not yet walking at three years of age (Figure 16.5). It is this patient who appears

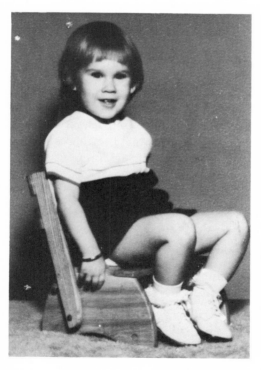

FIGURE 16.5. Five-year-old girl diagnosed at a psychiatric clinic as autistic and found to have lactic acidosis on later metabolic evaluation at a neurological clinic. Preliminary evidence suggests she may have a deficiency of pyruvate dehydrogenase complex (PDHC).

to have a deficiency in one of the enzymes of carbohydrate metabolism-pyruvate dehydrogenase complex (PDHC). One of the male patients has neurological abnormalities (clonus) and a concomitant hyperurico-suria. Since lactic acidosis tends to reduce urinary uric acid excretion, this combination is particularly striking and this patient is under further investigation.

Other patients with syndromes of developmental delay have been found to have lactic acidosis (Kuroda 1979; Haworth et al. 1967). A patient with Down's syndrome has even been reported with lactic acidosis (Hartmann et al. 1962).

The area of carbohydrate metabolism in autistic children has been studied very little. DeMyer et al. (1971) studied plasma free fatty acid metabolism in a mixed group of autistic and schizophrenic children and demonstrated greater variability than controls. We have constantly seen this pattern of greater variability in studies of autistic children, demonstrating that we are dealing with a biochemically heterogeneous group.

The recently described syndrome of hyperlactatemia in autistic patients is an area of future research investigation. If such a patient is identified, an evaluation of the carbohydrate pathway, particularly the pyruvate dehydrogenase complex (PDHC), is indicated. Identification of the specific enzyme in a patient could lead to research for a treatment; there are a number of such metabolic treatments currently being studied in other patient groups with lactic acidosis.

OTHER POSSIBLE METABOLIC PROBLEMS IN AUTISTIC CHILDREN

In addition to the metabolic diseases which are beginning to be defined, there are other documented biochemical abnormalities found in small subgroups of autistic children that remain, for the moment, not understood. For example, a large number of autistic patients have low levels of calcium, primarily in the urine. In the Children's Brain Research Clinic in 1976, 72 autistic patients were studied with reference to serum and urinary calcium levels. Sixteen of the autistic patients had urinary calcium levels below two standard deviations (Coleman et al. 1976b). These levels are also considered abnormal by the fact that they were below any level recorded in the control children in the study. One of the 16 children also had a low serum calcium level. As for inorganic phosphate levels, there was only one child with a level that appeared low in the urine but this child also had blood and ketones in the urine specimen, so the result is difficult to interpret (see Table 8.2).

In an attempt to identify the causes of hypocalcinuria, a number of autistic patients in the Children's Brain Research Clinic have had extensive testing for calcitonin, parathormone and 1,25 dihydroxy vitamin D_3. To date, no patient has been found to have an abnormal value. Studies of ionized versus non-ionized calcium have also been non-revealing. Since as many as one out of every five autistic children may have a depression of urinary calcium, and since calcium levels may be of critical importance in the central nervous system, this should be a prime area of investigation in autism to determine whether or not it is an incidental finding.

In the original Children's Brain Research Clinic study of 1976, it was reported that five of the patients with low calcium levels had a diagnosis of celiac disease given to them by their pediatricians. Since injury to the bowel can cause malabsorption of vitamins, including fat-soluble vitamin D which controls calcium absorption, it seemed like a reasonable possibility for the cause of the hypocalcinuria in these patients. Detailed evaluations of the patients' records determined, however, that the diagnosis of celiac disease had been made because of the presence of steatorrhea and anecdotal evidence of improvement of diarrhea with removal of gluten-containing foods. In none of the patients had a jejunal bowel biopsy been performed, the only satisfactory way, in the 1970s, of definitely diagnosing celiac disease.

Therefore, in 1979, McCarthy and Coleman (1979) performed jejunal bowel biopsies on some of these and other autistic patients who had the diagnosis of celiac disease and hypocalcinuria. All the patients chosen were those in which there was anecdotal evidence of improvement of diarrhea in patient symptomology with the removal of gluten foods. Therefore, the patients were placed on gluten prior to the jejunal biopsy. The result of this study demonstrated absolutely no evidence of celiac disease in any of the patients.

In an earlier study, Walker-Smith and Andrews (1972) had investigated eight children for the possibility of celiac disease, but did not find direct evidence of the disease in their patients. It is interesting, however, that they did report that the autistic children shared one phenomenon with untreated celiacs—a reduction of serum alpha-1-anti-trypsin. Although the data to support it are not considered convincing to many investigators, celiac disease also has been proposed as a model for one subgroup of schizophrenia. Dohan (1983) summarizes the evidence in favor of this hypothesis.

This does not mean that there is not a possibility of a malabsorption or some other major bowel problem in a subgroup of autistic patients. Goodwin and Goodwin (1969) observed a six-year-old boy who had autism and what they believed to be celiac disease. Goodwin et al. (1971) reported a benefit to this child when placed on a gluten free diet, and a relapse, with exacerbation of autistic symptoms, when placed on a normal diet. Rutter (1967) found some symptoms which could implicate gastrointestinal functions in some way for those with autistic symptoms.

Lis et al. (1976) also raised the question of malabsorption in autistic patients as a result of finding a reversal of the hippurate:4-hydroxyhippurate ratio in their urine, a finding also seen in malabsorption caused by bypass surgery.

In addition, there is preliminary evidence to suggest an increase of gastrointestinal symptoms in close relatives of autistic children. Raiten and Massaro (in press) found that 10 percent of the mothers of the autistic children they were studying suffered from colitis. Herzberg (1976) did a study of 106 siblings of autistic children compared with 137 age- and sex-matched children from control families. She found both stomachaches (28 percent compared with 17 percent) and "loose bowels" (9 percent compared with 2 percent) more common in siblings of autistic children.

Food allergies and intolerance to specific foods are reported by some parents of these children. In an attempt to study this problem, Bird et al. (1977) were unable to demonstrate that suspected dietary substances affected clinical behavior, although in the same study they were able to demonstrate that behavior-conditioning techniques were useful.

In our own clinical experience, we have a small subgroup of autistic patients who have an intermittent chronic problem with diarrhea; many of these patients also have concomitant steatorrhea. Usually they have hypocalcinuria. This is a group in which further research regarding possible etiological factors could be useful, since the cause of steatorrhea and hypocalcinuria remains unexplained. At the same time, it should be noted that such patients should be checked for ova and parasites, since autistic children are notorious for consuming inappropriate foods and objects and handling contaminated items.

Magnesium is also of interest in the study of autistic children for several reasons. There have already been studies of magnesium levels in autistic children (see chapter 8). Magnesium, the fourth most abundant metal in living organisms, is distributed in three major parts of the body: 65 percent in the mineral phase of the skeleton, 34 percent in the intracellular space and only one percent in the extracellular fluid. Serum magnesium levels are controlled primarily by the kidneys. Also it is known that intracellular magnesium remains relatively stable despite wide fluctuations in serum magnesium (Levine and Coburn 1984). Magnesium, in its oxide form, is used to treat constipation, and there is another subgroup of autistic patients with bowel problems quite the opposite of those with diarrhea and steatorrhea. In this second subgroup of patients, severe constipation with wide diameter bowel movements can be a serious problem.

One of the enzymes reported to be abnormal in some autistic patients, PRPP synthetase, uses magnesium in the enzyme complex.

Magnesium also is used in conjuction with the pyridoxine treatment given to autistic patients (see chapter 20). The question has been asked if it is the pyridoxine or the magnesium which has led to the clinical improvement noted in these children.

Magnesium has an extremely complex relationship to calcium in the body—it both mimics and antagonizes calcium. As in the case with calcium metabolism, magnesium metabolism is another important area of research in autism.

The subgroup of autistic children with various metabolic diseases is just beginning to be defined. This should be a major research area in the future.

17   Structural Entities Associated with Autism

One of the very first autistic cases described in the medical literature with reference to biochemical evaluation was a patient mentioned by Schain and Yannet (1960). The diagnosis was arrested hydrocephalus and the finding was a high blood serotonin level (Schain and Yannet 1960). Other cases with mild or moderate hydrocephalus caused by the Dandy Walker syndrome (Knobloch and Pasamanick 1975), or with papilloma of the choroid plexus (Knobloch and Pasamanick 1975), also have been described. A further patient has been included in the literature who has hydrocephalus secondary to a case of meningitis (Knobloch and Pasamanick 1975). Damasio et al. (1980) reports a hydrocephalic autistic in his CT series. Garreau et al. (1984) also report a hydrocephalic autistic child. Such a patient of ours is pictured in Figure 17.1.

Although most CT scans described in autistic patients offer no gross evidence of structural abnormalities, a subgroup of patients has been described with evidence of decreased cerebral tissue thought to be either secondary to increased pressure or caused by atrophy (see chapter 11). In a CT study utilizing special volumetric measurements of the ventricles and subarachnoid spaces, the presence of an occasional autistic child with ventricular enlargement again has been confirmed (Rosenbloom et al. 1984).

Patients with previously undiagnosed hydrocephalus should, of course, have a neurosurgical consultation. Also, medical therapies, such as diuretics, sometimes are an option for these patients.

Malignant tumors have not yet been reported in autistic children, although they are searched for in the small subgroup of patients where cranial circumferences cross upward into higher and higher percentiles

FIGURE 17.1. Nine-year-old boy who had a shunt at three months of age because of a diagnosis of hydrocephalus. Moderately mentally retarded, he has lack of reciprocity, extreme echolalia, toe-walking and hand-flapping. Eye contact now improved. Psychomotor epilepsy began at four years of age.

with increasing age—a group whose etiology presently often remains undefined. This group includes both patients with evidence of increased intracranial pressure and children with completely normal serial CT scans.

Occasionally, lesions such as porencephaly (see Figures 17.2 and 17.3) and other gross abnormalities (see Figure 17.4) are seen in CT scans of autistic patients.

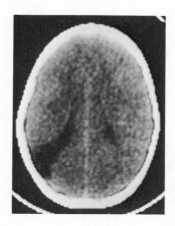

FIGURE 17.2. Large left parietal/occipital porencephaly seen in the CT scan of a three-year-old boy with social withdrawal, gaze avoidance, total lack of speech, lack of response to strong auditory stimuli (normal audiometry), severe tantrums if demands are made upon him, obsession with running water, insistence on bizarre rituals and superior talent with jigsaw puzzles. Diagnosis at age 2 of infantile autism and moderate mental retardation (IQ <50).

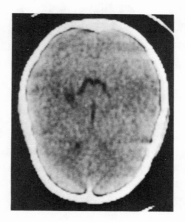

FIGURE 17.3. Loss of substance in the area of the right lateral geniculate in the CT scan of a nine-year-old boy with lack of reciprocity in "play" with other children, avoidance of gaze contact, resistance to touch, toe-gait, repetitive speech, head-banging, failure to understand human facial expression and strong resistance to change of routines. Diagnosis of infantile autism and mild mental retardation (IQ 65).

166

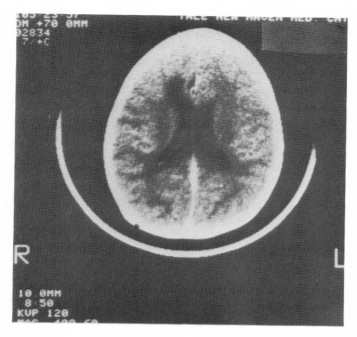

FIGURE 17.4. Right frontal porencephaly connecting to the ventricular system is seen in the CT scan of a nine-year-old boy who had severe dehydration in infancy. He has poor eye contact, stares at lights and sunbeams, has tactile defensiveness, rocks, has very poor peer relationships, hand-flapping when excited and is obsessed with clocks and photographs. He lines up toys rather than plays with them. Speech is no longer echolalic. Diagnosis of infantile autism (IQ 82).

CT scans are only a diagnostic tool of value in a limited number of autistic patients. Even where abnormalities are found, the relevance to the patient must be considered individually in light of the history and the physical examination.

At this point, the only structural lesion which has been consistently reported in a number of patients is arrested, mild, or moderate hydrocephalus. But this group accounts for only a small percentage of patients with autistic symptoms. It does however need to be ruled out in autistic patients, particularly those with the larger cranial circumferences.

18   Other Disease Entities

In addition to the disease entities which definitely fit into specific categories, such as metabolic or structural or genetic, there are several others which appear in combination with autistic features that must be considered in a differential diagnosis of a child showing autistic symptoms.

Autism is seen much more commonly in males. However, when the autistic syndrome is seen in females, Rett's syndrome should be considered in the differential diagnosis. Rett's syndrome, to date, is exclusively described in female patients (Figure 18.1).

Before this syndrome was described, these cases (in Sweden and elsewhere) were previously diagnosed as "early infantile autism" or "disintegrative childhood psychosis." In Vienna in 1966 and again in 1968, Rett described a syndrome of "cerebral atrophy and hyperammonemia" which he had observed in girls and was characterized by autistic behavior and dementia, apraxia of gait, loss of facial expression and stereotypical use of the hands. In 1977, the same author reported in greater detail on 21 cases. Unaware of Rett's descriptions, Hagberg in 1980 reported a similar pattern found in 16 girls from Sweden. Recently, a review of the syndrome, combining a report of 35 cases from several countries, was published (Hagberg et al. 1983).

The review of the syndrome shows that the girls have normal physical and psychomotor development up to the age of between seven and 18 months. Then psychomotor development slows and is followed by rapid deterioration. Eighteen months after onset of the disease, acquired microcephaly, loss of purposeful use of the hands, jerky truncal ataxia, and severe dementia are seen. It is during this period of the disease that autism is often diagnosed. The patients lose their interest in persons and toys, even though they are able to see and visually to follow things. Their responses are stereotypic, and interper-

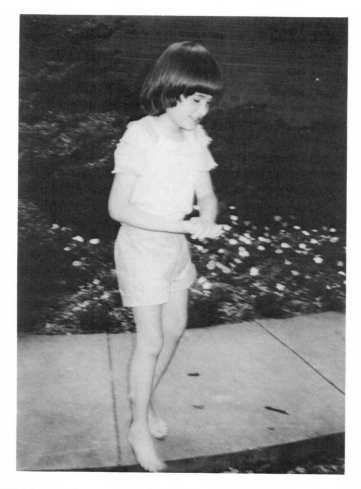

FIGURE 18.1. This ten-year-old girl has the classic symptoms and clinical course of Rett's syndrome. Here she is seen wringing her hands and toe-walking.

sonal contact becomes very limited or totally absent. Changes or other alterations in their routine cause great anxiety and apparent fear, sometimes associated with bouts of hyperpnea and sometimes with vasomotor reactions and profuse sweating.

One of the striking aspects of this syndrome is that grasping and other purposeful hand movements disappear by the age of three and are replaced by characteristic, stereotypic hand movements, especially "hand washing movements" in front of the mouth or chest, or rubbing motions of the hands. The median age of walking is 25 months, but this ability is later lost, often around the age of seven years. Truncal ataxia is present in the girls who are able to sit unsupported and has a peculiar jerky quality. The jerks have been compared either with intention or action myoclonus.

The electroencephalogram is almost always abnormal by three years of age. The girl then enters a plateau period which may last for decades. Gradually, additional insidious neurological abnormalities appear, such as epilepsy, vasomotor disturbances of the lower limb, and spastic paraparesis.

The etiology of this progressive disorder remains unknown. CT scans give an appearance of cortical atrophy with enlarged sulci, suggesting the preferential involvement of grey matter. Although Rett originally described the syndrome in association with hyperammonemia, most patients do not have it. Other biochemical studies have, to date, not disclosed the etiology of the syndrome. Only one familial case (Hagberg et al. 1983) is known and consists of two half-sisters. Because of the absence of males with the syndrome, it is unlikely that this is an acquired disease. The genetic data are consistent with a dominant mutation on one X chromosome which then becomes lethal for males.

Degenerative diseases that are sometimes known to have autistic symptoms also include the neurocutaneous disorders. In the case of this group of diseases, most of the patients reported do not have autistic symptoms, but a small subgroup do have pronounced autistic symptomology. The neurocutaneous diseases are thought to develop during a neuronal proliferation period in human gestation which has its peak between the second and fourth month of gestation when thickening of the neuroectoderm results in the development of the central nervous system. In several of these neurocutaneous disorders, there is evidence for excessive cellular proliferation within the central nervous system and occasionally there may be excessive proliferation of mesodermal structures as well as ectodermal structures. In tuberous sclerosis, both the neurons and glia are involved, while in neurofibromatosis, it is primarily the glia that have a dysplastic tendency with proclivity to tumor formation in the central nervous system, the skin, and the viscera. In 1923, van der Hoeve introduced the term "phakomatoses" to identify the neurocutaneous syndromes and they are sometimes called by that name. Most of these disease entities are inherited.

One neurocutaneous syndrome, tuberous sclerosis, is a disease characterized by tubers in the brain which frequently occur within the gyri, but can also be imbedded within the thalamus or caudate. Patients with concomitant syndromes of tuberous sclerosis and autism have been described by Valente (1971), lotter (1974) and Wing (1975). In these patients, the behavioral syndrome of autism usually is diagnosed prior to the physical syndrome of tuberous sclerosis. Tuberous sclerosis patients also form a small subgroup of the infants with the infantile spasm syndrome who later show autistic features. (See chapters 4 and 13.)

Neurofibromatosis, or von Recklinghausen disease, is another neurocutaneous syndrome, marked by a proclivity to tumor formation. In contrast with tuberous sclerosis in which the central lesions are the primary pathology and mental deficiency is much more frequent, in neurofibromatosis the lesions tend to involve peripheral outflow of the central nervous system and many more patients have normal intelligence. A seizure disorder may occur in both, but it is a common complication of tuberous sclerosis and relatively rare in neurofibromatosis (Figure 18.2). In a review of neurofibromatosis, patients have been described

FIGURE 18.2. Thirteen-year-old girl with autistic syndrome and mild to moderate mental retardation. Neurofibromatosis was diagnosed at age ten. Benign focal epilepsy since the age of ten years. Extreme echolalia.

who had very low IQs and were "exceedingly disturbed" (Crowe et al. 1956).

In 1984, Gillberg and Forsell described a nine-year-old boy and a ten-year-old girl who had the autistic syndrome concomitant with neurofibromatosis. The girl, who is at the special treatment center for autistic children has acquired some speech, while the boy remains aloof and mute (Gillberg and Forsell 1984). One of the authors of this monograph (M.C.) also has a girl who has been treated as an autistic child all her life. At the age of 19, she was diagnosed as having neurofibromatosis at the same time as her mildly retarded brother received a similar diagnosis. The girl is mute, profoundly retarded with self-stimulation, and even in the late teenage years continues to have severe tactile defensiveness.

From time to time the presence of the behavioral syndrome of autism is reported in a child who has another specific medical diagnosis. Since these are individual case reports, it may be coincidence, or in the future there may be found an increased frequency of the autistic syndrome in association with diagnostic categories. For the moment, however, one can merely list the case reports.

In the medical literature, two papers document simultaneous diagnoses of infantile autism and the Tourette syndrome, with the Tourette symptoms beginning around the time of puberty (Barabas and Matthews 1983, Realmuto and Main 1982). Also, the induction of the Tourette syndrome in an autistic patient after long-term neuroleptic medication has been reported (Stahl 1980). In 1975, Knobloch and Pasamanick reported that a child with the deLange syndrome met the criteria for autism, and one of the authors of this monograph (C.G.) also has a deLange autistic in his practice. A male with Noonan's syndrome and autistic behavior has been reported as well (Paul et al. 1983). Hersh et al. (1982) have reported a six-year-old girl with Coffin Siris syndrome, and Hauser et al. (1975) included a child with the fetal alcohol syndrome in their report of pneumoencephalograms in autistic patients. Classic autistic symptoms also have been described in a patient with the Biedl-Bardet syndrome (Gillberg and Wahlström 1984) and in a child with Duchenne muscular dystrophy (Komoto et al. 1984). Achondroplasia and concurrent autistic symptoms have also been described (Gillberg & Andersson 1984).

The Moebius syndrome has been described in several cases of autism (Ornitz et al. 1972, Gillberg and Winnergård 1984). Both of the authors of this monograph have such a patient in their practice. Considering the rarity of this brain damage syndrome, we could argue that the concurrence with autism appears to be more than coincidence (see chapter 22).

This spectrum of children with autistic symptoms and other diagnosable disease entities reminds the clinician that each child showing autistic symptomology must have a thorough clinical and laboratory evaluation. Autism is not a final diagnosis; it is a syndrome of many etiologies. Identifying the behavioral symptoms of autism is only the first step in diagnosis and treatment. When a known disease entity affecting the brain is then identified in a child with the autistic syndrome, the question then arises as to whether the disease is relevant or incidental to the autistic symptoms.

19   Blindness and Deafness

Autistic symptoms have been noted as sequelae of general neurological problems such as the infantile spasms syndrome (discussed in
chapter 4). They also are seen in many blind and deaf children. It is
important to note that although many patients with these handicaps do
not have autistic symptomology, a significant subgroup does in fact
develop the autistic syndrome (Chase, 1972).

It has been known for some time that the autistic syndrome is seen
in children with both congenital blindness and congenital deafness. An
excellent review of the effects of early blindness and deafness on cognition
by Isabel Rapin (1979) emphasizes that a majority of these children do
become competent adults when the severity of their handicap is taken
into consideration. She points out that the blind are viewed as having
few barriers to full cognitive competence, but the situation with the deaf
child is different. The detrimental consequences of deafness intensify
with age for all children because communication about events remote in
time or place and about abstract principles and sophisticated ideas is
contingent on the availability of a common symbolic system. Thus,
although both blind and deaf children suffer from a profound informa-
tional deprivation, the deaf often become deficient in reading skills and
in the knowledge one acquires in school, with the exception of mathe-
matical computation and spatial skills. It appears that a larger proportion
of the congenitally blind than the congenitally deaf go to college.

The literature reports a number of both congenitally blind and
congenitally deaf children with the autistic syndromes (Valente 1971,
Garreau et al. 1984)(see chapter 14 on rubella children). What distin-
guishes these children from others who are congenitally blind and deaf
is far from clear. More detailed investigation is needed of the etiology of
both the sensory handicap and the autistic syndrome in each of these
patients in an attempt to sort out the factors that may be responsible.

In a preliminary clinical survey of autistic blind children in Sweden, it is suggested that the underlying brain damage rather than the blindness in itself may be etiologically responsible for autistic symptomology (Bensch and Gillberg, unpublished data).

A study of multihandicapped deaf children, which compared them with deaf children without additional handicaps and hearing children with and without additional handicaps, found that one of the main items separating multihandicapped deaf children from the other three groups was avoidance of eye contact (Meadow 1984). Of course, for a child having no auditory contact with the environment, failure to maintain visual contact is equivalent to non-interaction, and is completely isolating for the deaf child. Thus, autistic symptoms may add a major handicap to a deaf child since they may impair the usual modes of overcoming the deafness handicap.

In the same way, a visually handicapped child with the autistic syndrome, who has difficulty tolerating sounds and "appears deaf" at times, also has a compounding variable which challenges the most resourceful educator in terms of teaching such a patient. Konstantareas et al. (1982) have reported on a successful program relying primarily on tactile-kinesthetic and auditory modalities for teaching sign language to a blind autistic child. This paper is an example of how a creative, intelligent group of professionals can meet the most difficult of challenges in communicating with a multihandicapped child.

Thus, from an educational point of view, the blind or deaf handicapped child with autistic symptomology is a major challenge. Each child needs a specially designed individualized program which builds on whatever channels of communication are possible. From a medical point of view, diagnosis and whatever medical treatments are appropriate to lessen autistic symptomology are critically needed by the child. The challenge of these multihandicapped children needs to be met by competent, dedicated professionals in both fields. The physician has a particularly significant responsibility to do everything possible to decrease tactile defensiveness, lack of eye contact, and poor attention span through medical therapies, so that the child may benefit from educational programming. These children present one of the ultimate challenges when working in the field of autism.

Part IV

Treatments Currently Under Investigation

20   Non-Drug Medical Therapies

Medical treatment of autistic patients is in its infancy. However, there is a small and growing medical literature regarding attempts both at specific and non-specific treatments for patients with one of the autistic syndromes.

The ideal medical treatment for this patient group would be first of all a specific identification of the etiology of the syndrome, and then a treatment based on that specific diagnosis. For example, if the diagnosis points toward a metabolic problem, then a treatment designed to correct the metabolic error would be indicated; if the diagnosis is of a structural nature, for example, moderate hydrocephalus, then neuro-surgical intervention might be appropriate for a given patient.

Because autism is a syndrome of multiple etiologies, the best medical treatment will be one that is specifically designed for the individual patient based on the individual diagnosis.

However, this ideal cannot be achieved in all patients because of our lack of understanding of the etiological mechanisms in many children. Thus, there are two other categories of therapy in autism. First, there are treatments that attempt to correct the non-specific biochemical abnormalities found in the child's blood, urine, cerebrospinal fluid or stool, which may have some relevance to the child's disorder, but are not identified as the underlying etiology of the disorder. And second, there are totally non-specific treatments, such as most drug therapies, that are designed to halt clinical symptoms, no matter what the underlying factors may be. In this chapter, non-drug therapies will be reviewed; drug therapies are reviewed in the next chapter.

Treatment for an autistic child needs to make use of a team approach. The physician, the teacher, and the parent all must work smoothly together to provide a consistent approach to the child's therapy. The best program combines a specific medical therapy with a specific educational plan. Such a combination yields the optimal results in these patients. There is no simple blueprint for therapy for all autistic children. Each one is a very special, fragile, sensitive, unusual human being and must be treated on an individualized basis built from adequate medical workup and intelligent, creative educational/psychological evaluations. The unwillingness on the part of the autistic child to cooperate in testing only enhances the problem. It takes an experienced and gifted observer to understand an autistic child. Often the parents, who know the child best, can help to guide professionals in dealing with the patient.

The goals of all treatments, both medical and educational, are to ameliorate circumstances for the individual child. In the majority of patients who give evidence of developmental delay, a goal of treament would be to encourage the development of language, social skills, self-care and academic skills. Another area where most patients will need assistance, whether they are developmentally delayed or not, is in the improvement of behavioral symptoms, such as hyperactivity, withdrawal, stereopathies, self-stimulation, external aggression, or the myriad of other socially unacceptable behaviors of this patient group. Medical therapies must work in conjunction with social training and educational programs.

It is the job of medical therapies to provide an optimal central nervous system environment for these educational interventions.

THERAPIES TO CORRECT BIOCHEMICAL ABNORMALITIES

In this section, attempts at correcting identified biochemical abnormalities in autistic patients will be reviewed, and studies of efforts to correct specific amine, enzyme or co-enzyme abnormalities will be described. Since no studies are done in the living brain itself, this entire chapter is based on the assumption that studies in the periphery may possibly have some relevance to the central nervous system. This assumption, in any single case, may or may not be true.

Catecholamines

One of the areas with the most extensive investigation to date in autistic patients has been studies of catecholamines and their metabolites. (For a review of the biochemistry and the studies in the medical literature see chapter 8.) Reviewing this literature, we must keep in mind that no neurotransmitter acts in the brain as a sole agent; it is always in an extremely complicated balance with many other neuro-transmitters operating through an incredibly complex feedback system.

In the case of the catecholamines, two enzymes of this pathway have been shown to be blocked in some children with autistic symptoms. These blockages may cause backup of the precursor metabolite to abnormally high levels with overflow into minor pathways. Such blocks in this particular pathway appear to have relevance for autistic symp-tomology in some patients, and therapies designed to relieve the abnormal functioning of this pathway are reviewed. Regarding evidence of endo-genous blockage of the pathway by decreased enzyme levels, we know that patients with phenylketonuria and autistic symptoms have a block at the first step of the pathway, the phenylalanine hydroxylase step (Figure 8.1), which results in the spillover of minor metabolites (see Figure 16.1). Also, there are two studies documenting some depression of the enzyme in the third step of the pathway (see Figure 8.1), dopamine-beta-hydroxylase (Goldstein et al. 1976; Lake et al. 1977), although another study (Young et al. 1980) showed a lowered level that was not statistically significantly depressed.

The review of attempts to therapeutically affect the catecholamine pathway is now described.

The therapy affecting the first step of the pathway—decreasing the effect of very low levels of the enzyme, phenylalanine-4-hydroxylase, by a low phenylalanine diet—is described elsewhere, since it is a specific treatment for a specific disease entity—phenylketonuria (PKU)(see chapter 16).

Next come the attempts to enhance the amount of DOPA available in the catecholamine pathway. Two studies have been conducted on the results of the administration of L-DOPA in autism, which was given presumably to enhance dopamine levels. The first one, by Ritvo et al. (1971a), studied the effect of L-DOPA over a six-month period on four hospitalized autistic children. No changes were observed in the clinical course, the amount of motility disturbances, the percentage of REM sleep time, or in measures of endocrine function. The second study of the administration of L-DOPA also included the administration of dopamine agonists: D-amphetamine and L-amphetamine. Again, no clinical improvement was found; in fact, there was worsening and development of new stereotypes (Campbell et al. 1972b, 1976b). On the other hand, dopamine antagonists, such as the phenothiazines and haloperidol, appear to be of value (see chapter 21).

Next in the catecholamine pathway comes the enzyme, L-aromatic amino acid decarboxylase (L-AAAD), which creates dopamine; it is followed by the enzyme, dopamine-beta-hydroxylase, which creates norepinephrine. Both of these enzymes have pyridoxine as their co-enzyme.

There have been several studies of the effect on autistic patients of administering vitamin B_6 or B_6/magnesium. In discussing this work we must remember that vitamin B_6 is the co-enzyme not only of the enzyme L-aromatic amino acid decarboxylase (L-AAAD)(affecting the serotonin and catecholamine pathway) and DBH (in the catecholamine pathway), but also of all non-oxidative enzymatic transformations of the other amino acid pathways, catalyzing such reactions as decarboxylation, transamination, racemization, β-elimination and γ-elimination. Pyridoxine also is involved in the biosynthesis of lipids, protein, carbohydrates, nucleic acids and spingosine bases. Pyridoxine also could have a detoxification role which is not yet well defined. Thus, the effect of the vitamin is ubiquitous.

Trials of pyridoxine on autistic children grew out of several observations. Initially, Dr. Bernard Rimland reported on the treatment by their physicians of 200 children having autistic symptoms with an experimental multiple-vitamin regimen (an initial multivitamin supplement with 11 vitamins and iron, followed by vitamin C, nicotinamide, pantothenic acid, pyridoxine in a sequential manner)(Rimland 1973 and 1974). Rimland observed that a subgroup of patients on the experimental vitamin regimen appeared to respond to pyridoxine with clinical improvement and that some of the children relapsed on withdrawal of vitamin B_6 and improved when the vitamin was given again.

Thus, together with Callaway and Dreyfus, Rimland undertook a double-blind crossover evaluation of the effectiveness of pharmacological doses of vitamin B_6 on this subgroup of previously identified autistic children who had shown previous behavioral responses to vitamin B_6 in the earlier open trials (Rimland et al. 1978). In this study they were able correctly to identify 11 out of 15 periods when autistic children were either on placebo or vitamin B_6, using only the behavioral data.

In a study by the Lelord group (Lelord et al. 1978, 1981, 1982)— again a double-blind crossover study—it was confirmed for a second time that a subgroup of autistic patients responded to vitamin B_6. The Lelord group had added magnesium to their protocol because in a separate study by the French group (Barthelemy et al. 1981) a trial of B_6 alone and of magnesium alone was found ineffective compared with the combination of pyridoxine and magnesium together. The Lelord study group, in addition to adding magnesium, also examined the effect of pyridoxine on averaged evoked potentials in the patients and reported an increase in amplitude of middle latency evoked potentials in the children receiving vitamin B_6 (Martineau et al. 1981).

A third group (Ellman et al. 1981) also sought to replicate the findings of a subgroup of autistic children who responded to pyridoxine. In their double-blind crossover study, they measured the urinary ratio of hydroxyanthranilic acid (HAA) to hydroxy-kynurenine (HK), one measure of pyridoxine status in humans. They reported that 25 percent of the autistic children could be identified correctly by blind raters as having received B_6 and having responded to it clinically. But they reported that in their study the urinary ratios of HAA/HK did not distinguish responders from non-responders to B_6, suggesting possibly that these tryptophan metabolites may not be involved in the pathway directly related to autistic symptoms.

Thus, there are three double-blind studies demonstrating that pyridoxine, with or without magnesium, may be effective in suppressing clinical symptoms in a subgroup of autistic children. It should be noted that it is a subgroup, not the entire autistic population, which responded in these studies. Since the side effects of water-soluble vitamins tend to be less toxic than the side effects of drugs, further work is now indicated to answer a number of questions:

1. Is there any way to anticipate the pyridoxine responders versus the non-responders?

2. What is the role of magnesium? Is it or is it not part of the therapy, and does it have a separate therapeutic effect?

3. What clinical symptoms are specifically helped by the therapy?

4. What are the short-term and long-range side effects of giving pharmacological doses of the vitamin over long periods to autistic children?

Animal studies indicate in rats (Cohen et al. 1973) and beagle dogs (Phillips 1978) that pharmacological doses of pyridoxine can be associated with greater growth than is seen in controls, with normal protein content but lowered fat content. Muscle phosphorylase increases, as a reservoir for the vitamin (Black et al. 1977). In humans, sun blisters (Coleman et al. in press) and peripheral neuropathy (Schaumburg et al. 1983; Coleman et al. in press) have been reported. Presumably these side effects can be monitored and controlled by careful dose regulation in the same way clinicians try to prevent tardive dyskinesia in patients on some of the psychotropic drugs. Since the peripheral neuropathy described in pyridoxine megadoses is caused in some cases by niacin deficiency, we recommend that metabolites of this vitamin should be monitored in patients on large doses of pyridoxine.

Magnesium is the second most prevalent intracellular cation. It has many important functions, including key steps in intermediary metabolism, protein synthesis and DNA synthesis and transcription, regulation of mitochondrial function, and regulation of various processes at the cell membrane. Magnesium metabolism is closely allied to calcium metabolism, since magnesium may either bind competitively, or compete with calcium, or alter calcium flux across cell membranes (Levine and Coburn 1984). One of magnesium's neurological effects is related to its role at cell membrane levels. As a co-factor, magnesium is essential for utilization of other compounds, and clinical deterioration has been reported in malnourished patients when vitamin replenishment is undertaken without adequate magnesium available (Zieve 1975). Because only 1 percent of magnesium is present outside the cell in the extracellular fluids, magnesium deficiency is difficult to estimate in patients, and the effect of magnesium supplementation in clinical syndrome such as autism is difficult to evaluate.

In addition to the studies described above, the Lelord group (Lelord et al. 1978, 1979; Garreau et al. 1980) also did an interesting study attempting to tease out a mechanism of action of pyridoxine and/or pyridoxine and magnesium in autistic children. In a study of homovanillic acid (HVA)(a principal end-product of dopamine) in the urines of 37 autistic children, the authors found that the addition of pharmacological doses of pyridoxine, presumably to enhance both L-AAAD and DBH function, to the diet of these children, improved the autistic behavior in 15 out of 37 of the children. However, the pyridoxine simultaneously reduced the HVA levels in all the autistic children while increasing them in all the control children (Lelord et al. 1978)! This suggests that in autistic children pyridoxine may be having a major effect on DBH rather than on L-AAAD as far as this particular pathway is concerned. It also suggests that pyridoxine may lower the functional level of dopamine by increasing its catabolic enzyme (DBH).

Attempts at lowering or blocking dopamine in autistic children also have been tried both with the phenothiazines and the butyrophenone drugs. Butyrophenones are more specific dopamine blockers (although they also have multiple other effects) and the butyrophenone, haloperidol, has emerged as a drug that can be tried in autistic children (see chapter 21).

In connection with norepinephrine, the next step in the pathway, a study has been tried with the drug clonodine, which is a norepinephrine agonist that reduces the activity of the principal nucleus of norepinephrine cells in the locus ceruleus in the brain stem. This reduction of selective norepinephrine function is thought to occur at the pre-synaptic, inhibitory alpha-2-norepinephrine receptor. The report of elevated plasma norepinephrine levels in autism (Lake et al. 1977) led to a trial of clonodine in three autistic adolescents, but did not lead to any significant clinical improvement (Young et al. 1981a).

Serotonin

Studies of serotonin metabolism have been another active area of research in the field of autism (for a review, see Figure 8.1). Therapeutic trials have been designed, in some cases, to decrease and, in other cases, to raise serotonin levels in autistic patients. Because of the complexities of interrelationships of neurotransmitters, and the multiple etiologies of the autistic syndrome, it is not surprising to find such contradictory studies.

The attempts designed to raise serotonin in autistic patients fall into two categories: those using the precursor amino acid, 5-hydroxytryptophan (5-HTP), and those using vitamin B_6 (with or without magnesium), the co-enzyme of the decarboxylase step that forms serotonin. 5-hydroxytryptophan was administered to eight patients in a single-blind crossover study over a 24-month period. Half the patients received placebo and the other half received 5-HTP during the first year and then were crossed over to the other medication during the second research year. Cessation of 5-HTP, whether it occurred at the end of the first or the second year, was associated with deterioration of the clinical course, lasting up to three weeks, with insomnia, increased aggressive behavior, increased temper tantrums and acceleration of hand-flapping, rocking or twirling, and increased jerking in patients who had myoclonic jerks. However, in spite of 5-HTP withdrawal phenomena, nothing in the study suggested that the amino acid was of long-term value to this group of autistic patients (Coleman 1978a).

Pharmacological doses of pyridoxine, the co-enzyme of L-AAAD, which makes serotonin, have been shown in other disease entities (Bhagavan et al. 1975; Coleman et al. 1979) to raise serotonin levels in the whole blood. Since a small percentage of autistic children have subnormal levels of serotonin (see chapter 8) this is a subgroup that could benefit from pyridoxine therapy. However, it should be noted that present information suggests that the value of pyridoxine in autism is more likely owing to its effect on catecholamines (as reviewed before in this chapter) rather than on serotonin. In truth, it may be unrelated to either of these pathways but to amine systems as yet unstudied in the syndrome.

The drug fenfluramine, which is a serotonin depletor, appears to be of value to a subgroup of autistic children. This drug was originally given to patients with high blood serotonin levels (a significantly large group of autistic children). However, the high blood serotonin levels do not necessarily identify the patients who may benefit from the drug (see chapter 21 for more detail).

Other Therapies

A variety of other diet and vitamin therapies are currently under investigation in autistic patients but none are yet published with adequate double blind studies. Folic acid therapy in fragile X patients may be soon reported in the literature as helpful or not.

21
Medical Treatments Using Drugs

If no treatment modalities are indicated based on a study of the patient's biochemistry, or if such individualized treatment modalities do not significantly help the patient and may in that particular case be irrelevant to the problem, the next step is to move on to the non-specific treatments that are available for autistic children. These drug therapies will be reviewed in two section. First, the many trials of different drugs that occurred up to 1980 without any kind of general agreement that any particular drug was superior will be reviewed. However in recent years a consensus is developing about therapies which may be beneficial to a significant number of patients and have been established by well-documented, double-blind studies.

BEFORE 1980

For several decades, researchers attempted, by trial and error, to find drugs that might alleviate some of the clinical symptoms seen in autistic children. However, the state of the art was best summed up by Dr. Magda Campbell, a major researcher in drug therapy in autism, in 1978 when she stated as follows:

> Psychopharmacology of autistic and schizophrenic children and adolescents is still in a primitive state. Drug studies with large samples of diagnostically homogeneous populations, controlled for age, IQ, and other pertinent variables, are almost nonexistent. There is no evidence, based on well-controlled, double-blind studies, in large samples of children, that pharmacotherapy is more effective than administration of placebo or any other treatment. (Campbell 1978)

The story of drug experimentation with autistic children goes back to the early 1950s when it was discovered that chlorpromazine was very useful in the treatment of adult psychiatric patients. Because of the success in adult schizophrenia, investigators began exploring the use of the various psychoactive agents with children who also had psychiatric symptomology, including subgroups of autistic children in some studies. There are many difficulties with these studies because the populations of children usually were not homogeneous. Many studies were done without adequate controls, many were done without blind or crossover techniques, and often there was no random assignment of subjects to treatment conditions. Moreover, the samples studied tended to include small numbers of patients, which made statistical analysis even more difficult. Often, initially promising drugs on a few patients would turn out to be of little more than placebo value when studied on larger groups. A review of the drugs tried in the last 30 years on autistic patients, which have yet to be established as of significant value on a large scale, are listed in Table 21.1. This table, where possible, has been limited to studies that used at least some attempt at research design, as opposed to completely open, unblinded studies.

One factor to keep in mind is that age ranges in some of these studies were excessively wide, so that children prior to puberty and those over puberty were included in the same research category—a quite inappropriate procedure in evaluating drugs in children, particularly in autistic children. Many of the phenothiazines, for example, appear to be relatively ineffective in young children, but appear to be of limited value in young autistic adults in the control of some symptomology.

Also, in evaluating any drug studies, we must remember the diagnostic confusion that existed in selecting patients as autistic as described in earlier chapters.

In a group of patients who have a syndrome rather than a single disease entity, it is important to emphasize that the failure of any individual drug to be established in a large group study does not mean that the drug might not be of value for a small subgroup of patients within the syndrome who have a specific disease process which differs from other patients with the autistic syndrome. Also, many of the drugs listed in Table 21.1 have not been stringently subjected to necessary research criteria which would either establish or rule out their usefulness, and thus the failure of these drugs to become accepted as standard treatment at this time does not mean that future development is ruled out.

TABLE 21.1. Some Drugs Tried in Autistic Patients.

Class	Drug	Sample reference studies
Phenothiazines	chlorpromazine	Korein et al. 1971
		Campbell et al. 1972a
	trifluoperazine	Fish et al. 1966
		Wolpert et al. 1967
	fluphenazine	Faretra et al. 1970
		Engelhardt et al. 1973
Thioxanthenes	thiothixene	Wolpert et al. 1967
		Campbell et al. 1970
		Waizer et al. 1972
Tricyclics	imipramine	Campbell et al. 1971
	loxapine	Pool et al. 1976
Amphetamines	dextroamphetamine	Campbell et al. 1972b
	levoamphetamine	Campbell et al. 1976b
Ergot alkaloids	methysergide	Fish et al. 1969
	lysergic acid	Bender et al. 1963
Indole derivative	molindone	Campbell et al. 1971
Antihistamines	diphenhydramine	Korein et al. 1971
Ion	lithium	Campbell et al. 1972a
		Gram & Rafaelsen 1972

In the early years, many of these drugs were given on a purely empirical basis, based on a trial and error procedure, with the hope that symptoms might be reduced. Often the studies did not employ blind and objective-rating instruments that would be sensitive to the specific changes both of autistic children in general, and of the particular autistic child under treatment.

For this reason, although many of the drugs tested in the 1960s and 1970s have failed to demonstrate efficacy by strict scientific criteria, a review of the literature listed in Table 21.1 will show that many of the drugs have not had really adequate studies among homogeneous subgroups of autistic children and that a great deal more work remains to be done in this area.

In the treatment of autism, the same principle applies to drug therapy as to all other forms of therapy: the younger the child, the better the results. Therefore, until a drug has been tried in very young, two-and three-year-old autistic children, it cannot be ruled out as a possible therapy.

In discussing methodological issues and problems with drug studies during the 1960s and 1970s, Magda Campbell presented several excellent reviews (1978, 1975).

Before leaving the subject of unestablished treatments for autistic patients, we should mention the attempt at hemodialysis as a treatment for autism. In 1979, Varley et al. (1979) proposed a study of hemodialysis as a treatment for early infantile autism, since at the time there had been some evidence to suggest that such dialysis might have been helpful in some adults with chronic schizophrenia. However, by 1980, this research group reported a course of ten weekly hemodialyses conducted on a young adult female with autism, and, since no significant changes were noted in mood, behavior or cognitive functioning, they concluded that hemodialysis in a larger group of autistic individuals was not justified (Varley et al. 1980). A trial on one individual is ordinarily not considered an adequate trial for any therapy. However, the amount of intervention, the time and expense of such therapy, and the inconclusive results do not make it a promising area for research at this time.

As is true with any treatment, the price of therapeutic attempts are often short- or long-term side effects. For instance a number of untoward effects have been reported in association with psychopharmacological drugs. These effects can be classified into three groups: (1) immediate short-term side effects, (2) long-term side effects, and (3) side effects that occur as a result of withdrawal of the drug. In addition, when used with children, the drugs can have effects outside the central nervous system, including effects on height, weight, skin, the ocular system, and the cardiovascular and autonomic system. One report of hospitalized children, four to 16 years of age, found thioridazine a major cause of weight gain and possibly a factor in decelerating learning (McAndrew et al. 1972).

References detailing the side effects of psychoactive agents in some autistic children are available in the literature (McAndrew et al. 1972; Paulson et al. 1975; Polizos and Engelhardt 1980; Gualtieri et al. 1982; Campbell et al. 1983a). In side effects, imipramine has been shown to produce seizures in several autistic children. Therefore, it should be used most judiciously with this group of patients, which contains a significant number of seizure-prone individuals (Petti and Campbell 1975). The longer one has experience with drugs, the more often one encounters unusual side effects. For example, the tardive Tourette syndrome has now been reported in an autistic patient as a result of gradual tapering off of long-term therapy with thioridazine (Stahl 1980).

Very few research studies have been done with autistic children in the use of thioridazine. This is unfortunate since, in a 1974 study, in response to a mailed questionnaire sent out by the Institute for Child Behavior Research in San Diego (in a survey reporting that non-drug treatments were more effective), parents reported that from their point of view thioridazine was the most effective of the available drugs (Rimland 1974). A later questionnaire mailed out in the 1980s, however, suggested that another drug, haloperidol, was more effective than thioridazine. Thus, we move to current drug research.

AFTER 1980

As years of experience went by and increasingly sophisticated research trials of drugs were undertaken, the issues of drug therapy in autistic children began to clarify. Factors of efficacy and safety began to be sorted out by experience and published studies. The use of specific drugs for specific age groups and for specific targeted symptoms is presently one of the goals of such current research.

In the first half of the 1980s, interest was concentrated primarily on two drugs—haloperidol and fenfluramine. Interestingly enough, these two pharmacological agents are both drugs that depress an important neurotransmitter in the central nervous system. In the case of haloperidol, dopamine is blocked, and in the case of fenfluramine, serotonin is lowered. As is the case with all drugs that are effective, there is good evidence to suggest that any major action on specific neurotransmitters is only one of a multitude of effects of each of these drugs. Nevertheless, it is interesting that of the medicines in the pharmacopoeia, two of the most powerful in blocking the action of a specific neurotransmitter have emerged as the most successful drugs to date in this patient group.

Haloperidol, a butyrophenone rather than a phenothiazine, had been under investigation since the beginning of the previous decade. Faretra et al. (1970) and Englehardt et al. (1973) had published initial studies with drugs that looked promising. Also, Campbell et al. (1972a) published the results with another butyrophenone compound, triflupe-ridol, and observed some initially encouraging results.

In 1978(a), Campbell et al. published a large study of 40 autistic children in a carefully designed, double-blind study with random assignment of subjects. An interesting aspect of this study was that it also compared two levels of language training (response-contingent reinforcement group and response-independent or placebo reinforcement group). The major finding of this study was that haloperidol was more efficacious than placebo in reducing two cardinal symptoms of autism—withdrawal and stereotypies. Another major finding of the study was that the combination of haloperidol and behavioral language training was more effective than either haloperidol or language training alone. In a later study (Campbell et al. 1982b; Campbell et al. in press; Anderson et al. in press), the previous design was continued, with the improvement that each child served as his or her own control. Again 40 children were studied. In this study, haloperidol was again found to be effective, this time in 8 out of 14 abnormal behaviors. The authors felt that one of the most important results of the study was that haloperidol appeared to be influencing the attention span and perhaps other cognitive factors in the children, rather than merely suppressing stereotypies. Since this is a finding that goes against the literature in other patient groups (Werry and Aman 1975), this result must be duplicated by additional studies. If duplicated, it is an important finding for the treatment of autistic children. Another finding from the Campbell et al. 1983b study was that short-term side effects such as sedation could be controlled by adjustment of the dosage.

It appears, however, that haloperidol has many long-term side effects which are undesirable. This is well documented in adult populations (Faurbye et al. 1964). One approach to preventing long-term side effects is to limit trials of the drug to four or so months at a time and then perform crossover studies, both to decrease the long-term side effects and to check at regular intervals that the drug is still efficacious in treating that particular child.

The main side effect of haloperidol is tardive dyskinesia, that is, an abnormal, involuntary movement disorder, most frequently involving the facial, buccal, lingual, and masticatory muscles, and often extending to the upper and lower extremities, fingers, toes, trunk, and neck. The typical movements of the mouth, tongue and face are slow and rhythmical; they include opening and closing of the mouth, chewing, licking, sucking, puckering, smacking, panting, protruding the tongue, tongue movements outside and inside the mouth (bon-bon sign), and fine vermicular movements of the tongue. However, any part of the body can be involved, in the form of choreiform, athetotic, myoclonic, dystonic, rolling, tic-like, and ballistic-type movements. These include diaphragmatic involvement in the form of respiratory dyskinesia, peculiar vocalizations, grunts, and dysarthria. Ataxia of upper and lower extremities is also reported. These movements can be rhythmic or irregular, repetitive, persistent, or transient, and, at times, bizarre. They can be activated or temporarily suppressed by voluntary movements, specific tasks, muscle activities, or emotional factors. During sleep they disappear; they may be seen more readily in the standing position (Campbell et al. 1983a).

One of the problems of evaluating this side effect is that many autistic children have pre-existing movement disorders such as stereotypies and mannerisms which can be suppressed with the drug but re-emerge when the drug is discontinued. Campbell et al. (1983b) assessed the safety of haloperidol in careful studies and report that 22 percent of autistic children in their study developed abnormal movements which then later ceased between 16 days and 9 months. They recommend the drug, in spite of its side effects, because of its clinical efficacy.

The other drug that has risen to prominence in the 1980s is fenfluramine. In 1982, Geller and his associates published a preliminary report on three autistic hospitalize boys who had elevated blood levels of serotonin. They pointed out that the fenfluramine decreased the blood serotonin level in the children, an effect similar to what had been seen in animals where the drug is effective in decreasing levels of serotonin in the brain. However, in at least one child with a rare leukodystrophy, it has been demonstrated that *high* serotonin in the blood is associated with *low* serotonin in the central nervous system (Coleman et al. 1977). This raises the question as to whether the efficacy of fenfluramine may be related to another neurotransmitter pathway rather than to serotonin. In any event, Geller et al. (1982) reported improvements both in behavior and in intelligence tests in these three initial patients on fenfluramine.

In 1983, Ritvo et al. (1983a) initiated a double-blind crossover study in 14 autistic outpatients. Six of the 14 had serotonin levels above 300 ng/ml—significantly elevated levels of serotonin. The serotonin levels fell an average of 51 percent in both normal and hyperserotonemic patients after one month on fenfluramine. When discontinuing the drug, 10 of 14 patients had a rebound effect, and the blood serotonin levels two months later were higher than baseline. According to the authors, during the four-month period of active treatment, all the parents noted decreased restlessness, improved sleep patterns, increased eye contact and increased spontaneous use of language during the study. More socialization and increased social awareness were also reported. During the washout period when the patients were crossed over off fenfluramine, the symptoms began to recur within two weeks after the placebo was begun. A repeat study produced the same results (Ritvo et al. in press).

A larger study from many medical centers (the fenfluramine multicenter study) was reviewed by the investigators in October, 1984. Although final results were not yet available, the consensus of opinion at the time indicated that about one out of every four autistic patients tried on the drug appeared improved compared with placebo periods. Increased attention span and social skills along with decreased hand flapping and twirling was found in patients who were helped (Multicenter Study 1984).

Fenfluramine was originally developed as an anorexogenic agent, so one side effect of this drug may be weight loss or diminished appetite. Other side effects reported so far include irritability, restlessness, and sleep disruption. Since the drug is relatively new at the time of this writing in its use in autism, long-term side effects are not yet determined.

In conclusion, many different types of drugs have been tried with autistic children. These include phenothiazines, thioxanthenes, tricyclics, amphetamines, ergot alkaloids, antihistamines and butyrophenones. In spite of a number of drug studies done over a 25-year period, no single drug has emerged as a drug of choice for autism, probably because autism is a syndrome of multiple etiologies and medication must be more individualized. In the last few years, haloperidol and fenfluramine have been extensively studied, and both appear to be promising drugs for at least some young children with autism who have no specific therapies available.

Part V

Conclusion

22   Theoretical Considerations: CNS Mechanisms Underlying the Autistic Syndrome

INTRODUCTION

One of the fascinating challenges of autism is to try to understand the mechanisms in the central nervous system that underlie autistic symptomatology. In this chapter we review and explore some of the theories regarding the final common pathway that leads to symptoms of autism.

There are autistic children who show no major signs or history indicative of a neurological disorder, particularly when they are young. Are they brain dysfunctional at all? We would submit that indeed they are, but our instruments used in detecting brain dysfunction are too crude. The proportion of autistic patients without associated neurological dysfunction dwindles rapidly as our evaluation methods increase in sophistication. Autistic children with and without detectable neurological disorder do not differ from the behavioral point of view (Garreau et al. 1984).

When one looks at brain dysfunction in an individual, one asks essentially two primary questions: "What is the lesion?" and "Where is the lesion?" The earlier chapters of this book reviewed a number of the etiologies of the autistic syndrome, so we are beginning to tease out the answer to the first question: "What is the lesion?" Some possible answers are that it is an abnormally functioning enzyme or a brain infection, or the chronic effects of mildly increased pressure inside the brain.

However, the answer to the question "Where is the lesion?" or "Where is the final common pathway that leads a child to have autistic

197

symptoms rather than other types of brain symptoms?" is more elusive. The human brain comprises 14 billion neurons with a density of approximately 1 trillion synapses per cubic centimeter of cortex. The staggering complexity and multiple redundancies that exist in the brain make even the boldest investigator hesitant to attempt to explain fully a disease process in the central nervous system.

What is wrong with the brain of autistic children? Based on current research, a number of tantalizing clues present themselves. Regarding the rate of metabolism in the brain, the PET studies (Rapoport et al. 1983) indicate an increased rate of metabolism. The currently most promising drugs, haloperidol and fenfluramine, are drugs that block or dampen down metabolic pathways (see chapter 21).

Is the brain of the autistic individual immature or advanced? In one autopsy study of an adult, a profound immaturity of the brain was suggested by the retention of the lamina desicans zone which is usually found only in very young children (chapter 12). Also, certain REM sleep studies are found to resemble those of very young children, as young as 18 months of age or less (chapter 10). Endocrine studies demonstrate lack of circadian rhythm for corticosteroids in older patients when such a pattern is usually seen only in children well under four years of age (chapter 9). Yet, on the other hand, there is evidence from studies of cortical auditory and visual evoked potentials that suggest that some of the higher levels of function could be either normal or advanced (chapter 10). And it appears that an occasional autistic child may, as an adult, even become a member of a society for geniuses (Sofaer and Emery 1981).

In connection with localization in the brain, autistic patients offer a number of clues to direct our attention toward certain areas. First and foremost, they all appear to have a type of cognitive defect which delays the development of natural, progressive, hierarchic integration of the brain which is so essential for the maturation of the young brain. But, in contrast to many retarded children, autistic children have a profound social immaturity. In addition, they also have sensory processing problems primarily studied in the auditory system, but clearly evident in the visual and tactile systems if investigated. Relatively spared is the visual spatial system (Shah and Frith 1982); this sparing is related primarily only to the spatial area per se and not to temporal visual processing. Children also have evidence of basal ganglia disease and there are a number of studies suggesting brainstem dysfunction.

How have past investigators interpreted these symptoms in terms of anatomy? In 1964, Rimland hypothesized that the error in these patients lay in the reticular formation of the brainstem and he propounded a theory suggesting that the cognitive dysfunction was secondary to this brainstem problem. Hutt and Hutt (1970) also suggested that a hyperactive reticular activating system could underlie symptoms of autism with a reactive effort by the brain in an effort to reduce the sensory input. Simon (1975) also suggested a brainstem location, this time in the inferior colliculus. Cohen et al. (1976) raised the question of brainstem and mid-brain dysfunction involving catecholamine pathways. Damasio and Maurer (1978) related symptoms to the mesolimbic cortex and the anterior and medial nuclear groups of the thalamus. Coleman (1979) raised the possibility of birth injury affecting the thalamus in some cases. There were theorists suggesting that the left side of the brain was damaged (Aarkrog 1968; Prior 1979; Hier et al. 1979; Dawson et al. 1982) while Myklebust et al. (1972) suggested a right-sided lesion and was backed up by some evidence by Baltaxe (1981), Ross (1981) and Weintraub et al. (1981).

However, most authorities today agree that a bilateral—not unilateral—brain dysfunction would be required for autism to develop (see Ornitz 1983 for a review). In an attempt to conceptualize the problem, a working hypothesis will be presented which selectively integrates some of the studies and theories of other investigators into a comprehensive theoretical model.

A THEORY LINKING BRAINSTEM/MESOLIMBIC DYSFUNCTION WITH AUTISTIC SYMPTOMS

Brainstem Dysfunction

There is evidence from several groups and studies that in autistic patients the brainstem has dysfunctional sections. In 1963, Bonvallet and Allen noted increased heartrate variability, failure to habituate to respiratory responses, and enhancement of vascular reaction to visual input. These could be taken as evidence of unusual functioning of the reticular formation in the brainstem.

The UCLA research team has performed a number of studies of vestibular function and have noted that a large portion of autistic children have either a decrease or absence of post rotary nystagmus. They also typically display a lack of dizziness or nausea after spinning and rotation. This too can be interpreted as brainstem dysfunction (see Ornitz 1983 for overview).

Electrophysiological studies have also suggested brainstem dysfunction. Even though baseline EEGs áre not specific, the findings on these EEGs are suggestive of centrencephalic rather than circumscribed telencephalic damage (Gladwell et al. 1979; Gillberg and Schauman 1983). Also, auditory brainstem evoked response studies have indicated brainstem dysfunction in a subgroup of autistic children (see chapter 10). This examination is most sensitive to *structural* brainstem damage, thus it is quite possible that even among those with normal results, there are children who have abnormal brainstem *function*.

The autopsy studies of Williams et al. (1980), who studied the autopsies of four autistic children and limited those studies to the cortex, also indirectly support this concept since they found no, or minimal, evidence of structural abnormalities in the cortex.

Thus, the evidence of autonomic dysfunction, the vestibular studies, and the electrophysiological studies all point in the direction of brainstem dysfunction in this patient group.

As is seen in Figure 22.1, the first part of this comprehensive theory assumes brainstem dysfunction or damage. The theory then

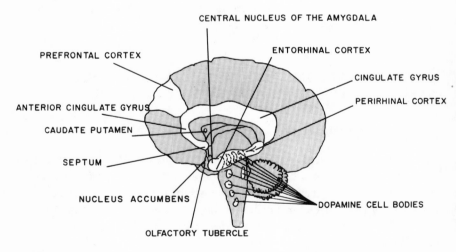

FIGURE 22.1. Mesolimbic damage could arise de novo or secondary to damage (or failure of development?) of dopamine cell bodies in the brainstem. Although the dopamine system is pictured here, there is also evidence of dysfunction of other, related brainstem nuclei–such as the serotonergic and endorphin systems.

assumes that one way brainstem dysfunction can present is as an abnormal dopaminergic state that might arise throughout the brain wherever dopaminergic nerve fibers project because of injury to the central neurons in the brainstem either through structural or metabolic injury.

Dopamine Dysfunction

The cell bodies for the dopamine neurons are located in the brainstem and the diencephalon and there are studies which indicate a relatively abnormal function of dopamine in autistic patients. To review the evidence that there may be an absolute or relatively excessive amount of dopamine in autistic patients, one finds the following data in support of that hypothesis:

1. The enzyme that hydroxylyzes (lowers the level of) dopamine beta hydroxylase (DBH) is depressed in the serum of patients in several studies (Goldstein et al. 1976; Lake et al. 1977).

2. A minor metabolite of dopamine (homoprotocatechuic acid), which is only found in significant amounts when there is a backup of the dopamine pathway (with excessive dopamine being metabolized into minor pathways), has been demonstrated in 88 percent of autistic patients (Landgrebe and Landgrebe 1976).

3. Dopamine agonists, such as amphetamines, tend to make patients worse, while dopamine antagonists, such as haloperidol, clinically help some autistic children (Campbell et al. 1976b; Campbell et al. 1978a).

4. The end product of dopamine is homovanillic acid (HVA) which is elevated in both the cerebral spinal fluid (Cohen et al. 1977b; Winsberg et al. 1980; Gillberg et al. 1983) and the urine (Garreau et al. 1980; Lelord et al. 1978).

5. The elevated HVA level in autistic children can be lowered by giving them pyridoxine (or vitamin B_6)—the co-enzyme of both the step before and after dopamine (Lelord et al. 1978). Since the vitamin lowers HVA, presumably it may be selectively enhancing DBH function whose job it is to lower the level of dopamine. (However, in normal children, the opposite effect is reported. Their normal levels of HVA go up, presumably by enhancing L-AAAD, the enzyme creating more dopamine.) Thus, the cate-

cholamine pathway is affected by pyridoxine differently in autistic patients compared with normal children. Double-blind studies show that pyridoxine is helpful clinically to one subgroup of autistic children.

The fact that these dopamine-related results are consistent with each other in different laboratories is encouraging, but it is important to note several limitations at this time. The studies listed above are primarily concerned with measuring compounds from the periphery and, only by analogy, from the brain. Even cerebral spinal fluid contains a large ultrafiltrate of blood. Also, these are early studies, some of which have not been confirmed independently.

In fact, abnormal functional levels of dopamine could be due to a number of reasons. As suggested, it could be due to a relative block in the enzyme, DBH, whose job is to catabolize the amine. It also could be due to a normal function of the dopamine pathway with depressed levels of other neurotransmitters with which dopamine is in delicate balance. It also could be due to denervation hypersensitivity of dopamine neurons themselves, making them hypersensitive and hyperfunctional. Or it could be due to other reasons not yet understood.

In contrast, there is also a very small literature which is compatible with depression of dopamine functioning. For example, in PKU patients we know that there is a block in the catecholamine pathway ahead of dopamine which prevents a normal amount of the compound from being formed (see chapter 16). Also, the gait in some autistic patients has been carefully analyzed and called a childhood equivalent of Parkinson's disease (Vilensky et al. 1981). Parkinson's disease is a documented dopamine deficiency disease seen in older age groups.

In our comprehensive model, we therefore postulate that dopamine neurons in the dopamine pathways from the brainstem up into the cortex are functioning abnormally—overdoing or underdoing their job—in many of these patients. Other pathways originating in the brainstem, as yet unexplored, probably are also dysfunctional. This area also contains enkephalin substances so dysfunction of enkephalin-containing neurons also is a possibility.

Where do dopaminergic neurons send their axons? The target area of dopaminergic mesencephalic neurons is the mesolimbic cortex which is architectonically and neurochemically distinct and, along with the striatum, constitutes the target area for these neurons. According to Damasio and Maurer (1978), "bilateral neural structures that include the ring of mesolimbic cortex located in the mesial frontal and temporal lobes, the neostriatum and the anterior and medial nuclear groups of the thalamus,'' may be specifically dysfunctional in autistic patients.

Mesolimbic Cortex and Striatum

With reference to the cerebral cortex, where are the areas that symptoms of autism suggest might be damaged? Several authors have indicated left hemisphere damage and dysfunction, and there are studies of disturbed interhemisphere relationship or relative left hemisphere dysfunction, such as non-right-handedness, special musical skills, special artistic skills and superior visual/spatial skills in autistic children. There are also laboratory studies implying a link between autism and left hemisphere dysfunction (e.g. left temporal lobe damage that is evident in pneumoencephalography: cf. Aarkrog 1968; Hauser et al. 1975, though Ornitz [1978] and others have criticized the conclusion of that study), left parietal occipital reduction of brain parenchyma (Hier et al. 1979), and a deficient left hemisphere specialization for language functions (Dawson et al. 1982). With reference to right hemisphere dysfunction, the dysprosodic characteristics of autistic speech (Baltaxe 1981) and the failure to convey emotions can be attributed to right, rather than left, hemisphere dysfunction (Ross 1981; Weintraub et al. 1981).

If both sides of the brain are involved, that is, if it is a bilateral problem, which portions of the cortex would one expect to find with abnormal functioning? The mesial portions of the temporal lobe is an obvious choice owing to the nature of autistic symptoms (Hetzler and Griffin 1981). In this area and the immediately adjacent areas are the centers for controlling motor language functions, emotion, autonomous functions, auditory processing centers and modulation centers for sensory stimuli and voluntary movements. Damage to this region could lead to many of the symptoms typical of autism, while dysfunction in this area might lead to less pronounced problems of a similar kind.

Medial temporal structures are among those most likely to be damaged by reduced optimality in the prenatal period (Griffiths and Laurence 1974). Furthermore, the studies connecting postnatal herpes encephalitis with reversible autistic symptoms also point in the direction of the temporal lobe being affected, since herpes viruses are known to have a predilection for just those areas (Haymaker et al.). In the Klüver-Bucy syndrome (Klüver and Bucy 1938 and 1939) in which temporal lobe structures are bilaterally destroyed there is severe incapacity in the fields of recognizing the emotional significance of objects and in social relationships. These symptoms also are typical of autism. Further, in the adult Korsakoff's syndrome there is a well-known loss of recall for recent events, which results from bilateral hippocampal lesions in the temporal lobe. This problem, too, can be characteristic of autism (Boucher 1981). The language problem in autism, at one point thought to be similar to that of developmental dysphasia but now shown not to be identical, could be interpreted to favor bilateral temporal lobe damage. Bryson (1970) has presented evidence that association fibers connecting the temporal and occipital lobes may be dysfunctional or damaged in autism. The autistic children in that study showed poorer auditory visual or vice versa, than visual visual performances. Psychomotor epilepsy is probably more common in autism than other kinds of epilepsy (Corbett 1982). This, too, would suggest temporal lobe affliction.

What about the mesial frontal lobe area? The mesial frontal cortex has an exceptionally high concentration of dopamine. Originally it was thought to be a silent pre-frontal area. Frontal lobes scarcely exist in laboratory animals and are fully developed only in human beings. However, new findings suggest that it helps to integrate information from both sides of the brain and that it has particularly close connections with three deeper brained areas, the thalamus (the site of perception, constant or inconstant), the caudate nucleus (one of the basal ganglia), and the brainstem. Goldman-Rakic and Brown (1982) have shown that, in the frontal lobes, columns of axons from cell bodies in the cortex of one hemisphere alternate with columns of axons from cells of the other hemisphere, and that the silent prefrontal area which was believed to be undifferentiated and diffused actually has an exquisite and precise organization. Additional evidence for frontal lobe dysfunction in autism has been provided by Rumsey (1984) who found significant deficits in the formulation of rules and also severe preservative tendencies in nine highly verbal, autistic adult males.

With reference to the thalamus, the anterior group of thalamic nuclei are involved in recent memory processing and they are also involved in the balance between stereotyped and exploratory behavior. The thalamus is the main nucleus for perceptual integration, and the perceptual inconstancy described so graphically by Ornitz and Ritvo (1968a) could represent a thalamic (or third neuron up) lesion, rather than primary or secondary deficits seen in disease entities where perception is consistently impaired.

The neostriatal area is involved in the extrapyramidal motor balance system of the body. Dysfunction of this area conceivably could account for the variations of tone that are seen in autistic children, which result in toe-walking or in other minor motor problems (see discussion by Vilensky et al. 1981).

Comprehensive Model

Thus, in Figure 22.1, we summarize this comprehensive model that could possibly account for some autistic symptomology. If the ascending dopaminergic nerve fibers from the brainstem/diencephalon are coming from neurons that are dysfunctional or injured, then their target cell areas, such as the mesolimbic area, might be dysfunctional and, in a growing child, underdeveloped. It is well established that sensory input is necessary in young children for the development of certain "end interpretation loci."

Therefore, our comprehensive model suggests that brainstem dysfunction or damage through the mechanism of the dopaminergic pathways (and probably other pathways arising from the brainstem area) may cause loss of tropic sensory input necessary for optimal development in the mesolimbic and striatal systems of the central nervous system. Thus, autistic symptoms might develop in cortex secondary to brainstem disease processes or, in other cases, de novo in mesolimbic cortex itself.

CONCLUSION

Interesting as these theories of biochemical and anatomical localization may be, in the living child whose brain is constantly maturing, specific localization may be misleading. In the young child, dynamic rather than static anatomical approaches often underlie the truest interpretations of symptoms. For example, although autism is thought to be primarily a bilateral phenomenon (as described above), the suggestion has been made by DeLong et al. (1981) that there may be both a bilateral and a unilateral form, with the unilateral being, in general, milder, more reversible and associated with preserved islands of normal function.

We would like to end by discussing the study of dichotic listening tests by Wetherby et al. (1981). A group of autistic subjects ranging from eight to 24 years of age, who had normal hearing on monaural speech tests, were studied. It was found that only for those subjects displaying echolalia was there an indication of central auditory nervous system dysfunction in the language dominant hemisphere, as determined from the dichotic tests. Autistic children who were no longer echolalic had normal dichotic test results. One subject who was tested over the course of a year gradually lost echolalia. At the same time, the child showed a normalization in the dichotic test of central auditory function. Thus, in this autistic child, a clinical improvement was documented by an improvement in a functional laboratory test.

It is important to remember that the child's brain is a dynamic, growing organism capable of change. In young children the brain, with maddening ability to switch locations, simply refuses to follow the anatomical rules that were worked out in adult patients. Any theoretical model of brain function in autism based on studies in children needs to keep this fundamental point in mind.

23   Summary

This book examines the evidence in the medical literature indicating that the symptoms of autism originate in disease processes in the child rather than in his parents or in other environmental factors. After initially reviewing the history of the development of the concept of autism as a psychologically caused illness, we have reviewed studies of parents of autistic children suggesting that these parents do not have personalities different from parents of other children.

After a review of diagnostic criteria in the literature, we present five criteria used to diagnose autism. The behavioral syndrome of autism can be diagnosed in a child in whom the following five character-istics are found:

1. Early onset—before two-and-a-half years of age.
2. Severe disturbance of social relatedness.
3. Abnormalities of development of communication, usually prominently noted in abnormalities of language development.
4. Elaborate repetitive routines.
5. Abnormal response to sensory stimuli.

Autism is a behavioral syndrome, but the majority of the patients also have a mental retardation syndrome. The clinical course of autistic children through the various age groups is reviewed and the variety of outcomes detailed. Epilepsy, a common complication of the autistic syndrome, is discussed in a separate chapter.

The epidemiology of the autistic syndromes is reviewed, and the fact that there are between four and five autistic children per 10,000 live births in most studies is noted. The relationship of other handicaps, such as mental retardation, blindness, and deafness is discussed.

A chapter on twin and family studies documents the concordance for autism in monozygotic twins and discusses the presence of autism in family groupings. To date, a sex-linked pattern of inheritance, an autosomal recessive pattern of inheritance and, in a few cases, a possible dominant problem are suggested by these studies.

Preconception, prenatal and perinatal studies indicate that maternal uterine bleeding is the prenatal event most likely to be significantly associated with the subsequent development of infantile autism. Perinatal studies show that there is an increased at-risk factor for many infants who later develop autism, but birth injury per se is difficult to establish.

Biochemical studies of these patients find that a majority have a high level of serotonin in their blood and an elevation of the end-product of dopamine (homovanillic acid) in urine and spinal fluid. Endocrine studies indicate that many autistic children have immature patterns of normal circadian rhythm for corticosteroids.

With respect to electrophysiological studies, the literature on brainstem auditory evoked responses is suggestive of abnormalities with a longer brainstem transmission time, while cortical evoked potentials tend to show amplitudes that are, if anything, small. REM sleep studies have indicated deficiencies in the tonic aspects of REM sleep, and the eye-movement activity during REM sleep often resembles that of normal children who are much younger in age.

Brain imaging studies have been disappointing in identifying specific locations for disease processes in autistic children, but there does appear to be a small subgroup of such children who have evidence of mild or moderate hydrocephalus. Autopsy studies, however, are in their infancy.

Several specific disease entities with a subgroup of autistic patients have now been identified. This includes the chromosomal syndrome (fragile-X), prenatal rubella encephalitis and metabolic diseases such as phenylketonuria, purine autism, and lactic acidosis.

In the discussion of medical therapies, it is pointed out that because autism is a syndrome of multiple etiologies, the best medical treatment will be specifically designed for the individual patient based on individual diagnosis. In addition, the general therapies currently under investigation in autism include pyridoxine, haloperidol and fenfluramine.

The book ends by discussing a theoretical model linking early brainstem damage affecting dopaminergic neurons with improper development of the mesolimbic portion of the cortex leading to autistic symptoms.

Autism is a syndrome of multiple etiologies and every patient needs an adequate medical workup and appropriate medical therapy in combination with the educational programs now available that are developed specifically for autistic children. Areas where future research is indicated are identified throughout this book.

Appendix

NEUROPSYCHIATRIC ASSESSMENT

A. History
—detailed structured assessment in respect to autism using standardized questionnaire, including handedness
—review of optimality in pre-, peri-, and neonatal period (medical records required)
—review of postnatal, potentially brain-damaging events (medical records if needed)
—review of previous medical illnesses, growth patterns, etc.
—detailed psychiatric history:
—family factors and psychosocial milieu
—temperament and attention span of child
—heredity (especially autism, childhood schizophrenia, learning disorders, affective disorders, all other psychiatric disorders including anorexia nervosa, geniuses)

B. General Physical
—measurement of cranial circumference, height, weight, auricle length and interpupillary distance
—assessment with respect to minor physical anomalies, meticulous somatic examination (often needs repeating) including search for café-au-lait spots, adenoma sebaceum or depigmented spots
—(after puberty only) inspection of testicles for size
—assessment of heart beat variation

C. Neurological—age-appropriate pediatric neurological examination

D. Psychological Evaluation—performed by an experienced psychologist who knows how to do cognitive testing in autistic children and uses appropriate test batteries

E. Laboratory Examinations
    Essential (unless clinical examination has already revealed etiology)
    1. Blood
        —Phenylalanine
        —Serotonin and platelet count
        —Uric acid
        —Calcium
        —Phosphorus
        —Magnesium
        —Lactic acid
        —Pyruvic acid
        —Herpes titer
        —Cytomegalovirus titer
        —Mumps titer
        —Chromosomal culture—folate deficient media (males with
          large ears only)
        —BUN
    2. 24-hour Urine
        —Uric acid
        —Magnesium
        —Calcium
        —Phosphorus
        —Metabolic screen (including test for mucopolysaccharides)
        —Creatinine
        —HVA
    3. Other laboratory tests
        —EEG
        —CT or NMR
        —Ophthalmological
        —Auditory evaluation (including brainstem auditory evoked
          potential if the child is mute)
        —Otological examination, including test of vestibular function
          such as Barany's rotation test for elicitation of nystagmus

    Optional
        —72-hour stool for lipid and occult blood
        —24-hour urine for amino acids, organic acids, urinary peptide
          excretion, succinyl purines, niacin metabolites and zinc.
        —Cerebrospinal fluid-protein, cell count, glucose, monoamine
          and endorphin content
        —Brainstem and cortical auditory evoked potential

Comment: This neuropsychiatric assessment of an autistic person is the current one suggested by the authors at the time of publication of this monograph. Such assessments are, of course, constantly upgraded as new data are available.

Bibliography

Aarkrog, T. (1968) "Organic factors in infantile psychoses and borderline psychoses." *Danish Medical Bulletin* 15:283–288.

Abbassi, V., T. Linscheid, and M. Coleman. (1978) "Triiodothyronine (T3) concentration and therapy in autistic children." *Journal of Autism and Childhood Schizophrenia* 8:383–387.

Addae, S.K., and F.I.D. Konotey-Ahulu. (1971) "Renal handling of uric acid in homozygous haemoglobin C disease." *African Journal of Medical Science* 2:1.

Allanen, Y.O., T. Arajarvi, and R.O. Viitamaki. (1964) "Psychoses in childhood." *Acta Psychiatrica Scandinavica.* Suppl. 174.

American Psychiatric Association, (1980) *DSM-III, Diagnostic and Statistical Manual of Mental Disorders:* Washington, D.C.

Anast, C.S., and D.W. Gardner. (1981) "Magnesium metabolism." In *Disorders of Mineral Metabolism: Pathophysiology of Calcium, Phosphorus and Magnesium*, edited by F. Bronner and J.W. Coburn, pp. 423–522. New York: Academic Press.

Anderson, L.T., M. Campbell, D.M. Grega, R. Perry, A.M. Small, and W.H. Green. "Infantile Autism II. Effects of Haloperidol on Learning." In press.

Andersson, L., and K. Wadensjö (1981) *Early childhood psychosis in Malmöhus län—a descriptive study.* Research report. Social Welfare Authorities, County of Malmöhus län (in Swedish).

Anthony, J. (1958) "An experimental approach to the psychopathology of childhood. Autism." *British Journal of Medical Psychology* 31:211–225.

Asperger H. (1944) "Die Autistischen Psychopathen im Kindesalter." *Archiv für Psychiatrie und Nervenkrankheiten* 117:76–136.

August, G.J., M.A. Stewart, and L. Tsai. (1981) "The incidence of cognitive disabilities in the siblings of autistic children." *British Journal of Psychiatry* 138:416–422.

Avery, G.B., G.R.G. Monif, J.L. Sever, and S.L. Leikin. (1965) "Rubella syndrome after inapparent maternal illness." *American Journal of Diseases of Children* 110:444–446.

Bakwin, H. (1954) "Early infantile autism." *Journal of Pediatrics* 45:492–497.

Bakwin, R.M., E.H. Mosbach, and H. Bakwin. (1961) "Concentration of copper in serum of children with schizophrenia." *Pediatrics* 27:642–644.

Baltaxe, C.A.M. (1981) "Acoustic characteristics of prosody in autism." In *Frontiers of knowledge in mental retardation. Vol. 1: Social, educational and behavioral aspects*, edited by P. Mittler. Proceedings of the International Association for the Scientific Study of Mental Deficiency.

Barabas, G., and W.S. Matthews. (1983) "Coincident infantile autism and Tourette syndrome: A case report. *Developmental and Behavioral Pediatrics* 4(4):280–281.

Barnet, A.B. (1979) "Sensory evoked potentials in autism." In *Workshop on the Neurobiological Basis of Autism*, edited by L.A. Lockman, K.F. Swaiman, J.S. Drage, K.B. Nelson, and H.M. Marsden, National Institute of Neurological and Communicative Disorders and Stroke, National Institute of Health. Monograph No. 23.

Bartak, L., M. Rutter, and A. Cox. (1977) "A comparative study of infantile autism and specific developmental receptive language disorders. III: Discriminant function analysis." *Journal of Autism and Childhood Schizophrenia* 7:383–396.

Bartak, L., M. Rutter, and A. Cox. (1975) "A comparative study of infantile autism and specific developmental language disorder. I. The Children. " *British Journal of Psychiatry* 126:127–145.

Barthelemy, C., B. Garreau, I. Leddet, D. Ernouf, J.P. Muh, and G. Lelord. (1981) "Behavioral and biological effects of oral magnesium, vitamin B_6 and combined magnesium–vitamin B_6 administration in autistic children." *Magnesium Bulletin* 2:150–153.

Bartholome, K., D.J. Byrd, S. Kaufman, and S. Milstein. (1977) "Atypical phenylketonuria with normal phenylalanine hydroxylase and dihydropteridine reductase activity in vitro." *Pediatrics* 59:575–761.

Bartlik, B.D. (1981) "Monthly variation in births of autistic children in North Carolina." *J. American Medical Women's Assoc.* 36:363–368.

Bauman, M., and T.L. Kemper. (in press) "Histoanatomic observations of the brain in early infantile autism." *Neurology.*

Becker, M.A., K.O. Raivio, B. Bakay, W.B. Adams, and W.L. Nyhan. (1980) "Variant human phosphoribosylpyrophosphate synthetase altered in regulatory and catalytic functions." *J. Clin. Invest.* 65:109–120.

Belmaker, R.H., J. Hattab, and R.P. Ebstein. (1978) "Plasma dopamine-beta-hydroxylase in childhood psychosis." *Journal of Autism and Childhood Schizophrenia* 8:293–298.

Benda, C.E., and J.C. Melchoir. (1959) "Childhood schizophrenia, childhood autism and Heller's disease." *International Record of Medicine* 172:137–154.

Bender, L., E. Fry, B. Pennington, M. Puck, J. Salbenblatt, and A. Robinson. (1983) "Speech and language development in 41 children with sex chromosome abnormalities." *Pediatrics* 71:262–267.

Bender, L., G. Faretra, and L. Cobrinik. (1963) "LSD and UML treatment of hospitalized disturbed children." In *Recent Advances in Biological Psychiatry*, Vol. 5, edited by J. Wortis, pp. 84–92. New York: Plenum Press.

Bensch, A., and C. Gillberg. "A study of blind autistic children in Sweden." In preparation.

Bergström, K., and B. Bille. (1980) "Computed tomography of the brain in children with minimal brain damage: a preliminary study of 46 children." *Neuropädiatrie* 9:378–384.

Berneis, K.H., M. DaPrada, and A. Pletscher. (1969) "Micelle formation between 5-hydroxytryptamine and adenosine triphosphate in platelet storage organelles." *Science* 165:913–914.

Berry, H.K., D.J. O'Grady, L.J. Perlmutter, and M.K. Bofinger. (1979) "Intellectual development and academic achievement of children treated early for phenylketonuria." *Developmental Medicine and Child Neurology* 21:311–320.

Bertaccini, G. (1960) "Tissue serotonin and urinary 5-HIAA after partial or total removal of gastrointestinal tract in the rat." *J. Physiol.* (London) 153:239.

Bettelheim, B. (1959) "Feral children and autistic children." *Am. J. Sociology* 64:455–467.

Bhagavan, H.N., M. Coleman, and D. Coursin. (1975) "Distribution of pyridoxal-5-phosphate in human blood between the cells and plasma: effect of oral administration of pyridoxine on the ratio of Down's and hyperactive patients." *Biochem. Med.* 14:201–208.

Bickel, H., J. Gerrard, and E. Hickman. (1953) "Influence of phenylalanine intake on phenylketonurics." *Lancet* 2:812.

Biesele, G.G., W. Schmid, and M. Lawless. (1962) "Mentally retarded schizoid twin girls with 47 chromosomes." *Lancet* 1:403–405.

Bird, B.L., D.C. Russo, and M.F. Cataldo. (1977) "Considerations in the analysis and treatment of dietary effects on behavior: a case study." *Journal of Autism and Childhood Schizophrenia* 7:373–382.

Bishop, D. (1980) "Handedness, clumsiness and cognitive ability." *Developmental Medicine and Child Neurology* 22:569–579.

Black, A.L., B.M. Guirard, and E.E. Snell. (1977) "Increased muscle phosphorylase in rats fed high levels of vitamin B₆." *J. Nutri.* 107:1962.

Blattner, R.J. (1966) "Congenital rubella: Persistent infection of the brain and liver." *Journal of Pediatrics* 68:997–999.

Bleuler, E. (1911) *Dementia praecox or the group of schizophrenias.* Vienna. Translated by J. Zinkin (1950). New York: International University Press.

Bliumina, M.G. (1975) "A schizophrenic-like variant of phenylketonuria." *Zh. Nevropatrol Psikhiatr.* 75:1525–1529.

Blomquist, H. K:son, M. Bohman, S.-O. Edvinsson, C. Gillberg, K.-H. Gustavson, G. Holmgren, and J. Wahlström. (1984) "Frequency of the fragile

X-syndrome, in infantile autism. A Swedish multicenter study." *Clinical Genetics*. In press.

Blomquist, H. K:son, K.-H. Gustavson, G. Holmgren, I. Nordenson, and U. Palsson-Strale. (1983) "Fragile X syndrome in mildly mentally retarded children in a northern Swedish county." *Clinical Genetics* 24:393–398.

Blomquist, H. K:son, K.-H. Gustavson, G. Holmgren, I. Nordenson, and A. Sweins. (1982) "Fragile site X-chromosomes and X-linked mental retardation in severely retarded boys in a northern Swedish county. A clinical study." *Clinical Genetics* 21:209–214.

Boesen, U., and T. Aarkog. (1967) "Pneumoencephalography of patients in a child psychiatric department." *Danish Medical Bulletin* 14:210–218.

Bohman, M., P.O. Björk, I.L. Bohman, and E. Sjöholm. (1981) "Barndoms-psykoserna—försummade handikapp?—Epidemiologi och habilitering i ett glesbygdslän." *Läkartidningen* 78:2361–2364 (in Swedish, summary in English).

Bonvallet, M., and M.B.D. Allen. (1963) "Prolonged spontaneous and evoked activation following discrete bulbar lesions." *Electroencephalography and Clinical Neurophysiology* 15:969.

Böök, J.A., G. Nichtern, and F. Gruenberg. (1963) "Cytogenetical investigation in childhood schizophrenia." *Acta Psychiatrica Scandinavica* 39:309–323.

Born, G.V.R., and R.E. Gillson. (1959) "Studies on the uptake of 5-hydroxytryptamine by blood platelets." *J. Physiol.* (London) 146:472.

Boss, G.R., and J.E. Seegmiller. (1982) "Genetic defects in human purine and pyrimidine metabolism." *Ann. Rev. Genet.* 16:297–328.

Boucher, J. (1981) "Memory of Recent Events in Autistic Children." *Journal of Autism and Developmental Disorders* 11:293–302.

Boullin, D.J., and R.A. O'Brien. (1972) "Uptake and loss of 14-C-dopamine by platelets from children with infantile autism." *Journal of Autism and Childhood Schizophrenia* 2:67–74.

Boullin, D.J., H.N. Bhagavan, R.A. O'Brien, and M.B.H. Youdim. (1976) "Platelet monoamine oxidase in children with infantile autism." In *The Autistic Syndromes*, edited by M. Coleman, pp. 51–56. Amsterdam: North-Holland.

Boullin, D.J., M. Coleman, R.A. O'Brien, and B. Rimland. (1971) "Laboratory predictions of infantile autism, based on 5-hydroxytryptamine efflux from platelets, and their correlation with the Rimland E-2 scores." *Journal of Autism and Childhood Schizophrenia* 1:63–71.

Boullin, D.J., M. Coleman, and R.A. O'Brien. (1970) "Abnormalities in platelet 5-hydroxytryptamine efflux in patients with infantile autism." *Nature* 226:371–372.

Boyer, J.-P., A. Deschatrette, and M. Delwarde. (1981) "Autisme convulsif?" *Pédiatrie* 5:353–368 (in French).

Brask, B.H. (1970) "A prevalence investigation of childhood psychosis." Paper given at the 16th Scandinavian Congress of Psychiatry.

Brask, B.H. (1967) "The need for hospital beds for psychotic children: An analysis based on a prevalence investigation in the county of Århus." *Ugeskrift for Leger* 129:1559–1570.

Brøndum-Nielsen, K. (1983) "Diagnosis of the fragile X syndrome (Martin-Bell syndrome). Clinical findings in 27 males with the fragile site at X_q28." *Journal of Mental Deficiency Research* 27:211–226.

Brown, W.T. (1969) "Adolescent development of children with infantile psychosis." Seminars in Psychiatry 1:79–89.

Brown, W.T., E.C. Jenkins, E. Friedman, J. Brooks, K. Wisniewski, S. Raguthu, and J. French. (1982) "Autism is associated with the fragile X syndrome." *Journal of Autism and Developmental Disorders* 12:303–308.

Bryson, C.Q. (1972) "Short-term memory and cross-model information processing in autistic children." *Journal of Learning Disabilities* 5:81.

Bryson, C.Q. (1970) "Systematic identification of perceptual disabilities in autistic children." *Perceptual and Motor Skills* 31:329–346.

Butler, I.J., S.H. Koslow, A. Krumholz, N.A. Holtzman, and S. Kaufman. (1978) "A disorder of biogenic amines in dihydropteridine reductase deficiency." *Annals of Neurol.* 3:224–230.

Byassee, J.E., and S.A. Murrell. (1975) "Interaction patterns in families of autistic, disturbed and normal children." *American Journal of Orthopsychiatry* 45:473–478.

Caddell, J.L. (1974) "Magnesium in the nutrition of the child." *Clin. Pediatrics* 13:263–272.

Caldwell, D.F., D. Oberleas, J.J. Clancy, and A.S. Prasad. (1970) "Behavioral improvement in adult rats following zinc deficiency." *Proc. of Soc. Exp. Biol. Med.* 133:1417–1421.

Campbell, D.G. (1983) "The cruel trick that nature played on young Duffy Mayo: candida victim was believed to be autistic." *The Los Angeles Times*, Sept. 25, Part VIII.

Campbell, M. (1978) "Pharmacotherapy." In *Autism. A reappraisal of concepts and treatment*, edited by M. Rutter and E. Schopler, pp. 337–355. New York: Plenum Press.

Campbell, M. (1975) "Pharmacotherapy in early infantile autism." *Biological Psychiatry* 10:399–423.

Campbell, M., and B. Fish. (1974) "Triiodothyronine in schizophrenic children." In *The Thyroid Axis, Drugs, and Behavior*, edited by A.J. Prange, Jr., pp. 87–102. New York: Raven Press.

Campbell, M., L.T. Anderson, A.M. Small, R. Perry, D.M. Grega, and W.H. Green. (in press) "Infantile Autism I. Effects of Haloperidol on Behavioral Symptoms." In press.

Campbell, M., D.M. Grega, W.H. Green, and W.G. Bennett. (1983a) "Neuroleptic-induced dyskinesias in children." *Clin. Neuropharm.* 6:207–222.

Campbell, M., R. Perry, and W.G. Bennett. (1983b) "Long-term therapeutic efficacy and drug-related abnormal movements: a prospective study of haloperidol in autistic children." *Psychopharmacology Bulletin* 19:80–83.

Campbell, M., S. Rosenbloom, R. Perry, A,E. George, I.I. Kricheff, L. Anderson, A.M. Small, and S.J. Jennings. (1982) "Computerized axial tomography in young autistic children." *American Journal of Psychiatry* 139:510–512.

Campbell, M., T. Petti, W. Green, I. Cohen, N. Genieser, and R. David. (1980) "Some physical parameters of young autistic children." *J. Am. Acad. Child Psychiatry* 19:193–212.

Campbell, M., L.T. Anderson, M. Meier, I.L. Cohen, A.M. Small, C. Samit, and E.J. Sachar. (1978a) "A comparison of haloperidol, behavior therapy and their interaction in autistic children." *J. Am. Acad. Child Psychiatry* 17:640–655.

Campbell, M., A.S. Hardesty, E.I. Burdock. (1978b) "Demographic and perinatal profile of 105 autistic children: A preliminary report." *Psychopharmacology Bulletin* 14:36–39.

Campbell, M., C.S. Hollander, S. Ferris, and L.W. Greene. (1978c) "Response to thyrotropin-releasing hormone stimulation in young psychotic children: a pilot study." *Psychoneuroendocrinology* 3:195–201.

Campbell, M., B. Geller, A. Small, T. Petti, and S. Ferris. (1978d) "Minor physical anomalies in young psychotic children." *American Journal of Psychiatry* 135:573–575.

Campbell, M., A.M. Small, C.S. Hollander, J. Korein, I.L. Cohen, M. Kalmijn, and S. Ferris. (1978e) "A controlled crossover study of triiodothyronine in autistic children." *Journal of Autism and Childhood Schizophrenia* 8:371–381.

Campbell, M., E. Friedman, W.H. Green, A.M. Small, and E.I. Burdock. (1976a) "Blood platelet monoamine oxidase activity in schizophrenic children and their families." *Neuropsychobiology* 2:239–246.

Campbell, M., A.M. Small, P.J. Collins, E. Friedman, R. David, and N. Genieser. (1976b) "Levodopa and levoamphetamine: A crossover study in young schizophrenic children." *Current Therapeutic Research* 19:70–86.

Campbell, M., E. Friedman, W. Breen, P. Collins, A. Small, and H. Breuer. (1975) "Blood serotonin in schizophrenic children." *International Pharmacopsychology* 10:213–221.

Campbell, M., E. Friedman, E. DeVito, L. Greenspan, and P. Collins. (1974) "Blood serotonin in psychotic and brain damaged children." *Journal of Autism and Childhood Schizophrenia* 4:33–41.

Campbell, M., B. Fish, R. David, T. Shapiro, P. Collins, and C. Koh. (1973) "Liothyronine treatment in psychotic and nonpsychotic children under 6 years." *Archives of General Psychiatry* 29:602–608.

Campbell, M., B. Fish, T. Shapiro, and A. Floyd, Jr. (1972a) "Acute responses of schizophrenic children to a sedative and a 'stimulating' neuroleptic: a pharmacologic yardstick." *Current Therapeutic Research* 14:759–766.

Campbell, M., B. Fish, R. David, T. Shapiro, P. Collins, and C. Koh. (1972b) "Response to triiodothyronine and dextroamphetamine: A study of pre-school schizophrenic children." *Journal of Autism and Childhood Schizophrenia* 2:343–358.

Campbell, M., B. Fish, T. Shapiro, and A. Floyd, Jr. (1971) "Study of molindone in disturbed preschool children." *Current Therapeutic Research* 13:28–33.

Campbell, M., B. Fish, T. Shapiro, and A. Floyd, Jr. (1970) "Thiothixene in young disturbed children: a pilot study." *Archives of General Psychiatry* 23:70–72.

Cantwell, D.P., and L. Baker. (1978) "The language environment of autistic and dysphasic children." *J. Am. Acad. Child Psychiatry* 17:604–613.

Cantwell, D.P., L. Baker, and M. Rutter. (1978) "Family factors." In *Autism: A Reappraisal of Concepts and Treatments*, edited by M. Rutter and E. Schopler, pp. 269–296. New York: Plenum Press.

Caparulo, B.K., D.J. Cohen, S.L. Rothman, J.G. Young, J.D. Katz, S.E. Shaywitz, and B.A. Shaywitz. (1981) "Computed tomographic brain scanning in children with developmental neuropsychiatric disorders." *J. Am. Acad. Child Psychiatry* 20:338–357.

Chase, J.B. (1972) *Retrolental Fibroplasia and Autistic Symptomatology.* New York: American Foundation for the Blind, Inc.

Chase, H.P., and D. O'Brien. (1970) "Effect of excess phenylalanine and of other amino acids on brain development in the infant rat." *Pediatric Research* 4:95–102.

Chess, S. (1977) "Follow-up report on autism in congenital rubella." *Journal of Autism and Childhood Schizophrenia* 7:68–81.

Chess, S., S.J. Korn, and P.B. Fernandez. (1971) *Psychiatric Disorders of Children with Congenital Rubella.* New York: Brunner/Mazel.

Churchill, D.W. (1978) *Language of Autistic Children.* New York: John Wiley & Sons, Ltd.

Chutkow, J.G. (1974) "Metabolism of magnesium in central nervous system." *Neurology* 24:780–787.

Ciaranello, R., S. VandenBerg, and T. Anders. (1982) "Intrinsic and extrinsic determinants of neuronal development: relation to infantile autism." *Journal of Autism and Developmental Disorders* 12:115–145.

Clark, P., and M. Rutter. (1981) "Autistic Children's Responses to Structure and to Interpersonal Demands." *Journal of Autism and Developmental Disorders* 11:201–218.

Clark, P., and M. Rutter. (1979) "Task difficulty and task performance in autistic children." *Journal of Child Psychology and Psychiatry* 20:271–285.

Cohen, D.J., and J.G. Young. (1977) "Neurochemistry and child psychiatry." *J. Am. Acad. Child Psychiatry* 16:353–411.

Cohen, D.J., J.G. Young, T.L. Lowe, and D. Harcherik. (1980) "Thyroid hormone in autistic children." *Journal of Autism and Developmental Disorders* 10:445–450.

Cohen, D.J., B. Caparulo, and B. Shaywitz. (1977a) "Primary childhood aphasia and childhood autism." *J. Am. Acad. Child Psychiatry* 16: 604–645.

Cohen, D.J., B.K. Caparulo, B.A. Shaywitz, and M.B. Bowers. (1977b) "Dopamine and serotonin metabolism in neuropsychiatrically disturbed children: CSF homovanillic acid and 5-hydroxyindoleacetic acid." *Archives of General Psychiatry* 34:545–550.

Cohen, D.J., W.T. Johnson, and B.K. Caparulo. (1976) "Pica and elevated blood lead level in autistic and atypical children." *American Journal of Diseases of Children* 130:47–48.

Cohen, D.J., B.A. Shaywitz, W.T. Johnson, and M.B. Bowers, Jr. (1974) "Biogenic amines in autistic and atypical children. Cerebrospinal fluid measures of homovanillic acid and 5-hydroxyindoleacetic acid." *Archives of General Psychiatry* 31:845–853.

Cohen, R.A., K. Schneidman, F. Ginsberg-Fellner, J.A. Sturman, J. Knittle, and G.E. Gaull. (1973) "High pyridoxine in rats." *J. Nutri.* 103:143–151.

Coleman, M. (1981a) "Congenital brain syndromes." In *Neonatal Neurology*, edited by M. Coleman, pp. 371–384. Baltimore: University Park Press.

Coleman, M. (1981b) "Genetic metabolic diseases." In *Neonatal Neurology*, edited by M. Coleman, pp. 333–360. Baltimore: University Park Press.

Coleman, M. (1978a) "The effects of 5-hydroxytryptophan in Down's syndrome and other diseases of the central nervous system." In *Serotonin in Mental Abnormalities*, edited by D.J. Boullin, pp. 225–240. New York: John Wiley & Sons, Ltd.

Coleman, M. (1978b) "Serotonin in behavioral and intellectual dysfunction of children." In *Serotonin in Health and Disease vol. III: The Central Nervous System*, edited by W.B. Essman, pp. 293–316. New York: Spectrum Publishers.

Coleman, M., ed. (1976) *The Autistic Syndromes*. Amsterdam: North-Holland.

Coleman, M. (1974) "A crossover study of allopurinol administration to a schizophrenic child." *Journal of Autism and Childhood Schizophrenia* 4:231–240.

Coleman, M. (1970) "Serotonin levels in infant hypothyroidism." *Lancet* 2:235.

Coleman, M., and J.P. Blass. (1985) "Autism and lactic acidosis." *Journal of Autism and Developmental Disorders*. 15:1–8.

Coleman, M., and B. Rimland. (1976) "Familial autism." In *The Autistic Syndromes*, edited by M. Coleman, pp. 175–182. Amsterdam: North-Holland.

Coleman, M., and F. Hur. (1973) "Platelet serotonin in disturbances of the central nervous system." In *Serotonin in Down's Syndrome*, edited by M. Coleman, pp. 149–164. Amsterdam: North-Holland.

Coleman, M., and D. Mahanand. (1973) "Baseline serotonin levels in Down's syndrome patients." In *Serotonin in Down's Syndrome*, edited by M. Coleman, pp. 5–24. Amsterdam: North-Holland.

Coleman, M., and D. Mahanand. (unpublished) "A diet controlled study of zinc levels in 12 autistic patients and controls."

Coleman, M., S. Sobel, H.N. Bhagavan, D.B. Coursin, A. Marquardt, M. Guay, and C. Hunt. (in press) "A double blind study of vitamin B_6 in Down's Syndrome infants. Part I—clinical and biochemical results." J. Neural Deficiency Research.

Coleman, M., G. Steinberg, J. Tippett, H.N. Bhagavan, D.B. Coursin, M. Gross, C. Lewis, and L. DeVeau. (1979) "A preliminary study of the effect of pyridoxine administration in a subgroup of hyperkinetic children: a double-blind crossover comparison with methylphenidate." *Biological Psychiatry* 14:741–751.

Coleman, M., P.N. Hart, J. Randall, J. Lee, D. Hijada, and C.G. Bratenahl. (1977) "Serotonin levels in the blood and central nervous system of a patient with sudanophilic leukodystrophy." *Neuropädiatrie* 8:459–466.

Coleman, M., M.A. Landgrebe, and A.R. Landgrebe. (1976a) "Purine autism. Hyperuricosuria in autistic children: does this identify a subgroup of autism?" In *The Autistic Syndromes*, edited by M. Coleman, pp. 183–195. Amsterdam: North-Holland.

Coleman, M., M.A. Landgrebe, and A.R. Landgrebe. (1976b) "Calcium studies and their relationship to celiac disease in autistic patients." In *The Autistic Syndromes*, edited by M. Coleman, pp. 197–205. Amsterdam: North-Holland.

Coleman, M., M. Landgrebe, and A. Landgrebe. (1974) "Progressive seizures with hyperuricosuria reversed by allopurinol." *Archives of Neurology* 31:238–242.

Cooper, L.Z., A.L. Florman, P.R. Ziring, and S. Krugman. (1971) "Loss of rubella hemagglutination inhibition antibody in congenital rubella." *American Journal of Diseases of Children* 122:397–403.

Corbett, J. (1983a) "An epidemiological approach to the evaluation of services for children with mental retardation." In *Epidemiological Approaches in Child Psychiatry, II*, edited by M. Schmidt and H. Remschmidt. New York: Thieme-Stratton Inc.

Corbett, J. (1983b) "Epilepsy and mental retardation—a follow up study." In *Advances of Epileptology*, edited by M. Parsonage, pp. 207–214. XIVth Epilepsy International Symposium, New York.

Corbett, J. (1982) "Epilepsy and the electroencephalogram in early childhood psychoses." In *Handbook of Psychiatry. Volume III*, edited by J.K. Wing and L. Wing, pp. 198–202. London: Cambridge University Press.

Corbett, J. (1981) *Epilepsy and mental retardation in epilepsy and psychiatry.* Edited by E.J. Reynolds and M.R. Trimble. London & New York: Churchill Livingston.

Cowdry, R.W., M. Ebert, D.P. van Kammen, R. Post, and F. Goodwin. (1983) "Cerebrospinal fluid probenecid studies: a reinterpretation." *Biological Psych.* 18:1287–1299.

Cox, A., M. Rutter, S. Newman, and L. Bartak. (1975) "A comparative study of infantile autism and specific developmental receptive language disorder: II. Parental characteristics." *British Journal of Psychiatry* 126:146–159.

Creak, M. (1964) "Schizophrenic syndrome in childhood. Further progress report of a working party (April 1964)." *Developmental Medicine and Child Neurology* 6:530–535.

Creak, M. (1963) "Childhood Psychosis. A review of 100 cases." *British Journal of Psychiatry* 109:84.

Creak, M., and G. Pampiglione. (1969) "Clinical and EEG studies on a group of 35 psychotic children." *Developmental Medicine and Child Neurology* 11:218–227.

Creak, M. and S. Ini. (1960) "Families of psychotic children." *Journal of Child Psychology and Psychiatry* 1:156.

Crook, W.G. (1983) "Letter to the Editor." *J. Orthomolecular Psychiatry* 12(1):34–37.

Crowe, F.W., W.J. Schull, and J.W. Neil. (1956) *A Clinical Pathological and Genetic Study of Multiple Neurofibromatosis.* Springfield, Ill.: Charles C. Thomas.

Damasio, A.R., and R.G. Maurer. (1978) "A neurological model for childhood autism." *Archives of Neurology* 35:777–786.

Damasio, H., R.G. Maurer, A.R. Damasio, H.C. Chui. (1980) "Computerized tomographic scan findings in patients with autistic behavior." *Archives of Neurology* 37:504–510.

Darby, J.K. (1976) "Neuropathologic aspects of psychosis in children." *Journal of Autism and Childhood Schizophrenia* 6:339–352.

Darr, G.C., and F.G. Warden. (1951) "Case report 28 years after infantile autistic disorder." *American Journal of Orthopsychiatry* 21:559–570.

Dawson, G. (1983) "Lateralized brain dysfunction in autism: evidence from the Halstead-Reitan Neuropsychological Battery." *Journal of Autism and Developmental Disorders* 13:269–286.

Dawson, G., S. Warrenburg, and P. Fuller. (1982) "Cerebral lateralization in individuals diagnosed as autistic in early childhood." *Brain and Language* 15:353–368.

DeLong, G.R., S.C. Beau, and F.R. Brown. (1981) "III. Acquired reversible autistic syndrome in acute encephalopathic illness in children." *Archives of Neurology* 38:191–194.

DeMyer, M.K. (1979) *Parents and Children in Autism.* Washington, D.C.: Victor H. Winston & Sons.

DeMyer, M.K. (1975) "Research in infantile autism: a strategy and its results." *Biological Psychiatry* 10:433-452.

DeMyer, M.K., J.N. Hingtgen, and R.K. Jackson. (1981) "Infantile autism reviewed: A decade of research." *Schizophrenia Bulletin* 7:388-451.

DeMyer, M.K., S. Barton, W.E. DeMyer, J.A. Norton, J. Allen, and R. Steele. (1973) "Prognosis in autism: a follow-up study." *Journal of Autism and Childhood Schizophrenia* 3:199-246.

DeMyer, M.K., W. Pontius, J.A. Norton, S. Barton, J. Allen, and R. Steele. (1972) "Parental practices and innate activity in normal autistic and brain damaged infants." *Journal of Autism and Childhood Schizophrenia* 2:49-66.

DeMyer, M.K., H. Schwier, C.Q. Bryson, E.B. Solow, and N. Roeske. (1971) "Free fatty acid response to insulin and glucose stimulation in schizophrenic, autistic, and emotionally disturbed children." *Journal of Autism and Childhood Schizophrenia* 1:436-452.

Desmond, M.M., G.S. Wilson, J.L. Melnick, D.B. Singer, T.E. Zion, A.J. Rudolph, R.G. Pineda, M.H. Ziai, and R.J. Blattney. (1967) "Congenital rubella encephalitis." *Journal of Pediatrics* 71:311-331.

Despert, J.L. (1971) "Reflections on early infantile autism." *Journal of Autism and Childhood Schizophrenia* 1:363-367.

Despert, J.L. (1951) "Some considerations relating to the genesis of autistic behaviour in children." *American Journal of Orthopsychiatry* 21:335.

Deykin, E., and G. MacMahon. (1980) "Pregnancy, delivery and neonatal complications among autistic children." *American Journal of Diseases of Children* 134:860-864.

Deykin, E.Y., and G. MacMahon. (1979) "Viral exposure and autism." *American Journal of Epidemiology* 109:628-638.

Dobson, J.C., M.L. Williamson, C. Azen, R. Koch. (1977) "Intellectual assessment of 111 four-year-old children with phenylketonuria." *Pediatrics* 60:822-827.

Dohan, F.C. (1983) "More on celiac disease as a model for schizophrenia." *Biological Psychiatry* 18:561-564.

Duran, M., F.A. Beemer, C.v.d. Heiden, J. Korteland, P.K. deBree, M. Brink, and S.K. Wadman. (1978) "Combined deficiency of xanthine oxidase and sulphite oxidase. A defect of molybdenum metabolism or transport?" *J. Inher. Metab. Dis.* 1:175-178.

Eisenberg, L. (1956) "The autistic child in adolescence." *American Journal of Psychiatry* 112:607-612.

Ekstein, R., and S.W. Friedman. (1974) "Infantile autism: From entity to process." *Reiss-Davis Clinic Bulletin* 11:70-85.

Elek, S.D., and H. Stern. (1974) "Development of a vaccine against mental retardation caused by cytomegalovirus infection in utero." *Lancet* 1:1-5.

Ellenberg, J., and K. Nelson. (1979) "Birth weight and gestational age in children with cerebral palsy or seizure disorders." *American Journal of Diseases of Children* 133:1044-1049.

Ellman, G., M. Zingarelli, T. Salfi, and B. Mendel. (1981) "Vitamin B$_6$: its role in autism." Presented at the meeting of the National Society for Autistic Citizens, San Diego.

Engelhardt, D.M., P. Polizos, J. Waizer, and S.P. Hoffman. (1973) "A double-blind comparison of fluphenazine and haloperidol in outpatient schizophrenic children." *Journal of Autism and Childhood Schizophrenia* 3:128–137.

Evans-Jones, L.G., and L. Rosenbloom. (1978) "Disintegrative psychosis in childhood." *Developmental Medicine and Child Neurology* 20:462–470.

Faretra, G., L. Dooher, and J. Dowling. (1970) "Comparison of haloperidol and fluphenazine in disturbed children." *American Journal of Psychiatry* 126:1670–1673.

Faurbye, A., R.J. Rosch, P.B. Petersen, G. Brandborg, and H. Pakkenberg. (1964) "Neurological symptoms in pharmacotherapy of psychosis." *Acta Psychiatrica Scandinavica* 40:10–27.

Fein, D., B. Skoff, and A.F. Mirsky. (1981) "Clinical correlates of brainstem dysfunction in autistic children." *Journal of Autism and Developmental Disorders* 11:303–315.

Feinberg, I., M. Braun, and E. Schulman. (1969) "EEG sleep patterns in mental retardation." *Electroencephalography and Clinical Neurophysiology* 27:128–141.

Felicetti, T. (1981) "Parents of autistic children: some notes on a chemical connection." *Milieu Therapy* 1:13–16.

Finnegan, J.A., and B. Quarrington, (1979) "Pre-, peri- and neonatal factors and infantile autism." *Journal of Child Psychology and Psychiatry* 20: 119–128.

Fish, B., and E. Ritvo. (1979) "Psychoses of childhood." In *Basic Handbook of Child Psychiatry*, Volume II, edited by V. Noshpitz, pp. 249–303, New York: Basic Books.

Fish, B., M. Campbell, T. Shapiro, and A. Floyd, Jr. (1969) "Schizophrenic children treated with methysergide (Sansert)." *Diseases of the Nervous System* 30:534–540.

Fish, B., T. Shapiro, and M. Campbell. (1966) "Long-term prognosis and the response of schizophrenic children to drug therapy: a controlled study of trifluoperazine." *American Journal of Psychiatry* 123:32–39.

Flannery, D.B., E. Hitchcock, and P. Mamunes. (1983) "Dietary management of phenylketonuria from birth using a phenylalanine-free product." *Journal of Pediatrics* 103:247–249.

Fölling, A. (1934) "Über Ausscheidung von Phenylbenztraubensaure in den Haarn als Stoffwechselanomalie in Verbindung mit Imbessillität." *Hoppe Seylers Z. Physiol. Chem.* 227:169.

Folstein, S., and M. Rutter. (1977) "Infantile autism: a genetic study of 21 twin pairs." *Journal of Child Psychology and Psychiatry* 18:297–321.

Forsius, H., U. Kaski, J. Schröeder, and A. de la Chapelle. (1972) "Is there a common psychopathology of XXX boys? A clinical report on three cases of XYY and XY/XYY." *Acta Paedopsychiatrica* 39:28–41.

Fraiberg, S. (1977) *Insights from the Blind. Comparative Studies of Blind and Sighted Infants.* New York: Basic Books.

Fraknoi, J., and B.A. Ruttenberg. (1971) "Formulation of the dynamic economic factors underlying infantile autism." *J. Am. Acad. Child Psychiatry* 10:713–738.

Frank, S.M., D.A. Allen, L. Stein, and B. Myers. (1976) "Linguistic performance in vulnerable and autistic children and their mothers." *American Journal of Psychiatry* 133:909–915.

Freedman, D.A., B.J. Fox-Kolenda, and S.L. Brown. (1970) "A multihandicapped rubella baby: The first 18 months." *J. Am. Acad. Child Psychiatry* 9:298–317.

Freeman, B.J. (1976) "Evaluating autistic children." *Journal of Pediatric Psychology* 1:18–21.

Friedman, E. (1969) "The autistic syndrome and phenylketonuria." *Schizophrenia* 1:249–261.

Fuccillo, D.A., R.W. Steele, S.A. Hensen, M.M. Vincent, J.B. Hardy, and J.A. Bellanti. (1974) "Impaired cellular immunity to rubella virus in congenital rubella." *Infection and Immunity* 9:81–84.

Fulop, M., and A. Drapkin. (1965) "Potassium depletion syndrome secondary to neuropathy apparently caused by 'outdated tetracycline'." *New England J. Med.* 272:986.

Funderburk, S.J., J. Carter, P. Tanguay, B.J. Freeman, and J.R. Westlake. (1983) "Parental reproductive problems and gestational hormonal exposure in autistic and schizophrenic children." *Journal of Autism and Developmental Disorders* 13:325–332.

Fuxe, K., T. Hokfelt, and U. Ungerstedt. (1968) "Localization of indolealkylamines in CNS." *Advances Pharmacol.* 6A:235.

Garnier, C., C. Barthelemy, B. Garreau, J. Jouve, J.P. Muh, and G. Lelord. (1983) "Les anomalies des monoamines et leurs enzymes dans l'autisme de l'enfant." *Encephale* 9:201–262.

Garreau, B., C. Barthelemy, D. Sauvage, I. Leddet, and G. Lelord. (1984) "A comparison of autistic syndromes with and without associated neurological problems." *Journal of Autism and Developmental Disorders* 14:105–111.

Garreau, B., C. Barthelemy, D. Sauvage, J.P. Muh, G. Lelord, and E. Callaway. (1980) "Troubles du metabolisme de la dopamine chez des enfants ayant un comportement autistique. Résultats des examens cliniques et des dosages urinaires de l'acide homovanilique." *Acta Psychiatr. Belg.* 80:249–265.

Gastaut, H., J. Roger, R. Soulayrol, C.A. Tassinari, H. Regis, C. Dravet, R. Bernard, N. Pinsard, and M. Saint-Jean. (1966) "Childhood epileptic encephalopathy with diffused slow spike-waves." *Epilepsia* 7:139–179.

Geller, E., E.R. Ritvo, B.J. Freeman, and A. Yuwiler. (1982) "Preliminary observations on the effect of fenfluramine on blood serotonin and symptoms in three autistic boys." *New England J. Med.* 307:165–169.

Gesell, A. (1941) *Wolf Child and Human Child.* New York: Harper & Bros.

Gillberg, C. (1985) "Onset at age 14 of a typical autistic syndrome. A case report of a previously normal girl with herpes encephalitis." *Journal of Autism and Developmental Disorders.* Submitted for publication.

Gillberg, C. (1984a) "Infantile autism and other childhood psychoses in a Swedish urban region. Epidemiological aspects." *Journal of Child Psychology and Psychiatry* 25:35–43.

Gillberg, C. (1984b) "Asperger's syndrome and recurrent psychosis—a neuropsychiatric case study." *Journal of Autism and Developmental Disorders.* Accepted for publication.

Gillberg, C. (1984c) "Autism in the Laurence-Moon-Biedl syndrome." Unpublished manuscript.

Gillberg, C. (1984d) "On the relationship between epidemiological and clinical samples." *Journal of Autism and Developmental Disorders.* 14:214–217.

Gillberg, C. (1984e) "Autistic children growing up. Problems of puberty and adolescence." *Developmental Medicine and Child Neurology* 26:125–129.

Gillberg, C. (1984f) "A population-based twin study of autistic syndromes in Northern Europe." Research report (in Swedish).

Gillberg, C. (1983a) "Identical triplets with infantile autism and the Fragile X syndrome." *British Journal of Psychiatry* 143:256–260.

Gillberg, C. (1983b) "Psychotic behaviour in children and young adults in a mental handicap hostel." *Acta Psychiatrica Scandinavica* 68:351–358.

Gillberg, C. (1983c) "Perceptual, motor and attentional deficits in Swedish primary school-children. Some child psychiatric aspects." *Journal of Child Psychology and Psychiatry* 24:377–403.

Gillberg, C. (1981) "Infantile autism. Fact and fiction." *Läkartidningen* 78:4373–4376 (in Swedish, summary in English).

Gillberg, C. (1980) "Maternal age and infantile autism." *Journal of Autism and Developmental Disorders* 10:293–297.

Gillberg, C., and I. Winnergård. (1984) "Childhood psychosis in a case of Moebius Syndrome." *Neuropaediatrics* 15:147–149.

Gillberg, C., and J. Wahlström. (1984) "Chromosome abnormalities in infantile autism and other childhood psychoses. A population study of 66 cases." *Developmental Medicine and Child Neurology.* In press.

Gillberg, C., and C. Forsell. (1984) "Childhood psychosis and neurofibromatosis—more than a coincidence?" *Journal of Autism and Developmental Disorders* 14:1–8.

Gillberg, C., and S.O. Dahlgren. (1985) "Symptoms in the first two years of life: a preliminary population study of infantile autism." In preparation.

Gillberg, C., and L. Andersson. (1984) "Autism and achondroplasia. A case study." Unpublished manuscript.

Gillberg, C., and I.C. Gillberg. (1983) "Infantile autism: A total population study of reduced optimality in the pre-, peri- and neonatal period." *Journal of Autism and Developmental Disorders* 13:153–166.

Gillberg, C., and H. Schaumann. (1983) "Epilepsy presenting as infantile autism? Two case studies." *Neuropaediatrics* 14:206–212.

Gillberg, C., and P. Svendsen. (1983) "Childhood psychosis and computed tomographic brain scan findings." *Journal of Autism and Developmental Disorders* 13:19–32.

Gillberg, C., and H. Schaumann. (1982) "Social class and infantile autism." *Journal of Autism and Developmental Disorders* 12:223–228.

Gillberg, C., and H. Schaumann. (1981) "Infantile Autism and Puberty." *Journal of Autism and Developmental Disorders* 11:365–371.

Gillberg, C., L. Terenius, and G. Lönnerholm. (1984a) "Endorphin activity in childhood psychosis." *Archives of General Psychiatry.* Accepted for publication.

Gillberg, C., J. Wahlström, and E. Persson. (1984b) "The fragile-X syndrome in infantile autism. Intensive clinical study of 10 boys from a population study." *Journal of Mental Deficiency Research.* Submitted for publication.

Gillberg, C., I. Winnergård, and J. Wahlström. (1984c) "The sex chromosomes—one key to autism? An XYY case of infantile autism." *Applied Research in Mental Retardation* 5:327–334.

Gillberg, C., U. Rosenhall, and E. Johansson. (1983) "Auditory brainstem responses in childhood psychosis." *Journal of Autism and Developmental Disorders* 13:181–195.

Gillberg, C., O.E. Trygstad, and I. Foss. (1982) "Childhood psychosis and urinary excretion of peptides and protein-associated peptide complexes." *Journal of Autism and Developmental Disorders* 12:229–241.

Gillberg, C., P. Rasmussen, and J. Wahlström. (1982) "Minor neural developmental disorders in children born to older mothers." *Developmental Medicine and Child Neurology.* 24:437–447.

Gillberg, C., P. Rasmussen, and J. Wahlström. (1979) "Long-term follow-up of 80 children born to mothers who had amniocentesis." *Lancet* 1:1341.

Giller, E.L., Jr., G. Young, X.O. Breakefield, C. Carbonari, M. Braverman, and D.J. Cohen. (1980) "Monoamine oxidase and catechol-o-methyltransferase activities in cultured fibroblasts and blood cells from children with autism and the Gilles de la Tourette syndrome." *Psychiatry Research* 2:187–197.

Gladwell, S.R., K.R. Kaufman, and M.V. Driver. (1979) "Psychoses or epilepsy? Differentiation in a complex case." *Developmental Medicine and Child Neurology* 21:95–100.

Goldberg, M., J. Hattab, D. Meir, L. Ebstein and R. Belmaker. (1984) "Plasma cyclic AMP and cyclic GMP in childhood-onset psychoses." *Journal of Autism and Developmental Disorders* 14:159–164.

Goldfarb, W.A. (1970) "A follow-up investigation of schizophrenic children treated in residence." *Psychosocial Process* 1:9–64.

Goldfarb, W., R.L. Spitzer, and J.A. Endicott. (1976) "A study of psychopathology of parents of psychotic children by structured interview." *Journal of Autism and Childhood Schizophrenia* 6:327–338.

Goldfarb, W., E. Yudkovitz, and N. Goldfarb. (1973) "Verbal symbols to designate objects: An experimental study of communication in mothers of schizophrenic children." *Journal of Autism and Childhood Schizophrenia* 3:281–298.

Goldman-Rakic, P.S., and R.M. Brown. (1982) "Postnatal development of monoamine content and synthesis in the cerebral cortex of rhesus monkeys." *Brain Research* 256:339–349.

Goldstein, M., D. Mahanand, J. Lee, and M. Coleman. (1976) "Dopamine-beta-hydroxylase and endogenous total 5-hydroxyindole levels in autistic patients and controls." In *The Autistic Syndromes*, edited by M. Coleman, pp. 57–63. Amsterdam: North-Holland.

Goodwin, M.S., and T.C. Goodwin. (1969) "In a dark mirror." *Mental Hygiene* 53:550.

Goodwin, M.S., M.A. Cowen, and T.C. Goodwin. (1971) "Malabsorption and cerebral dysfunction: a multivariate and comparative study of autistic children." *Journal of Autism and Childhood Schizophrenia* 1:48.

Gorky, M. Nilushka. (1921) In *Through Russia*. London: Everyman's, Dent. English translation 1964.

Gram, L.F., and O.J. Rafaelsen. (1972) "Lithium treatment of psychiatric children and adolescents. A controlled clinical trial." *Acta Psychiatrica Scandinavica* 48:253–260.

Grave, G. (1977) "Introduction." In *Thyroid Hormones and Brain Development*, edited by G. Grave, pp. xiii–xv. New York: Raven Press.

Greenbaum, G.H.C. (1970) "An evaluation of niacinamide in the treatment of childhood schizophrenia." *American Journal of Psychiatry* 127:129–132.

Griffiths, A.D., and K.M. Laurence. (1974) "The effects of hypoxia or hypoglycemia on the brain of the newborn human infant." *Developmental Medicine and Child Neurology* 16:308–319.

Gruber, H.E., I. Jansen, R.C. Willis, and J.E. Seegmiller. (in press) "Regulation of the inosinate branchpoint enzymes in cultured human lymphoblasts." *J. Biol. Chem.*

Gruter, W. (1963) *Angeborene Stoffwechselstörungen und Schwachsinn am Beispiel der Phenylketonurie.* Stuttgart, Germany: F. Enke Verlag.

Gualtieri, C.T., S.E. Breuning, S.R. Schroeder, and D. Quade. (1982) "Tardive dyskinesia in mentally retarded children, adolescents and young adults: North Carolina and Michigan studies." *Psychopharmacology Bulletin* 18:62–65.

Guichano, M., M.G. Mattei, J.F. Mattei, and F. Giraud. (1982) "Genetic aspects of autosomal fragile sites: a study of 40 cases." *Journal de Génétique Humaine* 30:183–197 (in French).

Gustavson, K.-H., B. Hagberg, G. Hagberg, and K. Sars. (1977) "Severe mental retardation in a Swedish county. I. Epidemiology, gestational age, birth weight and associated CNS handicaps in children born 1959-70." *Acta Paediatrica Scandinavica* 66:373-379.

Gustavson, K.-H., B. Hagberg, G. Holmgren, and K. Sars. (1978) "Grav mental retardation hos barn: incidens, prevalens, etiologi och multihandikapp. *Läkartidningen* 75:434-438 (in Swedish, summary in English).

Hagberg, B. (1980) "Infantile autism, dementia and loss of hand use: a report of 16 Swedish girl patients." Paper presented at the Research Session of the European Federation of Child Neurology Societies, Manchester, England.

Hagberg, B., J. Aicardi, K. Dias, and O. Ramos. (1983) "A progressive syndrome of autism, dementia, ataxia and loss of purposeful hand use in girls: Rett's syndrome: report of 35 cases." *Annals of Neurol.* 14:471-479.

Hagberg, B., G. Hagberg, A. Lewerth, and U. Lindberg. (1981) "Mild mental retardation in Swedish children. I. Prevalence." *Acta Paediatrica Scandinavica* 70:441-444.

Halonen, P.E., R. Rimon, K. Arohonka, and V. Jantti. (1974) "Antibody level to herpes simplex type 1, measles and rubella viruses in psychiatric patients." *British Journal of Psychiatry* 125:461-465.

Hanley, H.G., S.M. Stahl, and D. Freeman. (1977) "Hyperserotonemia and amine metabolites in autistic and retarded children." *Archives of General Psychiatry* 34:521-531.

Hansson, D.R., and I.I. Gottesman. (1976) "The genetics, if any, of infantile autism and childhood schizophrenia." *Journal of Autism and Childhood Schizophrenia* 6:209-234.

Haracopos, D., and A. Kellstrup. (1978) "Psychotic behaviour in children under the institutions for the mentally retarded in Denmark." *Journal of Autism and Childhood Schizophrenia* 8:1-12.

Harlow, H.F., R.O. Dodsworth, and J.K. Harlow. (1955) "Total social isolation in monkeys." *Proceedings of the National Academy of Science* 54:90-97.

Harlow, H.F., and W.T. McKinney, Jr. (1971) "Nonhuman primates and psychoses." *Journal of Autism and Childhood Schizophrenia* 1:368-375.

Harper, J., and S. Williams. (1974) "Early environmental stress and infantile autism." *Medical Journal of Australia* 1:341-346.

Harris, I., and A.W. Wilkinson. (1971) "Magnesium depletion in children." *Lancet* 2:735.

Hartmann, A.F., H.S. Wohltmann, M.L. Purkerson, and M.E. Wesley. (1962) "Lactate metabolism—studies of a child with serious congenital deviation." *Journal of Pediatrics* 61:165.

Haslam, H.A., and D.B. Clark. (1971) "Progressive cerebellar ataxia associated with Hand-Schuller-Christian disease." *Developmental Medicine and Child Neurology* 13:174.

Haslam, R.H.A., J.T. Dalby, R.D. Johns, and A.W. Rademaker. (1981) "Cerebral asymmetry in developmental dyslexia." *Archives of Neurology* 38:679–682.

Hauser, S., G. DeLong, and N. Rosman. (1975) "Pneumographic findings in the infantile autism syndrome: A correlation with temporal lobe disease." *Brain* 98:667–688.

Haverback, B.J., and J.D. Davidson. (1958) "Serotonin and the gastrointestinal tract." *Gastroenterology* 35:570.

Haworth, J.C., J.D. Ford, and M.K. Younoszai. (1967) "Familial chronic acidosis due to an error in lactate and pyruvate metabolism." *Can. Med. Assoc. J.* 97:773.

Haymaker, W., A. Pentschew, C. Margoles, and W.G. Bingham. (1958) "Occurrence of lesions in the temporal lobe in the absence of convulsive seizures." In *Temporal Lobe Epilepsy*, edited by M. Baldwin and P. Bailey. Springfield, Illinois: Charles C. Thomas.

Hermelin, B. (1976) "Coding and the sense modalities." In *Early Childhood Autism*, edited by L. Wing, pp. 135–168. 2nd Edition. Oxford: Pergamon Press.

Hermelin, B., and N. O'Connor. (1970) *Psychological Experiments with Autistic Children*. Oxford: Pergamon Press.

Hersh, J., A. Bloom, and B. Weisskopf. (1982) "Childhood autism in a female with Coffin Siris syndrome." *Developmental and Behavioral Pediatrics* 3:249–251.

Hetzler, B.E., and J.L. Griffin. (1981) "Infantile autism and the temporal lobe of the brain." *Journal of Autism and Developmental Disorders* 11:317–330.

Herzberg, B. (1976) "The families of autistic children." In *The Autistic Syndromes*, edited by M. Coleman, pp. 151–172. Amsterdam: North-Holland.

Hier, D.E., M. LeMay, and P.B. Rosenberger. (1979) "Autism and unfavorable left-right asymmetries of the brain." *Journal of Autism and Developmental Disorders* 9:153–159.

Himwich, H.E., R.L. Jenkins, M. Fujimori, N. Narasimhachari, and M. Ebersole. (1972) "A biochemical study of early infantile autism." *Journal of Autism and Childhood Schizophrenia* 2:114–126.

Hingtgen, J.N., and C.Q. Bryson. (1972) "Recent developments in the study of early childhood psychoses: Infantile autism, childhood schizophrenia, and related disorders." *Schizophrenia Bulletin* 5:8–54.

Hobson, R.P. (1982) "The autistic child's concept of persons." *Proceedings of the 1981 International Conference on Autism, Boston, U.S.A.*, edited by D. Park. National Society For Children and Adults with Autism, Washington, D.C.

Holtzman, N.A., E.R.B. McCabe, G.C. Cunningham, and H.K. Berry. (1981) "Screening for phenylketonuria, a Letter to the Editor." *New England J. Med.* 304:1300–1301.

Hooft, C., C. Van Nevel, and A.F. De Schaepdryver. (1968) "Hyperuricosuric encephalopathy without hyperuricaemia." *Arch. Diseases in Childhood* 43:734–737.

Hoshino, Y., H. Kumashiro, M. Kaneko, Y. Numata, K. Honda, Y. Yashima, R. Tachibana, and M. Watanabe. (1979) "Serum serotonin, free tryptophan and plasma cyclic AMP levels in autistic children—with special reference to their relation to hyperkinesia." *Fukushima J. Med. Sci.* 26:79–91.

Howlin, P. (1982) "Echolalia and spontaneous phrase speech in autistic children." *Journal of Child Psychology and Psychiatry* 23:281–293.

Huether, G., V. Neuhoff, and R. Kaus. (1983) "Brain development in experimental hyperphenylalaninaemia: Disturbed proliferation and reduced cell numbers in the cerebellum." *Neuropaediatrics* 14:12–19.

Hughes, J.V., and T.C. Johnson. (1978) "Abnormal amino acid metabolism and brain protein synthesis during neural development." *Neurochem. Res.* 3:381–399.

Hunt, A. (1983) "Tuberous sclerosis: a survey of 97 cases." *Developmental Medicine and Child Neurology* 25:346–357.

Hutt, S., and C. Hutt. (1970) *Behavior Studies in Psychiatry.* Oxford: Pergamon Press.

Ishii, T., and O. Takahashi. (1982) "Epidemiology of Autistic Children in Toyota City, Japan. Prevalence." Paper read at the World Child Psychiatry Conference in Dublin.

Itokawa, Y., C. Tanaka, and M. Kimura. (1972) "Effect of thiamine on serotonin levels in magnesium-deficient animals." *Metabolism* 21:375–379.

Jackson, M.J., and P.J. Garrod. (1978) "Plasma zinc, copper and amino acid levels in the blood of autistic children." *Journal of Autism and Childhood Schizophrenia* 8:203–208.

Jaeken, J., and van den Berghe, G. (1984). "An infantile autistic syndrome characterised by the presence of succinylpurines in body fluids." *Lancet* 2:1058–1061.

Jeavons, P.M., and B.D. Bower. (1964) *Infantile Spasms.* Savenham, Suffolk: The Lavenham Press, Ltd.

Jenkins, E.C., W.T. Brown, C.J. Duncan, J. Brooks, M. Ben-Yishay, F.M. Giordano, and H.M. Nitowsky. (1981) "Feasibility of fragile X chromosome prenatal diagnosis demonstrated. Letter to the Editor." *Lancet* 2:1292.

Jervis, G. (1953) "Phenylpyruvic oligophrenia: Deficiency of phenylalanine oxidizing system." *Proc. of Soc. Exp. Biol. Med.* 82:514.

Johnson, R.J., V. Wiersema, and I.A. Kraft. (1974) "Hair amino acids in childhood autism." *Journal of Autism and Childhood Schizophrenia* 4:187–188.

Jörgensen, O.S., K. Brøndum-Nielsen, T. Isager, and S.E. Mouridsen. (1984) "Fragile X chromosome among child psychiatric patients with disturbances of language and social relationships." *Acta Psychiatrica Scandinavica* 70:510–514.

Judd, L.L., and A.J. Mandell. (1968) "Chromosome studies in early infantile autism." *Archives of General Psychiatry* 18:450–457.

Kanner, L. (1973) *Childhood Psychosis. Initial Studies and New Insights.* Washington, D.C.: Winston.

Kanner, L. (1972) *Proceedings of the Annual Meeting of the National Society of Autistic Children* (available from NSAC, 1234 Massachusetts Avenue, N.W., Suite 1017, Washington, D.C. 20005).

Kanner, L. (1971) "Follow-up study of 11 autistic children originally reported in 1943." *Journal of Autism and Childhood Schizophrenia* 1:119–145.

Kanner, L. (1954) "To what extent is early childhood autism determined by constitutional inadequacies?" In *Genetics and the Inheritance of Neurological and Psychiatric Patterns*, edited by D. Hooker and C.C. Hope. Baltimore: Williams and Wilkins.

Kanner, L. (1952) "Emotional interference with intellectual functioning." *Am. J. Ment. Def.* 56:701–707.

Kanner, L. (1949) "Problems of nosology and psychodynamics in early childhood autism." *American Journal of Orthopsychiatry* 19:416.

Kanner, L. (1948) *Child Psychiatry.* 2nd ed. Springfield, Illinois: Charles C. Thomas.

Kanner, L. (1943) "Autistic disturbances of affective contact." *Nervous Child* 2:217–250.

Kanner, L. (1941a) "Cultural implications of children's behavior problems." *Mental Hygiene* 25:353–362.

Kanner, L. (1941b) *In Defense of Mothers.* Springfield, Ill.: Charles C. Thomas.

Kanner, L., and I. Lesser. (1958) "Early infantile autism." *Pediatric Clinics of North America* 5:711–730.

Kanner, L., and L. Eisenberg. (1956) "Early infantile autism: 1943–1955." *American Journal of Orthopsychiatry* 26:55–65.

Kauffman, M. (1972) "Characteristics of the emotional pathology of the kibbutz child." *American Journal of Orthopsychiatry* 42:692–709.

Kaufman, S., G. Kapatos, W.B. Rizzo, J.D. Schulman, L. Tamarkin, and G.R. Van Loon. (1983) "Tetrahydropterin therapy for hyperphenylalaninemia caused by defective synthesis of tetrahydrobiopterin." *Annals of Neurol.* 14:308–315.

Kaufman, S., N. Holtzman, S. Milstein, I.J. Butler, and A. Krumholz. (1975) "Phenylketonuria due to a deficiency of dihydropteridine reductase." *N. England J. Med.* 293:785–789.

Keeler, W.R. (1958) "Autistic patterns and defective communication in blind children with retrolental fibroplasia." In *Psychopathology of Communication*, edited by P.H. Hoch and J. Zubin, pp. 64–83. New York: Grune and Stratton.

Khan, A.A. (1970) "Thyroid dysfunction." *British Medical Journal* 4:495.

King, P.D. (1975) "Early infantile autism: Relation to schizophrenia." *J. Am. Acad. Child Psychiatry* 14:666–682.

Kirman, B. (1977) "Mental retardation—medical aspects." In *Child Psychiatry Modern Approaches*, edited by M. Rutter and L. Hersov, p. 818. Oxford: Blackwell Scientific Publications.

Klüver, H., and P.C. Bucy. (1939) "Preliminary analysis of function of the temporal lobe in monkeys." *Archives of Neurology and Psychiatry* 42:979–1000.

Klüver, H., and P.C. Bucy. (1938) "An analysis of certain effects of bilateral temporal lobectomy in the rhesus monkey with special reference to psychic blindness." *Journal of Psychology* 5:33–54.

Knobloch, H., and B. Pasamanick. (1975) "Some etiologic and prognostic factors in early infantile autism and psychosis." *Journal of Pediatrics* 55:182–191.

Knobloch, H., R. Rider, P. Harper, and B. Pasamanick. (1956) "Neuropsychiatric sequelae of prematurity." *JAMA* 161:581–585.

Kolvin, I. (1971) "Psychoses in childhood—A comparative study." In *Infantile Autism: Concepts, Characteristics, and Treatment*, edited by M. Rutter, pp. 7–26. Edinburgh: Churchill Livingstone.

Kolvin, I., C. Ounsted, and M. Roth. (1971) "Studies in the childhood psychoses: Cerebral dysfunction and childhood psychoses." *British Journal of Psychiatry* 118:407–414.

Komoto, J., S. Usui, S. Otsuki, and A. Terao. (1984a) "Infantile autism and Duchenne muscular dystrophy." *Journal of Autism and Developmental Disorders* 14:191–195.

Komoto, J., S. Usui, and J. Hirata. (1984b) "Infantile autism and affective disorders." *Journal of Autism and Developmental Disorders* 14:81–84.

Konstantareas, M.M., D. Hunter, and L. Sloman. (1982) "Training a blind autistic child to communicate through signs." *Journal of Autism and Developmental Disorders* 12:1–12.

Korein, J., B. Fish, T. Shapiro, E.W. Gerner, and L. Levidow. (1971) "EEG and behavioral effects of drug therapy in children. Chlorpromazine and diphenhydramine." *Archives of General Psychiatry* 24:552–563.

Kotsopoulos, S. (1976) "Infantile autism in DZ twins: a case report." *Journal of Autism and Childhood Schizophrenia* 6:133–138.

Kotsopoulos, S., and K.M. Kutty. (1979) "Histidinemia and infantile autism." *Journal of Autism and Developmental Disorders* 9:55–60.

Kuroda, Y. (1979) "Abnormal pyruvate and alpha-ketoglutarate dehydrogenase complexes in a patient with lactic acidemia." *Pediatric Research* 13:928.

Kyllerman, M., B. Bager, J. Bensch, B. Bille, I. Olow, and H. Voss. (1982) "Dyskinetic cerebral palsy I. Clinical categories, associated neurological abnormalities and incidences." *Acta Paediatrica Scandinavica* 71:543–550.

Lake, C.R., M.G. Ziegler, M. Coleman, and J. Kopin. (1979) "Evaluation of the sympathetic nervous system in trisomy 21 (Down's syndrome)." *Psychiat. Res.* 15:1–6.

Lake, C.R., M.G. Ziegler, and D.L. Murphy. (1977) "Increased norepinephrine levels and decreased dopamine-beta-hydroxylase activity in primary autism." *Archives of General Psychiatry* 34:553–556.

Landgrebe, A.R., and M.A. Landgrebe. (1976) "Urinary catecholamine studies in autistic children." In *The Autistic Syndromes*, edited by M. Coleman, pp. 65–72. Amsterdam: North-Holland.

Lane, H. (1976) *The Wild Boy of Aveyron*. Cambridge, Mass.: Harvard University Press.

Leckman, J.F., D.J. Cohen, B.A. Shaywitz, B.K. Caparulo, G.R. Heninger, and M.B. Bowers, Jr. (1980) "CSF monamine metabolites in child and adult psychiatric patients." *Archives of General Psychiatry* 37:677–681.

Lelord, G., E. Callaway, J.P. Garreau, J. Martineau, and S. Roux. (in press) "Clinical data and homovanillic acid titration in urine from autistic children."

Lelord, G., E. Callaway, J.P. Muh, J. Martineau, B. Garreau, J.L. Adrien, and J. Domenech. (1983) "Urinary homovanillic acid and evoked potentials in autistic and normal children with respect to the different action of vitamin B_6 in each group." *Progress in Neuropsychopharmacology*.

Lelord, G., E. Callaway, J.P. Muh, and J. Martineau. (1982) "Clinical and biological effects of high doses of vitamin B_6 and magnesium on autistic children." *Acta Vitaminologica et Enzymologica* 4:27–44.

Lelord, G., J.P. Muh, C. Barthelemy, J. Martineau, B. Garreau, and E. Callaway. (1981) "Effects of pyridoxine and magnesium on autistic symptoms—initial observations." *Journal of Autism and Developmental Disorders* 11:219–230.

Lelord, G., J.P. Muh, J. Martineau, B. Garreau, and S. Roux. (1979) "Electrophysiological and biochemical studies in autistic children treated with vitamin B_6." In *Human Evoked Potentials*, edited by D. Lehmann and E. Callaway. New York: Plenum.

Lelord, G., E. Callaway, J.P. Muh, J.C. Arlot, D. Sauvage, B. Garreau, and J. Domenech. (1978) "L'acide homovanilique urinaire et ses modifications par ingestion de vitamine B6: exploration fonctionnelle dans l'autisme de l'enfant?" *Rev. Neurol.* 134:797–801.

Lelord, G., F. Laffant, P. Jusseaume, and J.L. Stephant. (1973) "Comparative study of conditioning of averaged evoked responses by coupling sound and light in normal and autistic children." *Psychophysiology* 10:415–425.

Lennox, W.G. (1945) "The petit mal epilepsies; their treatment with Tridione." *JAMA* 129:1069–1073.

Lesch, M., and W.L. Nyhan. (1964) "A familial disorder of uric acid metabolism and central nervous system function." *Amer. J. Med.* 36:561–570.

Levine, B.S., and J.W. Coburn. (1984) "Magnesium, the mimic antagonist of calcium." *New England J. Med.* 310:1253-1254.

Levitas, A., R.J. Hagerman, M. Braden, B. Rimland, and P. McBogg. (1983) "Autism and the fragile X syndrome." *J. Dev. Behavioral Pediatrics* 4:151-158.

Levy, H.L., V.E. Shih, and P.M. Madigan. (1974) "Routine newborn screening for histidinemia: clinical and biochemical results." *New England J. Med.* 291:1214.

Lewis, E. (1959) "The development of concepts in a girl after dietary treatment for phenylketonuria." *British Journal of Medical Psychology* 32:282-287.

Lindquist, L. (1981) "Autistiska barns integrering i förskola." The Swedish Save The Children Federation. Research report (in Swedish).

Lindsay, J., C. Ounsted, and P. Richards. (1979) "Long-term outcome in children with temporal lobe seizures. III: Psychiatric Aspects." *Developmental Medicine and Child Neurology* 21:630-636.

Links, P., M. Stockwell, F. Abichandani, and J. Simeon. (1980) "Minor physical anomalies in childhood autism." *JADD* 10:273-285.

Lis, A.W., D.I. McLaughlin, R.K. McLaughlin, E.W. Lis, and E.G. Stubbs. (1976) "Profiles of ultraviolet-absorbing components of urine from autistic children, as obtained by high-resolution ion-exchange chromatography." *Clin. Chem.* 22:1528-1532.

Lis, E.W., A.W. Lis, and K.F. de Hackbeil. (1970) "Ultraviolet-absorbing components of urine from mentally retarded children. III." *Clin. Chem.* 16:714.

Lobascher, M.E., P.E. Kingerlee, and S.S. Gubbay. (1970) "Childhood autism: An investigation of aetiological factors in twenty-five cases." *British Journal of Psychiatry* 117:525-529.

Loo, Y.H., L. Scotto, and M.G. Hornig. (1977) "Aromatic acid metabolites of phenylalanine in the brain of the hyperphenylalaninemic rat: effect of pyridoxamine." *J. Neurochem.* 29:411-415.

Lotter, V. (1978) "Follow-up studies." In *Autism: A Reappraisal of Concepts and Treatment*, edited by M. Rutter and E. Schopler, pp. 475-495. New York: Plenum Press.

Lotter, V. (1974) "Factors related to outcome in autistic children." *Journal of Autism and Childhood Schizophrenia* 4:263-277.

Lotter, V. (1967) "Epidemiology of Autistic Conditions in Young Children. II. Some Characteristics of the Parents and Children." *Social Psychiatry* 1:163-173.

Lotter, V. (1966) "Epidemiology of Autistic Conditions in Young Children. I. Prevalence." *Social Psychiatry* 1:124-137.

Lowe, T., D. Cohen, S. Miller, and J.G. Young. (1981) "Folic acid and B_{12} in autism and neuropsychiatric disturbances of childhood." *J. Am. Acad. Child Psychiatry* 20:104-111.

Lowe, T.L., K. Tanaka, M.R. Seashore, J.G. Young, and D.J. Cohen. (1980) "Detection of phenylketonuria in autistic and psychotic children." *JAMA* 243:126–128.

Lubs, H.A. (1969) "A marker X-chromosome." *American Journal of Human Genetics* 2:231–244.

MacCulloch, M.J., and C. Williams. (1971) "On the nature of infantile autism." *Acta Psychiatrica Scandinavica* 47: 295–314.

Macleod, M.D., J.F. Munro, J.G. Ledingham, and J.W. Farquhar. (1983) "Management of the extrapyramidal manifestations of phenylketonuria with L-dopa." *Arch. Diseases in Childhood* 58:457–466.

Mahanand, D., M.K. Wypych, and P.L. Calcagno. (1976) "Serum zinc and copper levels in autistic patients and matched controls." In *The Autistic Syndromes*, edited by M. Coleman, pp. 73–78. Amsterdam: North-Holland.

Mahler, M.S., and B.J. Gosliner. (1955) "On Symbiotic Child Psychosis: genetic, dynamic and restitutive aspects." *Psychoanalytic Study of the Child* 19:195–212.

Maltz, A. (1981) "Comparison of Cognitive Deficits Among Autistic and Retarded Children on the Arthur Adaptation of the Leiter International Performance Scale." *Journal of Autism and Developmental Disorders* 11:413–426.

Marcus, H., and S. Broman. "Preconception occupational exposure of parents of autistic children." In preparation.

Markowitz, P.I. (1983) "Autism in a child with congenital cytomegalovirus infection." *Journal of Autism and Developmental Disorders* 13:249–253.

Martineau, J., B. Garreau, C. Barthelemy, E. Callaway, and G. Lelord. (1981) "Effects of vitamin B_6 on averaged evoked potentials in infantile autism." *Biological Psychiatry* 16:627–641.

Massie, H.N. (1978) "Blind ratings of mother-infant interaction in home movies of pre-psychotic and normal infants." *American Journal of Psychiatry* 135:1371–1374.

Masterton, B.A., and G.B. Biederman. (1983) "Proprioceptive versus visual control in autistic children." *Journal of Autism and Developmental Disorders* 13:141–152.

Maurer, R., and A. Damasio. (1982) "Childhood autism from the point of view of behavioural neurology." *Journal of Autism and Developmental Disorders* 12:195–205.

McAdoo, W.G., and M. DeMyer. (1978a) "Personality characteristics of parents." In *Autism: A Reappraisal of Concepts and Treatment*, edited by M. Rutter and E. Schopler, pp. 251–268. New York: Plenum Press.

McAdoo, W.G., and M.K. DeMyer. (1978b) "Research related to family factors in autism." *Journal of Pediatric Psychology* 2:162–166.

McAndrew, J.B., Q. Case, and D.A. Treffert. (1972) "Effects of prolonged phenothiazine intake on psychotic and other hospitalized children." *Journal of Autism and Childhood Schizophrenia* 2:75–91.

McCabe, E.R., B. McCabe, G.A. Mosher, R.J. Allen, and J.L. Berman. (1983) "Newborn screening for phenylketonuria: Predictive validity as a function of age." *Pediatrics* 72:390-398.

McCann, B. (1981) "Hemispheric asymmetries and early infantile autism." *Journal of Autism and Developmental Disorders* 11:401-411.

McCarthy, D., and M. Coleman. (1979) "Response of intestinal mucosa to gluten challenge in autistic subjects." *Lancet* 2:877-878.

McKean, C.M. (1971) "Effects of a totally synthetic, low phenylalanine diet on adolescent phenylketonuria patients." *Arch. Diseases in Childhood* 46:608.

McKean, C.M., S.M. Schanberg, and N.J. Giarman. (1962) "A mechanism of the indole defect in experimental phenylketonuria." *Science* 137:604.

McQuaid, P.E. (1975) "Infantile autism in twins." *British Journal of Psychiatry* 127:530-534.

Meadow, K. (1984) "Social adjustment of preschool children: deaf and hearing, with and without other handicaps." In *Topics in Early Childhood Special Education*, edited by R. Fewell, pp. 27-40. Austin, Texas: Pro-Ed.

Melchoir, J.C., H.V. Dyggve, and H. Gylstorff. (1965) "Pneumoencephalographic examination of 207 mentally retarded patients." *Danish Medical Bulletin* 12:38-42.

Menkes, J.H. (1974) *Textbook of child neurology.* Philadelphia: Lea and Febiger.

Menkes, J.H. (1972) "Relationship of elevated blood tyrosine to the ultimate intellectual performance of premature infants." *Pediatrics* 49:218.

Meryash, D.L., L. Szymanski, and P. Gerald. (1982) "Infantile autism associated with fragile X syndrome." *Journal of Autism and Developmental Disorders* 12:295-301.

Miller, R.T. (1974) "Childhood schizophrenia: A review of selected literature." *International Journal of Mental Health* 3:3-46.

Mills, G.C., F.C. Schmalstieg, R.J. Koolkin, and R.M. Goldblum. (1982) "Urinary excretion of purines, purine nucleosides, and pseudouridine in immunodeficient children." *Biochem. Med.* 27:37-45.

Milstein, S., S. Orloff, S. Spielberg, S. Berlow, J. Schulman, and S. Kaufman. (1977) "Hyperphenylalaninemia due to phenylalanine hydroxylase cofactor deficiency." *Pediatric Research* 11:460.

Mirenda, P.L., A.M. Donnellan, and D.E. Yoder. (1983) "Gaze Behavior: A new look at an old problem." *Journal of Autism and Developmental Disorders* 13:397-409.

Money, J., N.A. Bobrow, and F.C. Clarke. (1971) "Autism and autoimmune disease: A family study." *Journal of Autism and Childhood Schizophrenia* 1:146-160.

Moynahan, E.J. (1976) "Zinc deficiency and disturbances of mood and visual behavior." *Lancet* 1:91.

Multicenter Study. (1984) Meeting of the fenfluramine multicenter group at the American Academy of Child Psychiatry, Toronto, October 1984.

Myklebust, H., J. Killen, and M. Bannochie. (1972) "Emotional characteristics of learning disability." *Journal of Autism and Childhood Schizophrenia* 2:151–159.

Narasimhachari, N., and H.E. Himwich. (1975) "Biochemical studies in early infantile autism." *Biol. Psych.* 10:425–432.

Nielsen, J., K.R. Christensen, U. Friedrich, E. Zeuthen, and O. Ostergaard. (1973) "Childhood of males with XYY syndrome." *Journal of Autism and Childhood Schizophrenia* 3:5.

Niswander, K.R., and M. Gordon. (1972) *The Women and Their Pregnancies*. (DHEW pub. no. 73-379.) Washington, D.C.: U.S. Government Printing Office.

Novick, B., G.H. Vaughn, Jr., D. Kurtzberg, and R. Simon. (1980) "An electrophysiologic indication of auditory processing defects in autism." *Psychiatry Research* 3:107–114.

Novick, B., D. Kurtzberg, and H.G. Vaughn, Jr. (1979) "An electrophysiologic indication of defective information storage in childhood autism." *Psychiatry Research* 1:101–108.

Nyhan, W.L., J.A. James, A.J. Teberg, L. Sweetman, and L.G. Nelson. (1969) "A new disorder of purine metabolism with behavioral manifestations." *Journal of Pediatrics* 74:20–27.

O'Brien, R.A., G. Semenuk, M. Coleman, and S. Spector. (1976) "Catechol-O-methyltransferase activity in erythrocytes of children with autism." In *The Autistic Syndromes*, edited by M. Coleman, pp. 43–50. New York: Elsevier.

Ogawa, T., A. Sugiyama, M. Suzuki, Y. Nakashita, and S. Ishiwa. (1982) "Hemispheric lateralization of EEG in early infantile autism." *Noto Shinkei* 34:981–988.

Omenn, G. (1973) "Genetic issues in the syndrome of minimal brain dysfunction." In *Minimal Cerebral Dysfunction in Children*, edited by S. Waltzer and P. Wolff, pp. 5–17. New York: Grune & Stratton.

O'Moore, M. (1972) "A study of the aetiology of autism from a study of birth and family characteristics." *J. Irish Med. Assoc.* 65:114–120.

Ornitz, E.M. (1983) "The functional neuroanatomy of infantile autism." *International Journal of Neuroscience* 19:85–124.

Ornitz, E.M. (1978) "Neurophysiologic Studies." In *Autism: A Reappraisal of Concepts and Treatment*, edited by M. Rutter and E. Schopler, pp. 117–139. New York: Plenum Press.

Ornitz, E.M. (1974) "The modulation of sensory input and motor output in autistic children." *Journal of Autism and Developmental Disorders* 4:197–215.

Ornitz, E.M. (1973) "Childhood autism: A review of the clinical and experimental literature." *California Medicine* 118:21–47.

Ornitz, E.M. (1971) "Childhood autism: a disorder of sensorimotor integration." In *Infantile Autism: Concepts, Characteristics and Treatment*, edited by M. Rutter, pp. 50–68. London: Churchill Livingstone.

Ornitz, E.M., and D.O. Walter. (1975) "The effect of sound pressure waveform of human brainstem auditory evoked responses." *Brain Research* 92:490-498.

Ornitz, E.M., and E.R. Ritvo. (1968a) "Neurophysiologic mechanism underlying perceptual inconstancy in autistic and schizophrenic children." *Archives of General Psychiatry* 19:22-27.

Ornitz, E.M., and E.R. Ritvo. (1968b) "Perceptual inconstancy in early infantile autism." *Archives of General Psychiatry* 18:76-98.

Ornitz, E.M., A. Mo, S.T. Olson, and D.O. Walter. (1980) "Influence of click sound pressure direction on brainstem responses in children." *Audiology* 19:245-254.

Ornitz, E.M., D. Guthrie, and A.J. Farley. (1977) "The early development of autistic children." *Journal of Autism and Childhood Schizophrenia* 7:207-229.

Ornitz, E.M., M.B. Brown, A. Mason, and N.H. Putnam. (1974) "Effect of visual input on vestibular nystagmus in autistic children." *Archives of General Psychiatry* 31:369-375.

Ornitz, E.M., A.B. Forsythe, and A. de la Pena. (1973a) "The effect of vestibular and auditory stimulation on the rapid eye movements of REM sleep in autistic children." *Archives of General Psychiatry* 29:786-791.

Ornitz, E.M., A.B. Forsythe, and A. de la Pena. (1973b) "The effect of vestibular and auditory stimulation on the rapid eye movements of REM sleep in normal children." *Electroencephalography and Clinical Neurophysiology* 34:379-390.

Ornitz, E.M., P.E. Tanguay, J.C.M. Lee, E.R. Ritvo, B. Silvertsen, and C. Wilson. (1972) "The effect of stimulus interval on the auditory evoked response during sleep in autistic children." *Journal of Autism and Childhood Schizophrenia* 2:140-150.

Ornitz, E.M., V. Wechter, D. Hartman, P.E. Tanguay, J.C.M. Lee, E.R. Ritvo, and R.D. Walter. (1971) "The EEG and rapid eye movements during REM sleep in babies." *Electroencephalography and Clinical Neurophysiology* 30:350-353.

Ornitz, E.M., E.R. Ritvo, M.B. Brown, S. LaFranchi, T. Parmelee, and R.D. Walter. (1969) "The EEG and rapid eye movements during REM sleep in normal and autistic children." *Electroencephalography and Clinical Neurophysiology* 26:167-175.

Ornitz, E.M., E.R. Ritvo, L.M. Panman, Y.H. Lee, E.M. Carr, and R.D. Walter. (1968) "The auditory evoked response in normal and autistic children during sleep." *Electroencephalography and Clinical Neurophysiology* 25:221-230.

Ornitz, E.M., E.R. Ritvo, and R.D. Walter. (1965) "Dreaming sleep in autistic and schizophrenic children." *American Journal of Psychiatry* 122:419-424.

Ottosson, J.-O. (1983) *Psychiatry*. Stockholm: Almqvist & Wiksell (in Swedish).

Paasonen, M.K. (1968) "Platelet 5-hydroxytryptamine as a model in pharmacology." *Amer. Med. Exp. Biol. Fenn.* 46:416.

Partington, M. (1961) "The early symptoms of phenylketonuria." *Pediatrics* 27:465.

Partington, M.W., J.B. Tu, and C.Y. Wong. (1973) "Blood serotonin levels in severe mental retardation." *Developmental Medicine and Child Neurology* 15:616.

Paul, R., D.J. Cohen, and F.R. Volkmar. (1983) "Autistic behaviors in a boy with Noonan Syndrome (letter)." *Journal of Autism and Developmental Disorders* 13:433–434.

Paulson, G.W., C.A. Rizvi, and G.E. Crane. (1975) "Tardive dyskinesia as a possible sequel of long-term therapy with phenothiazines." *Clin. Pediatrics* 14:953–955.

Pelliccione, N., J. Pinto, Y.P. Huang, and R.S. Rivlin. (1983) "Accelerated development of riboflavin deficiency by treatment with chlorpromazine." *Biochemical Pharmacology* 32:2949–2953.

Penrose, L., and J. Quastel. (1937) "Metabolic studies in phenylketonuria." *Biochem. J.* 31:266.

Perry, T., S. Hansen, and R.G. Christie. (1978) "Amino compounds and organic acids in CSF, plasma and urine in autistic children." *Biological Psychiatry* 13:575–586.

Peterson, M.R., and E.F. Torrey. (1976) "Viruses and other infectious agents as behavioral teratogens." In *The Autistic Syndromes*, edited by M. Coleman, pp. 23–42. Amsterdam: North-Holland.

Petre-Quadens, O., and C. De Lee. (1970) "Eye-movements during sleep: A common criterion of learning capacities and endocrine activity." *Developmental Medicine and Child Neurology* 12:730–740.

Petti, T.A., and M. Campbell. (1975) "Imipramine and seizures." *American Journal of Psychiatry* 132:538–539.

Phillips, P.A. (1978) "Effects of large doses of vitamin B_6 in beagle dogs." *Tox. Appl. Pharm.* 44:323.

Pittfield, M., and A. Oppenheim. (1964) "Child rearing attitudes of mothers of psychotic children." *Journal of Child Psychology and Psychiatry* 5:52–57.

Pletscher, A. (1968) "Metabolism, transfer and storage of 5-hydroxytryptamine in blood platelets." *Brit. J. Pharmacol.* 32:1.

Pliszka, S., and G. Rogeness. (1984) "Calcium and magnesium in children with schizophrenia and major depression." *Biological Psychiatry* 19:871–876.

Polizos, P., and D.M. Engelhardt. (1980) "Dyskinetic and neurological complications in children treated with psychotropic medication." In *Tardive Dyskinesia. Research and Treatment*, edited by W.E. Fann, R.C. Smith, J.M. Davis, and E.F. Domino, pp. 193–199. Jamaica, New York: Spectrum Publications.

Pool, D., W. Bloom, D.H. Mielke, J.J. Roniger, and D.M. Gallant. (1976) "A controlled evaluation of Loxitane in 75 adolescent schizophrenic patients." *Current Therapeutic Research* 19:99–104.

Prechtl, H.F.R. (1980) "The optimality concept." *Early Human Development* 4:201–205.

Prensky, A.L., M.A. Fishman, and B. Daftari. (1971) "Differential effects of hyperphenylalaninemia on the development of the brain in the rat." *Brain Res.* 33:181–191.

Prior, M.R. (1979) "Cognitive abilities and disabilities in infantile autism: a review." *J. Abnormal Child Psychology* 7:357–380.

Prior, M.R., B. Tress, W.L. Hoffman, and D. Boldt. (1984) "Computed tomographic study of children with classic autism." *Arch. Neurol.* 41:482–484.

"Profiles in Preventive Medicine." *Infant Screening* 5:1–2, April, 1983.

Pueschel, S.M., and J.E. Rynders, eds. (1982) *Down's Syndrome: Advances in Biomedicine and the Behavioral Sciences.* Cambridge, Mass.: The Ware Press.

Raiten, D.J., and T. Massaro. "Perspectives on the nutritional ecology of autistic children." *Journal of Autism and Developmental Disorders.* In press.

Rapin, I. (1979) "Effects of early blindness and deafness on cognition." In *Congenital and Acquired Cognitive Disorders*, edited by R. Katzman, pp. 189–245. New York: Raven Press.

Rapoport, J.L., J. Rumsey, R. Duavas, M. Schwartz, R. Kessler, N. Culten, and S.I. Rapoport. (1983) "Cerebral metabolic rate for glucose in adult autism as measured by positron emission tomography." *J. Cereb. Blood Flow Metab.* 3, Suppl. 1:264–265.

Realmuto, G.M., and B. Main. (1982) "Coincidence of Tourette's disorder and infantile autism." *Journal of Autism and Developmental Disorders* 12:367–372.

Reichelt, K.L., K. Hole, A. Hamberger, G. Saelid, P.D. Edminson, C.B. Braestrup, O. Lingjaerde, P. Ledaal, and H. Orbeck. (1981) In *Neurosecretion and Brain Peptides*, edited by J.B. Martin, S. Reichlin, and K.L. Bick. New York: Raven Press.

"Report of the New England Regional Screening Program and the New England Congenital Hypothyroidism Collaborative." (1982) *Pediatrics* 70:16–20.

Rett, A. (1977) "Cerebral atrophy associated with hyperammonaemia." In *Handbook of Clinical Neurology*, edited by P.J. Vinken and G.W. Bruyn. Vol. 29, pp. 305–329.

Rett, A. (1968) Über ein eigenartiges hirnatrophisches Syndrom bei Hyperammoniamie in Kindesalter. *Wien Med. Wochenschr.* 116:723–738.

Rett, A. (1966) *Über ein cerebral-atrophisches Syndrom bei Hyperammonamie.* Vienna: Bruder Hollinek.

Riikonen, R., and G. Amnell. (1981) "Psychiatric disorders in children with earlier infantile spasms." *Developmental Medicine and Child Neurology* 23:747–760.

Rimland, B. (1974) "An orthomolecular study of psychotic children." *J. Orthomolecular Psychiatry* 3:371–377.

Rimland, B. (1973) "High dosage levels of certain vitamins in the treatment of children with severe mental disorders." In *Orthomolecular Psychiatry*, edited by D. Hawkins and L. Pauling, pp. 513–538. New York: W.H. Freeman.

Rimland, B. (1965) *Infantile Autism*. London: Methuen.

Rimland, B. (1964) *Infantile Autism*. Englewood Cliffs, New Jersey: Prentice-Hall, Inc.

Rimland, B., E. Callaway, and P. Dreyfus. (1978) "The effects of high doses of vitamin B_6 on autistic children: A double-blind crossover study." *American Journal of Psychiatry* 135:472–475.

Ritvo, E.R., B.J. Freeman, A. Yuwiler, E. Geller, A. Yokota, P. Schroth, and P. Novak. "A 10 months' study of fenfluramine in 14 outpatients with the syndrome of autism." In press.

Ritvo, E.R., B.J. Freeman, A. Mason-Brothers, A. Mo, and A.M. Ritvo. (1984) "Concordance of the syndrome of autism in 40 pairs of afflicted twins." Submitted for publication.

Ritvo, E.R., B.J. Freeman, E. Geller, and A. Yuwiler. (1983a) "Effects of fenfluramine on 14 outpatients with the syndrome of autism." *J. Am. Acad. Child Psychiatry* 22:549–558.

Ritvo, E.R., M.A. Spence, B.J. Freeman, A. Mason-Brothers, A. Mo, and M.L. Marazita. (1983b) "Evidence for an autosomal recessive type of autism in 46 multiple incidence families." Submitted for publication.

Ritvo, E.R., E.C. Ritvo, and A. Mason-Brothers. (1982) "Genetic and Immunohematologic Factors in Autism." *Journal of Autism and Developmental Disorders* 12:109–114.

Ritvo, E.R., A. Yuwiler, E. Geller, A. Kales, S. Rashkis, A. Schicor, S. Plotkin, R. Axelrod, and C. Howard. (1971a) "Effects of L-dopa in autism." *Journal of Autism and Childhood Schizophrenia* 1:190–205.

Ritvo, E.R., D. Cantwell, E. Johnson, M. Clements, F. Benbrook, P. Slagle, P. Kelly, and M. Ritz. (1971b) "Social class factors in autism." *Journal of Autism and Childhood Schizophrenia* 1:297–310.

Ritvo, E.R., A. Yuwiler, E. Geller, E.M. Ornitz, K. Saeger, and S. Plotkin. (1970) "Increased blood serotonin and platelets in early infantile autism." *Archives of General Psychiatry* 23:566–572.

Rosenberg, A.L., L. Bergstrom, B.T. Troost, and B.A. Bartholomew. (1970) "Hyperuricaemia and neurologic deficits: a family study." *New England J. Med.* 282:992–997.

Rosenbloom, S., M. Campbell, A. George, I. Kricheff, E. Taleporos, L. Anderson, R. Reuben, and J. Korein. (1984) "High resolution CT scanning in infantile autism: a quantitative approach." *J. Am. Acad. Child Psychiatry* 23:72–77.

Rosenblum, S.M., J.R. Arick, D.A. Krug, E.G. Stubbs, N.B. Young, and R.O. Pelson. (1980) "Auditory brainstem evoked responses in autistic children." *Journal of Autism and Developmental Disorders* 10:215–225.

Ross, E.D. (1981) "The aprosodias: Functional-anatomic organization of the affective components of language in the right hemisphere." *Archives of Neurology* 38:561–569.

Ross, I.S. (1959) "An Autistic Child." *Pediatric Conferences, Babies Hosp. Units, United Hospitals of Newark, N.J.* 2:1–13.

Rostafinski, M.J. (1964) "The incidence of preventable forms of brain damage." *Virginia Med. Monthly* 91:22–26.

Roth, J.A., X.O. Breakefield, and C.M. Castiglione. (1976) "Monoamine oxidase and catechol-0-methyltransferase activities in cultured human skin fibroblasts." *Life Sciences* 19:1705.

Rothman, K., and S. Pueschel. (1976) "Birthweight of children with phenylketonuria." *Pediatrics* 58:842–844.

Rotman, A., R. Caplan, and G.A. Szekely. (1980) "Platelet uptake of serotonin in psychotic children." *Psychopharmacology* 67:245–248.

Rumsey, J.M. (1984) "Conceptual problem-solving in highly verbal, nonretarded, autistic men." *Journal of Autism and Developmental Disorders*. In press.

Rumsey, J.M., A.M. Grimes, A.M. Pikus, R. Duara, D.R. Ismond. "Auditory brainstem responses in pervasive developmental disorders." *Biological Psychiatry*. In press.

Rutt, C.N., and D.R. Offord. (1971) "Prenatal and perinatal complications in childhood schizophrenics and their siblings." *J. Nerv. Ment. Dis.* 152:324–331.

Rutter, M. (1983) "Cognitive deficits in the pathogenesis of autism." *Journal of Child Psychology and Psychiatry* 24:513–531.

Rutter, M. (1978a) "Diagnosis and definition." In *Autism: A Reappraisal of Concepts and Treatment*, edited by M. Rutter and E. Schopler, pp. 1–25. New York: Plenum Press.

Rutter, M. (1978b) "Diagnosis and definition of childhood autism." *Journal of Autism and Childhood Schizophrenia* 8:139–161.

Rutter, M. (1973) "Why are London children so disturbed?" *Proceedings of the Royal Society of Medicine* 66:1221–1225.

Rutter, M. (1972a) *Maternal Deprivation Reassessed*. Harmondsworth: Penguin.

Rutter, M. (1972b) "Clinical assessment of language disorders in the young child." In *The Child with Delayed Speech*, edited by M. Rutter and J.A.M. Martin. Clinics in Developmental Medicine, no. 43. London: SIMP/Heinemann Medical.

Rutter, M. (1971) "The description and classification of infantile autism." In *Infantile Autism*, edited by D.W. Churchill, G.D. Alpern, and M.K. DeMeyer. Springfield, Ill.: Charles C. Thomas.

Rutter, M. (1970) "Autistic children. Infancy of Adulthood." *Seminars in Psychiatry* 2:435–450.

Rutter, M. (1967) "Psychotic disorders in early childhood." In *Recent Developments in Schizophrenia*, edited by A. Cooper and A. Walk, pp. 133–158. British Journal of Psychiatry Special Publication. Ashford, Kent: Headley Bros.

Rutter, M. (1966) "Behavioural and cognitive characteristics of a series of psychotic children." In *Early Childhood Autism*, edited by J.K. Wing, pp. 51–81. Oxford: Pergamon.

Rutter, M. (1965) "The influence of organic and emotional factors on the origins, nature and outcome of childhood psychosis." *Developmental Medicine and Child Neurology* 7:518–528.

Rutter, M., and L. Bartak, (1971a) "Causes of infantile autism: Some considerations from recent research." *Journal of Autism and Childhood Schizophrenia* 1:20–32.

Rutter, M., and L. Lockyer. (1967) "A five to fifteen year follow-up study of infantile psychosis: I. Description of the sample." *British Journal of Psychiatry* 113:1169.

Rutter, M., L. Bartak, and S. Newman. (1971) "Autism—A central disorder of cognition and language." In *Infantile Autism: Concepts, Characteristics and Treatment*, edited by M. Rutter, pp. 148–171. London: Churchill-Livingstone.

Rutter, M., P. Graham, and W. Yule. (1970) *A Neuropsychiatric Study in Childhood*. Clinics in Developmental Medicine, No. 35/36. London: Heinemann Medical Books.

Rutter, M., S. Lebovici, L. Eisenberg, A.V. Sneznevskij, R. Sadoun, E. Brooke, and Tsung-Yi Lin. (1969) "A triaxial classification of mental disorders in childhood: an international study." *Journal of Child Psychology and Psychiatry* 10:41.

Rutter, M., D. Greenfield, and L. Lockyer. (1967) "A five to fifteen year follow-up study of infantile psychosis: II. Social and behavioural outcome." *British Journal of Psychiatry* 113:1183.

Saladino, C.F., Jr., and D.V. Sankar. (1973) "Studies on erythrocyte magnesium and potassium levels in children, schizophrenia and growth." *P.D.M.* 4–5 (9–12:1–8):107–110.

Samuelsson, B. (1981) "Neurofibromatosis (von Recklinghausen's disease). A clinical-psychiatric and genetic study." Thesis, University of Gothenburg.

Sanua, V.D. (1981) "Cultural changes and psychopathology in children: with special reference to infantile autism." *Acta Paedopsychiatrica* 47:133–142.

Satz, P. (1972) "Pathological left-handedness: an explanatory model." *Cortex* 8:121–135.

Schain, R., and D. Freedman. (1961) "Studies of 5-hydroxyindole metabolism in autistic and other mentally retarded children." *Journal of Pediatrics* 58:315–320.

Schain, R., and H. Yannet. (1960) "Infantile autism: an analysis of 50 cases and a consideration of certain relevant neuropsychological concepts." *Journal of Pediatrics* 57:560–567.

Schanberg, S.M., and N. Kirshner. (1976) "Serum DBH as an indicator of sympathetic activity and primary hypertension." *Biochemical Pharmacology* 25:617–621.

Schaumburg, H., J. Kaplan, A. Windebank, N. Vick, S. Rasmus, D. Pleasure, and M. Brown. (1983) "Sensory neuropathy from pyridoxine abuse: a new megavitamin syndrome." *New England J. Med.* 309:445–448.

Schönfelder, T. (1964) Über frühkindliche antriebsströrungen. *Acta paedopsychiatrica* 31:112–129.

Schopler, E. (1976) "Toward reducing behavior problems in autistic children." *Journal of Autism and Childhood Schizophrenia* 6:1–13.

Schopler, E. (1973) "Current approaches to the autistic child." *Pediatric Annals* 2(3):60–74.

Schopler, E., and G.B. Mesiboy. (1983) *Autism in Adolescents and Adults*. New York: Plenum Press.

Schopler, E., and R.J. Reichler. (1972) "How well do parents understand their own psychotic child?" *Jouurnal of Autism and Childhood Schizophrenia* 2:387–400.

Schopler, E., C.-E. Andrew, and K. Strupp. (1979) "Do autistic children come from upper-middle-class parents?" *Journal of Autism and Developmental Disorders* 9:139–152.

Schuett, V., R. Gurda, and E. Brown. (1980) "Diet discontinuation policies and practices of PKU clinics in the United States." *Am. J. Public Health* 70:498–503.

Seegmiller, J.E. (1967) "The clinical significance of hyperuricemia." *Med. Ann. of D.C.* 36:215.

Seegmiller, J.E., F.M. Rosenbloom, and W.N. Kelley. (1967) "Enzyme defect associated with a sex-linked human neurological disorder and excessive purine synthesis." *Science* 155:1682–1684.

Seeling, M.S. (1971) "Human requirements of magnesium; factors that increase needs." 1er Symposium International sur de Déficit Magnésique. In *Pathologie Humaine*. Vittel, p. 11.

Sells, C.J., R.L. Carpenter, and G.C. Ray. (1975) "Sequelae of central-nervous system enterovirus infections." *New England J. Med.* 293:1–4.

Sepe, J., H.L. Levy, and F.W. Mount. (1979) "An evaluation of routine follow-up blood screening of infants for phenylketonuria." *New England J. Med.* 300:606–609.

Shah, A., and V. Frith. (1983) "An islet of ability in autistic children: a research note." *Journal of Child Psychology and Psychiatry* 24:613–620.

Shah, A., N. Holmes, and L. Wing. (1982) "Prevalence of autism and related conditions in adults in a mental handicap hospital." *Applied Research in Mental Retardation* 3:303–317.

Shapiro, L.R., P.L. Wilmot, P. Brenholz, A. Leff, M. Martino, G. Harris, M. Mahoney, and J.C. Hobbins. (1982) "Prenatal diagnosis of fragile X chromosome." *Lancet* 1:99–100.

Shaywitz, B.A., D.J. Cohen, J.F. Leckman, J.G. Young, and M.B. Bowers, Jr. (1980) "Ontogeny of dopamine and serotonin metabolites in the cerebrospinal fluid of children with neurological disorders." *Developmental Medicine and Child Neurology* 22:748–754.

Shearer, T.R., K. Larson, J. Neuschwander, and B. Gedney. (1982) "Minerals in the hair and nutrient intake of autistic children." *Journal of Autism and Developmental Disorders* 12:25–34.

Sherwin, A.C., F.F. Flach, and P.E. Stokes. (1958) "Treatment of psychoses in early childhood with triiodothyronine." *American Journal of Psychiatry* 115:166–167.

Shirataki, S., S. Kuromaru, M. Hanada, Y. Sugiura, T. Yamada, S. Ushida, and S. Shimada. (1982) "Long-term following-up study of 13 autistic children." Paper read at International Conference on Child Psychiatry, Dublin, Ireland, July 1982.

Simon, N. (1975) "Echolalic speech in childhood autism: Consideration of possible underlying loci of brain damage." *Archives of General Psychiatry* 32:1439–1446.

Siva Sankar, D.V., N. Cates, H. Broer, and D.B. Sankar. (1963) "Biochemical parameters of childhood schizophrenia (autism) and growth." In *Recent Advances in Biological Psychiatry*, edited by J. Wortis, p. 76. New York: Plenum Press.

Skoff, B.F., A.F. Mirsky, and D. Turner. (1980) "Prolonged brainstem transmission time in autism." *Psychiatry Research* 2:157–166.

Small, J.G. (1975) "EEG and neurophysiological studies of early infantile autism." *Biological Psychiatry* 10:385–398.

Small, J.G., M.K. DeMyer, and V. Milstein. (1971) "CNV responses of autistic and normal children." *Journal of Autism and Childhood Schizophrenia* 1:215–231.

Sofaer, J.A., and A.E.H. Emery. (1981) "Genes for super-intelligence?" *J. Med. Genetics* 18:410–413.

Sorensen, L.B., and P.J. Benke. (1967) "Biochemical evidence for a distinct type of primary gout." *Nature* 213:1122–1123.

South, M.A., and C.A. Alford, Jr. (1973) "Congenital intrauterine infections." In *Immunologic Disorders in Infants and Children*, edited by E.R. Stiehm and V.A. Fulginiti, pp. 566–576. Philadelphia: Saunders.

Spector, R. (1977) "Vitamin homeostasis in the central nervous system." *New England J. Med.* 296:1393–1398.

Spitz, R.A. (1946) "Anaclitic depression—an inquiry into the genesis of psychiatric conditions in early childhood." In *The psychoanalytic study of the child*, edited by R.S. Eissler et al., Vol. II, pp. 313–342. New York: International University Press.

Stahl, S.M. (1980) "Tardive Tourette syndrome in an autistic patient after long-term neuroleptic administration." *American Journal of Psychiatry* 137:1267–1269.

Stanbury, J., J. Wyngaarden, and D. Fredrickson, eds. (1978) *The Metabolic Basis of Inherited Disease.* New York: McGraw-Hill Book Co.

Starr, J.G., R.D. Bart, and E. Gold. (1970) "Inapparent congenital cytomegalovirus infection: Clinical and epidemiologic characteristics in early infancy." *New England J. Med.* 282:1075–1078.

Steinhausen, H.C. (1985) "Community survey of infantile autism." *Journal of the American Academy of Child Psychiatry.* In press.

Steinhausen, H.-C., D. Göbel, M. Breinlinger, and B. Wohlleben. (1983) "Prevalence, social class, sex, and intelligence distribution in autism: a total population study." *Journal of Autism and Developmental Disorders.* Unpublished manuscript.

Stoop, J.W., B.J.M. Zegers, G.F.M. Hendrickx, L.H. Siegenbeek van Heukelom, G.E.J. Staal, P.K. deBree, S.K. Wadman, and R.E. Ballieux. (1977) "Purine nucleoside phosphorylase deficiency associated with selective cellular immunodeficiency." *New England J. Med.* 296:651–655.

Strelkauskas, A.J., R.T. Callery, J. Mcdowell, Y. Borey, and S.F. Schlossman. (1978) "Direct evidence for loss of human suppressor cells during active autoimmune disease." *Proceedings of the National Academy of Science* 75:5150–5154.

Stubbs, E.G. (1978) "Autistic symptoms in a child with congenital cytomegalovirus infection." *Journal of Autism and Childhood Schizophrenia* 8:37–43.

Stubbs, E.G. (1976) "Autistic children exhibit undetectable hemagglutination-inhibition antibody titers despite previous rubella vaccination." *Journal of Autism and Childhood Schizophrenia* 6:269–274.

Stubbs, E.G., E.R. Ritvo, and A. Mason-Brothers. "Autism and shared parental HLA antigens." *Journal of Child Psychiatry.* In press.

Stubbs, E.G., E.R. Ritvo, and A. Mason-Brothers. (1984) "Autism and shared parental HLA antigens." *J. Am. Acad. Child Psychiatry.* In press.

Stubbs, E.G., E. Ash, and C.P.S. Williams. (1984) "Autism and congenital cytomegalovirus." *Journal of Autism and Developmental Disorders* 14:183–189.

Stubbs, E.G., M. Litt, E. Lis, R. Jackson, W. Voth, A. Lindberg, and R. Litt. (1982) "Adenosine deaminase activity decreased in autism." *J. Am. Acad. Child Psychiatry* 21:71–74.

Stubbs, E.G., S.S. Budden, D.R. Burger, and A.A. Vandenbarg. (1980) "Transfer factor immunotherapy of an autistic child with congenital cytomegalovirus." *Journal of Autism and Developmental Disorders* 10:451–458.

Stubbs, E.G., M.L. Crawford, D.R. Burger, and A.A. Vandenbark. (1977) "Depressed lymphocyte responsiveness in autistic children." *Journal of Autism and Childhood Schizophrenia* 7:49–55.

Student, M., and H. Sohmer. (1978) "Evidence from auditory nerve and brainstem evoked responses for an organic brain lesion in children with autistic traits." *Journal of Autism and Childhood Schizophrenia* 8:13-20.

Suemitsu, S., T. Yoshikawa, and S. Otsuki, et al. (1974) "Serum serotonin levels of infantile autism." *Psychiat. Neurol. Paediat. Jap.* 14:105-109.

Sutherland, G.R. (1982) "Heritable fragile sites on human chromosomes. VIII. Preliminary population cytogenetic data on the folic-acid-sensitive fragile sites." *American Journal of Human Genetics* 34:452-458.

Szekely, G.A., R. Caplan, and A. Rotman. (1980) "Platelet dopamine uptake in autistic and other psychotic children. Inhibition by imipramine." *Prog. Neuro-Psychopharmacol.* 4:215-218.

Szurek, S.A. (1973) "Playfulness, creativity and schisis." In *Clinical Studies in Childhood Psychoses*, edited by S.A. Szurek and I.N. Berlin, pp. 10-28. New York: Brunner/Mazel.

Taft, L.T., and H.J. Cohen. (1971) "Hypsarrhythmia and childhood autism: a clinical report." *Journal of Autism and Childhood Schizophrenia* 1:327-336.

Taft, L.T., and W. Goldfarb. (1964) "Prenatal and perinatal factors in childhood schizophrenia." *Developmental Medicine and Child Neurology* 6:32-43.

Takahashi, S., H. Kanai, and Y. Miyamoto. (1976) "Reassessment of elevated serotonin levels in blood platelets in early infantile autism." *Journal of Autism and Childhood Schizophrenia* 6:317-326.

Tanguay, P.E. (1984) "Toward a new classification of serious psychopathology in children." Submitted for publication.

Tanguay, P.E. (1976) "Clinical and electrophysiological research." In *Autism. Diagnosis, Current Research and Management*, edited by E.R. Ritvo, pp. 75-84. New York: Spectrum Publications, Inc.

Tanguay, P.E., R.M. Edwards, J. Buchwald, J. Schwafel, and V. Allen. (1982) "Auditory brainstem evoked responses in autistic children." *Archives of General Psychiatry* 39:174-180.

Tanguay, P.E., E.M. Ornitz, A.B. Forsythe, and E.R. Ritvo. (1976) "Rapid eye movement (REM) activity in normal and autistic children during REM sleep." *Journal of Autism and Childhood Schizophrenia* 6:275-288.

Taylor, M.J., B. Rosenblatt, and L. Linschoten. (1982) "Auditory brainstem response abnormalities in autistic children." *Le Journal Canadien des Sciences Neurologiques* 9:429-434.

Terzian, H., and G. DelleOre. (1955) "Syndrome of Kluver and Bucy reproduced in man by bilateral removal of the temporal lobes." *Neurology* 3:373-380.

Therrell, B.L., L.O. Brown, P.E. Dziuk, and W.P. Peter, Jr. (1983) "The Texas newborn screening program." *Infant Screening* 5:1-3.

Tinbergen, E.A., and N. Tinbergen. (1976) "The aetiology of childhood autism: A criticism of the Tinbergens' theory: A rejoinder." *Psychological Medicine* 6:545-549.

Torrey, E.F., S.P. Hersh, K.D. McCabe. (1975) "Early childhood psychosis and bleeding during pregnancy: A prospective study of gravid women and their offspring." *Journal of Autism and Childhood Schizophrenia* 5: 287-297.

Touwen, B.C.L. (1979) "Examination of the child with minor neurological dysfunction." Clinical and Developmental Medicine, No. 71. London: SIMP/Heinemann Medical.

Towbin, A. (1969) "Cerebral hypoxic damage in fetus and newborn. Basic patterns and their clinical significance." *Archives of Neurol.* 20:35.

Treffert, D.A. (1970) "Epidemiology of infantile autism." *Archives of General Psychiatry* 22:431-438.

Trygstad, O.E., K.L. Reichelt, I. Foss, P.D. Edminson, G. Saelid, J. Bremer, K. Hole, H. Orbeck, J.H. Johansen, J.B. Böler, K. Titlestad, and P.K. Opstad. (1980) "Patterns of Peptides and Protein-associated Peptide Complexes in Psychiatric Disorders." *British Journal of Psychiatry* 136:59-72.

Tsai, L.Y., and M.A. Stewart. (1983) "Etiological implication of maternal age and birth order in infantile autism." *Journal of Autism and Developmental Disorders* 13:57-65.

Tsai, L.Y., and M.A. Stewart. (1982) "Handedness and EEG correlation in autistic children." *Biological Psychiatry* 17:595-598.

Tsai, L.Y., C.G. Jacoby, and M.A. Stewart. (1983) "Morphological cerebral asymmetries in autistic children." *Biological Psychiatry* 18:317-327.

Tsai, L.Y., C.G. Jacoby, M.A. Stewart, and J.M. Beisler. (1982) "Unfavourable left-right asymmetries of the brain and autism: A question of methodology." *British Journal of Psychiatry* 140:312-319.

Turner, B., and A.N. Jennings. (1961) "Trisomy for chromosome 22." *Lancet* 2:49-50.

Vaillant, G.E. (1963) "Twins discordant for early infantile autism." *Archives of General Psychiatry* 9:163-167.

Vaillant, G.E. (1962) "Historical notes: John Haslam on early infantile autism." *American Journal of Psychiatry* 119:376.

Valente, M. (1971) "Autism: symptomatic and idiopathic—and mental retardation." *Pediatrics* 48:495-496.

van der Hoeve, J. (1923) "Eye diseases in tuberous sclerosis of the brain and in von Recklinghausen disease." *Transophthal. Soc. U.K.* 43:534-540.

van Krevelen, A. (1952) "Early infantile autism." *Zeitschrift für Kinderpsychiat.* 19:91.

van Krevelen, D.A. (1971) "Early infantile autism and autistic psychopathy." *Journal of Autism and Childhood Schizophrenia* 1:82-86.

van Peenen, H.J. (1973) "Causes of hypouricemia." *Ann. Int. Med.* 78:547.

Varley, C., C. Kolff, E. Trupin, and R.J. Reichler. (1980) "Hemodialysis as a treatment for infantile autism." *Journal of Autism and Developmental Disorders* 10:399-404.

Varley, C., C. Kolff, E. Trupin, and R.J. Reichler. (1979) "Proposed study of hemodialysis as a treatment for early infantile autism." *Journal of Autism and Developmental Disorders* 9:305–306.

Victor, G. (1983) *The Riddle of Autism*. Toronto, Canada: D.C. Heath and Company.

Vilensky, J.A., A. R. Damasio, and R.G. Maurer. (1981) "Gait disturbances in patients with autistic behavior." *Archives of Neurology* 38:646–649.

Volpe, J.J. (1981) *Neurology of the Newborn*. Philadelphia: W.B. Saunders Co.

von Knorring, A.-L. (1983) "Adoption studies on psychiatric illness. Epidemiological, environmental and genetic aspects." Umeå University medical dissertations. New Series No. 101.

Waizer, J., P. Polizos, S.P. Hoffman, D.M. Engelhardt, and R.A. Margolis. (1972) "A single-blind evaluation of thiothixene with outpatient schizophrenic children." *Journal of Autism and Childhood Schizophrenia* 2:378–386.

Wakabayashi, S. (1979) "A case of infantile autism associated with Down's syndrome." *Journal of Autism and Developmental Disorders* 9:31–36.

Walker, H. (1976) "The incidence of minor physical anomalies in autistic children." In *The Autistic Syndromes*, edited by M. Coleman, pp. 95–116. Amsterdam: North-Holland.

Walker, G.H., and J. O'H. Tobin. (1970) "Cytomegalovirus infection in the northwest of England. A report on a two year study." *Arch. Diseases in Childhood* 45:513.

Walker-Smith, J., and J. Andrews. (1972) "Alpha-I-antitrypsin, autism and coeliac disease." *Lancet* 2:883.

Walter, W.G., V.J. Aldridge, R. Cooper, G. O'Gorman, C. McCallum, and A.L. Winter. (1971) "Neurophysiological correlates of apparent defects of sensori-motor integration in autistic children," In *Infantile Autism: Proceedings of the Indiana University Colloquium (1968)*, edited by D.W. Churchill, G.D. Alpern, and M. DeMyer, pp. 265–276. Springfield, Ill.: Charles C. Thomas.

Ward, T.F., and B.A. Hoddinott. (1962) "Early infantile autism in fraternal twins." *Canadian Psychological Association Journal* 7:191–195.

Waterhouse, L., D. Fein, J. Nath, and D. Snyder. (1984) "Pervasive schizophrenia occurring in childhood: a review of critical commentary." In *American Psychiatric Association, DSM-III: An Interim Appraisal*, APA. In press.

Watson, M.S., J.F. Leckman, B. Annex, W.R. Breg, D. Boles, F.R. Volkmar, and D.J. Cohen. (1984) "Fragile X in a survey of 75 autistic males." *New England J. Med.*

Webb, T., D. Butler, J. Insley, J.B. Weaver, S. Green, and C. Rodeck. (1981) "Prenatal diagnosis of Martin-Bell syndrome associated with fragile site Xq27-28." *Lancet* 2:1423.

Weintraub, S., M.M. Mesulam, and L. Kramer. (1981) "Disturbances in prosody: A right-hemisphere contribution to language." *Archives of Neurology* 38:742–744.

Weizman, A., R. Weizman, G.A. Szekely, H. Wijsenbeek, and E. Livni. (1982) "Abnormal immune response to brain tissue antigen in the syndrome of autism." *American Journal of Psychiatry* 139:1462–1465.

Werry, J.S., and M.G. Aman. (1975) "Methylphenidate and haloperidol in children." *Archives of General Psychiatry* 32:790–795.

Wetherby, A.M., R.L. Koegel, and M. Mendel. (1981) "Central auditory nervous system dysfunction in echolalic autistic individuals." *J. Speech and Hearing Research* 24:420–429.

White, P.T., W. DeMyer, and M. DeMyer. (1964) "EEG abnormalities in early childhood schizophrenia." *American Journal of Psychiatry* 120:950–958.

Whittam, H., G.B. Simon, and P.J. Mittler. (1966) "The early development of psychotic children and their sibs." *Developmental Medicine and Child Neurology* 8:552–560.

Wiedel, L., and M. Coleman. (1976) "The autistic and control population of this study. Demographic, historical and attitudinal data." In *The Autistic Syndromes*, edited by M. Coleman, pp. 11–20. Amsterdam: North-Holland.

Williams, R.S., S.L. Hauser, D.P. Purpura, G.R. DeLong, and C.N. Swisher. (1980) "Autism and mental retardation. Neuropathologic studies performed in four retarded persons with autistic behavior." *Archives of Neurology* 37:749–753.

Williams, S., and J. Harper. (1973) "A study of aetiological factors at critical periods of development in autistic children." *Australian and New Zealand Journal of Psychiatry* 7:163–168.

Wing, J.K. (1966) "Diagnosis, epidemiology, aetiology." In *Early Childhood Autism*, edited by J.K. Wing, pp. 3–49. Oxford: Pergamon Press.

Wing, L. (1983) "Social and interpersonal needs." In *Autism in Adolescents and Adults*, edited by E. Schopler and G.B. Mesibov, pp. 337–354. New York: Plenum.

Wing, L. (1982) "Infantile autism." Paper read at seminar in Gothenburg, Sweden. November 1982.

Wing, L. (1981a) "Sex ratios in early childhood autism and related conditions." *Psychiatry Research* 5:129–137.

Wing, L. (1981b) "Language, social and cognitive impairments in autism and severe mental retardation." *Journal of Autism and Developmental Disorders* 11:31–44.

Wing, L. (1981c) "Asperger's syndrome: a clinical account." *Psychological Medicine* 11:115–129.

Wing, L. (1980a) "Childhood autism and social class: A question of selection." *British Journal of Psychiatry* 137:410–417.

Wing, L. (1980b) *Early Childhood Autism*. 2nd edition. Oxford: Pergamon Press.

Wing, L. (1978) "Social, behavioural and cognitive characteristics." In *Autism. A Reappraisal of Concepts and Treatment*, edited by M. Rutter and E. Schopler, pp. 27–45. New York: Plenum.

Wing, L. (1976) "Epidemiology and theories of aetiology." In *Early Childhood Autism: Clinical, Educational and Social Aspects*, edited by L. Wing, pp. 65–92. Elmsford, New York: Pergamon Press.

Wing, L. (1975) "A study of language impairments in severely retarded children." In *Language, Cognitive Deficits and Retardation*, edited by N. O'Connor, pp. 87–116. London: Butterworths.

Wing, L. (1971) "Perceptual and language development in autistic children: a comparative study." In *Infantile Autism: Concepts, characteristics and treatment*, edited by M. Rutter, pp. 173–197. London: Churchill-Livingstone.

Wing, L., and J. Gould. (1979) "Severe impairments of social interaction and associated abnormalities in children: Epidemiology and classification." *Journal of Autism and Developmental Disorders* 9:11–29.

Wing, L., and J. Gould. (1978) "Systematic recording of behavior and skills of retarded and psychotic children." *Journal of Autism and Childhood Schizophrenia* 8:79–97.

Winsberg, B.G., J. Sverd, S. Castells, M. Hurwic, and J.M. Perel. (1980) "Estimation of monoamine and cyclic-AMP turnover and amino acid concentrations in spinal fluid of autistic children." *Neuropädiatrie* 11:250–255.

Wolpert, A., M.B. Hagamen, and S. Merlis. (1967) "A comparative study of thiothixene and trifluoperazine in childhood schizophrenia." *Current Therapeutic Research* 9:482–485.

Wolraich, M., B. Bzostek, R.L. Neu, L. Gardner. (1970) "Lack of chromosome aberrations in autism." *New England J. Med.* 283:1231.

Woo, S.L.C., A.S. Lidsky, F. Guttler, T. Chandra, and K.J.H. Robson. (1983) "Cloned human phenylalanine hydroxylase gene allows prenatal diagnosis carrier detection of classical phenylketonuria." *Nature* 306:151–155.

Yakovlev, P., M. Weinberger, and C. Chipman. (1948) "Heller's syndrome as a pattern of schizophrenic behavior disturbance in early childhood." *Am. J. Ment. Def.* 53:318–337.

Yamazaki, K., Y. Saito, F. Okada, T. Fujieda, and I. Yamashita. (1975) "An application of neuroendocrinological studies in autistic children and Heller's syndrome." *Journal of Autism and Childhood Schizophrenia* 5:323–332.

Young, J.G., M.E. Kavanagh, G.M. Anderson, B.A. Shaywitz, and D.J. Cohen. (1982) "Clinical Neurochemistry of Autism and Associated Disorders." *Journal of Autism and Developmental Disorders* 12:147–165.

Young, J.G., D.J. Cohen, S.E. Hattox, M.E. Kavanagh, G.M. Anderson, B.A. Shaywitz, and J.W. Maas. (1981a) "Plasma free MHPG and neuroendocrine responses to challenge doses of clonidine in Tourette's syndrome: Preliminary report." *Life Sciences* 29:1467–1475.

Young, J.G., D.J. Cohen, M.E. Kavanagh, H.D. Landis, B.A. Shaywitz, and J.W. Maas. (1981b) "Cerebrospinal fluid, plasma, and urinary MHPG in children." *Life Sciences* 28:2837–2845.

Young, J.G., R.M. Kyprie, N.T. Ross, D.J. Cohen. (1980) "Serum dopamine-beta-hydroxylase activity: Clinical applications in child psychiatry." *Journal of Autism and Developmental Disorders* 10:1–14.

Young, J.G., D.J. Cohen, B.K. Caparulo, S.-L. Brown, and J.W. Maas. (1979) "Decreased 24-hour urinary MHPG in childhood autism." *American Journal of Psychiatry* 136:1055–1057.

Young, J.G., D.J. Cohen, S.-L. Brown, and B.K. Caparulo. (1978) "Decreased urinary free catecholamines in childhood autism." *J. Am. Acad. Child Psychiatry* 17:671–678.

Young, J.G., B.K. Caparulo, B.A. Shaywitz, W.T. Johnson, and D.J. Cohen. (1977) "Childhood autism: cerebrospinal fluid examination and immunoglobulin levels." *J. Child Psychiatry* 16:174–179.

Yuwiler, A., E. Ritvo, E. Geller, R. Glousman, G. Schneiderman, and D. Matsuno. (1975) "Uptake and efflux of serotonin from platelets of autistic and nonautistic children." *Journal of Autism and Childhood Schizophrenia* 5:83–98.

Yuwiler, A., E.R. Ritvo, D. Bald, D. Kipper, and A. Koper. (1971) "Examination of circadian rhythmicity of blood serotonin and platelets in autistic and non-autistic children." *Journal of Autism and Childhood Schizophrenia* 1(4):421–435.

Yuwiler, A., S. Plotkin, E. Geller, and E. Ritvo. (1970) "A rapid accurate procedure for the determination of serotonin in whole human blood." *Biochemical Medicine* 3:426–436.

Zetterström, R. (1983) "Infantile autism—neuropsychological correlates." Paper read at Sävstaholm conference on autism, Uppsala, Sweden, May 1983.

Zieve, L. (1975) "Role of cofactors in the treatment of malnutrition as exemplified by magnesium." *Yale Journal of Biology and Medicine* 48:229–237.

Subject Index

Note: Page numbers in italic refer to tables or figures.

About the Authors

Mary Coleman is a pediatric neurologist who is the author of the book, The Autistic Syndromes. She is a member of the Department of Pediatrics of Georgetown University School of Medicine and Medical Director of the Children's Brain Research Clinic, Washington, D.C.

Christopher Gillberg, M.D. is a Professor of Child and Youth Handicap Research, East Hospital, University of Göteborg, Fellow of the Swedish Medical Research Council, and member of the Child Psychiatry Section of the Swedish Medical Research Council. He is the author of many papers reporting clinical and research data about autistic children.